SEEDS
of the
WORD

FINDING GOD IN THE CULTURE

ROBERT BARRON

Third edition published in 2017
by Word on Fire Catholic Ministries
Printed in the United States of America
All rights reserved.

Originally published in 2015.

23 22 21 20   9 10 11 12

ISBN: 978-0-988-52459-0

Library of Congress Control Number: 2015933319
Barron, Robert E., 1959-

www.wordonfire.org

CONTENTS

TAKE AND READ:
GOD IN BOOKS
89

CITY ON A HILL:
GOD IN POLITICS
135

RAYS OF TRUTH:
GOD IN THE CULTURE
171

FOREWORD

How should a Christian respond to popular forms of arts and entertainment found in our culture? Should a young woman striving for holiness avoid at all costs the latest movie or television show that may depict characters who act in ways contrary to the teachings of Jesus Christ, or who promote ideas contrary to the teachings of the Church? There are certainly some people who advise detachment and even rejection of the popular culture when it is at odds with the Church and would encourage that young woman to spend her time with explicitly Christian material. But while there may be times when certain things ought to be avoided, we can also look at this situation and see an opportunity—not to idly waste time, but to engage with the culture in a way that allows us to evangelize!

At times this can be a difficult question, but the good news is that Christians have been wrestling with it since the beginning of the Church and we can learn from their wisdom. In the second century we find Justin Martyr, a great defender of the Christian faith, explaining to the Roman Senate the similarities between the story of Socrates and the plight of Christians in Rome. We also find Clement of Alexandria, one of the great catechetical leaders of the early Church, explaining how philosophers, playwrights and poets who lived before Christ in pagan cultures nevertheless grasped some portion of the Christian message. Clement writes that the elements of truth in these works reflect the reality that "the force of truth is not hidden." Both of these men, evangelizers *par excellence*, were not afraid to use examples from the culture that surrounded them to explain and promote the teachings of Jesus Christ, whom we know is the Way, *the Truth*, and the Life.

Sometimes this task requires serious consideration and a little creativity, as the presence of Christian truths can be hard to detect in secular work. But the Christian message can be illuminated by turning to the fullness of the teachings of Christ found in the Church, the *Light of the Nations.* At the Second Vatican Council, the document *Lumen Gentium* acknowledged the good that exists in other religions as well as in those who have never heard of God, saying "whatever good or truth is found among them is looked upon by the Church as preparation for the Gospel" (*Lumen Gentium*, 16). So to bring this teaching together with the wisdom of Justin and Clement, we realize that not only are elements of truth found in popular works in our culture, but they even help to prepare the way for the full acceptance of the Gospel!

And that brings me to Bishop Robert Barron. His magnificent *Catholicism* DVD series showed how the beauty of the Catholic faith can deepen our understanding and draw us even closer to Christ. In addition to being a great teacher of the Catholic faith, Bishop Barron is also one of the best at finding the connection between twenty-first century culture and the timeless teachings of Catholicism. Whether it is the many movie reviews he offers on his YouTube channel or the essays that follow in this book, Bishop Barron has a wonderful ability to identify the ways that the message of Christ is present in places we might not always expect. This powerful witness makes him an exceptional evangelizer, and I am grateful for all his efforts! Bishop Barron reaches many people outside the Church through his ability to connect what *they know* about the culture around them with what *he knows* about the saving message of Jesus Christ.

Cardinal Timothy Michael Dolan
Archbishop of New York
December 4, 2014

PREFACE

Just below the Parthenon and the Acropolis in Athens is a rocky out-cropping called the Areopagus, which, in ancient times, functioned as a forum for the adjudication of legal disputes and the airing of philosophical opinions. To that place, some time around 55 AD, came a man who had been trained in both the Greek and the Jewish traditions and who had a novel message to share. The Apostle Paul commenced, not with the news itself, but rather with an observation about the religiosity on display in the city: "You Athenians, I see that in every respect you are very religious. For as I walked around look-ing carefully at your shrines, I even discovered an altar inscribed 'To an Unknown God'" (Acts 17:23). Christians have long taken Paul's strategy on the Areopagus as a model for the evangelization of cul-ture. Before sowing the Word, one looks for *semina verbi* (seeds of the word) already present among the people one seeks to evange-lize. The wager is that, once these are uncovered, the Word of Christ will not seem so strange or alien. In the best case, a nonbeliever might come to see that he had, in fact, been worshipping Christ all along, though under the guise of an Unknown God.

I have been actively involved in the work of evangelizing the culture for over ten years. Sometimes, I think it is necessary to chal-lenge deep moral dysfunction in the culture directly. For example, in the face of an abortion-on-demand philosophy, which permits a mother to eliminate a baby in her womb simply because she doesn't care for another child of that gender, one can and should only shout, "No!" However, especially in our relativistic postmodern frame-work, commencing with moral prohibitions is often an evangelical nonstarter. Therefore, I have tended to begin my work by presenting features of the high or low culture that, sometimes faintly and sometimes powerfully, echo the Gospel message. Monsignor. Robert Sokolowski, who taught me many years ago at Catholic University, shared an image that has long stayed in my mind. The integrated icon of Christian doctrine, he said, exploded at the time of the Reformation and the Enlightenment, and its charred and distorted fragments have landed here and there, littering the contemporary cultural environment. Accordingly, we are not going to find, at least very often, the whole Catholic thing on beautiful display, but we are indeed going to find bits and pieces of it practically everywhere, provided we have the eyes to see.

If the evangelist exercises his analogical imagination, he can see images of Jesus in Superman, Spider-Man, and Andy Dufresne; he can sense the play between divine love and divine mercy in the strong arms of Rooster Cogburn; he can hear an echo of Augustine's anthropology in the protagonist of *Eat, Pray, Love*; he can discern a powerful teaching on the danger of concupiscent desire in *The Great Gatsby*; he can sense a longing for the supernatural in *The Exorcist* and the *Twilight* series; he can pick up overtones of Jeremiah and Isaiah in Bob Dylan; he can hear the voice that spoke to Job out of the whirlwind in the Coen Brothers' *A Serious Man*; and he can appreciate one of the most textured presentations of Christian soteriology in Clint Eastwood's *Gran Torino*. Are any of these adequate presentations of the Word as such? Hardly. But are they all *semina verbi*, seeds of the Word?

Absolutely.

And thus can they, like the altar to the Unknown God in ancient Athens, provide a foundation for evangelization, a way in, a point of departure?

Emphatically yes.

The short pieces gathered in this collection represent one Catholic evangelist's attempt to sow the seed of the Gospel in the contemporary culture. There is a "journalistic" and therefore somewhat ephemeral quality to these essays, since they deal with issues, films, books, and events of a very particular time. But I hope that they nevertheless convey something of the timeless truth of the Good News and that they, however inadequately, provide a model for how proclaimers of the Gospel might go about their work on the Areopagus.

IMAGO DEI:
GOD IN FILM

Kierkegaard, Woody Allen, and the Secret to Lasting Joy

THE GREAT NINETEENTH-CENTURY PHILOSOPHER Søren Kierkegaard spoke of three stages that one passes through on the way to spiritual maturity: the aesthetic, the ethical, and the religious. During the aesthetic stage, a person is preoccupied with sensual pleasure, with the satisfaction of bodily desire. Food, drink, sex, comfort, and artistic beauty are the dominating concerns of this stage of life. The ordinary fellow drinking beer at the baseball game and the effete aristocrat sipping wine in his box at the opera are both fundamentally enjoying the aesthetic life in Kierkegaard's sense. The pleasures of this stage are pure and intense, and this is why it is often difficult to move to the next level, the ethical.

At this second stage, one transcends the preoccupation with satisfying one's own sensual desire and accepts the moral obligation that ties one in love to another person or institution. The young man who finally abandons his bachelor's life and enters into marriage with all of its practical and moral responsibilities is passing from stage one to stage two, as is the soldier who lets go of superficial self-interest and dedicates himself to the service of his country.

But finally, says Kierkegaard, there is a dimension of spiritual attainment that lies beyond even the ethical. This is the religious. At this stage of life, a person falls in love with God, and this means that she falls unconditionally in love, since she has found the infinite object that alone corresponds to the infinite longing of her heart.

For the religious person, even the objects of deepest ethical commitment—family, country, business, etc.—fall into a secondary position. When Thomas More said on the scaffold, "I die the King's good servant, but God's first," he gave evidence that he had passed from the ethical to the religious stage of life. This famous account of the stages on life's way came to my mind as I was watching Woody Allen's film *Vicky, Christina, Barcelona*. Like most of Allen's movies, this one concentrates on the mores and behaviors of the cultural elite: wealthy business executives, artists, poets, and writers. Vicky and Christina are two young New Yorkers who have resolved to spend a couple of summer months in Barcelona. While enjoying a late meal at an elegant restaurant, they are propositioned by Juan Antonio, an infinitely charming painter, who invites the women to join him for a romantic weekend. Despite Vicky's initial hesitation, they accept. Juan Antonio is a consummate bon vivant, and he introduces Vicky and Christina to the pleasures of the Spanish good life: the best restaurants, vistas, art galleries, music, etc. And then, of course, he seduces both of them. In order not to spoil the movie for you (and to keep a PG rating for this article), suffice it to say that they become involved in a love triangle—and eventually quadrangle. None of the lovers is capable of a stable commitment, and all make appeal continually to the shortness of life, the importance of enjoying the moment, and the restrictions of conventional morality.

What they all do—to varying degrees—is to reduce sexual relationship to the level of good food and music and art; something that satisfies at the aesthetic level. And what makes this reduction possible is precisely the disappearance of religion. All of the players in this film move in the world of the sophisticated European high culture; an arena from which God has been rather summarily ejected. Kierkegaard thought that the three stages are ordered to one another in such a way that the highest gives stability and purpose to the other two. When a person has fallen in love with God, both his ethical commitments and aesthetical pleasures become focused and satisfying. But when the religious is lost, ethics devolves into, first, a fussy legalism, and then is swallowed up completely by the lust for personal satisfaction.

This film is a vivid presentation of precisely this declension. And the end result of this collapse is deep unhappiness. What struck me throughout Woody Allen's film was just this: how unhappy, restless, and bored every single character is. So it goes when souls that are ordered to God are bereft of God.

There is, however, a sign of hope. As in so many of Allen's movies—*Hannah and Her Sisters* and *Crimes and Misdemeanors* come to mind—religion, especially Catholicism, haunts the scene. At the very commencement of their weekend together, Juan Antonio showed the two young women the sculpture that, in his own words, "inspired him the most." It was a medieval depiction of the crucified Jesus. It's as though even this postmodern bohemian, this thoroughly secularized sophisticate, realizes in his bones that his life will not hold together unless and until he can fall in love unconditionally. The joy that none of them finds can be had only when they order their aesthetic and ethical lives to the divine love made manifest in that cross of Jesus.

Angels, Demons, and Modern Fantasies about Catholicism

As I was coming to the end of Ron Howard's movie, *Angels and Demons*, I felt like shouting out to the screen, "No, no, you've got it precisely backward!" The central theme of the film, based on Dan Brown's thriller of the same name, is the battle between "science" and Catholicism. It appears as though an ancient rationalist society, the Illuminati, which had been persecuted by the Church in centuries past, is back for revenge. They've kidnapped four cardinals and placed a devastating explosive device under St. Peter's and they're threatening to obliterate the Vatican as a conclave gathers to elect a new pope. To the rescue comes Professor Robert Langdon, a cool agnostic from Harvard, who helps to unravel the mystery after he's given access to the archives to which the Vatican had heretofore denied him access (presumably for his mischief in *The Da Vinci Code*!). As the plot unfolds, and Langdon cleverly uncovers the sinister plot of the scientists, one is tempted to say, "Well, for once the bad guys are the rationalists and the victims are the faithful." Ah, but not so fast (spoiler alert). In fact, we discover the whole thing has been concocted by the evil *camerlengo*, an ultimate Vatican insider, who has revived the old tale of the Illuminati and organized the wicked scheme in order to create a scapegoat against which he could engage in heroic struggle and so engineer his own election as pope! (I swear I'm not making this up.)

Without going into any more of the goofy twists and turns of the story, can you see what prompted my *cri de coeur* about getting it backward? In point of fact, it is not Catholicism that feels the need constantly to revive the struggle between science and the faith, but rather secular modernity—and Ron Howard's movie itself is exhibit A. There is a stubbornly enduring myth that the "modern" world—especially in its scientific expression—emerged out of a terrible struggle with backward-looking Catholicism. And thus many avatars of modernity feel the need on a regular basis to bring out the Catholic Church as a scapegoat and punching bag, as if to reenact the founding myth. Of course, the central act in this drama is the story of Galileo's persecution at the hands of the ignorant and vindictive Church, and so Brown and Howard bring the great Renaissance scientist front and center: Langdon is almost suffocated by wicked Vaticanisti while he diligently researches in the Galileo archive, and at the end of the film, a grateful cardinal rewards the intrepid scientist with a long-hidden text of the master. Well.

Though these facts are well known, it appears that they bear repeating. Albert the Great and Thomas Aquinas were early advocates of Aristotelian science; Copernicus, the popularizer of the heliocentric understanding of the solar system, was a priest; Gregor Mendel, the father of genetics and a chief forerunner of Darwin, was a monk; many of the founders of modern science—Newton, Kepler, Tycho Brahe, Descartes, Pascal, Leibniz—were devoutly religious men; the formulator of the Big Bang theory of cosmic origins was a priest. Perhaps most importantly, the modern physical sciences emerged precisely in the context of a Christian culture, where the belief in creation and hence in universal intelligibility was taken for granted. And today, the supposedly sinister and anti-scientific Vatican sponsors a number of observatories and supports societies at its pontifical universities devoted to dialogue with the sciences at the very highest levels. In fact, in November 2014, Jesuit brother and Vatican astronomer Guy Consolmagno became the first clergyman to be awarded the prestigious Carl Sagan Medal "for outstanding communication by an active planetary scientist to the general public."

Despite the tragedy of the Galileo incident, prompted by the ignorance and in some cases ill will of certain churchmen at the time, Catholicism is not the enemy of science and feels absolutely no compulsion to define itself over against science as though the two are locked in a kind of zero-sum game. It is a longstanding conviction of the Church that since God is one and since all truth comes from God, there can finally be no conflict between the truths of revelation and the truths discoverable through the exercise of human reason. And so the Church rejoices in whatever the empirical sciences uncover and expects no conflict between those discoveries and its own faith, rightly interpreted.

What I found particularly galling about *Angels and Demons* is that Robert Langdon not only solves the mystery but also effectively protects the Church from itself. This, of course, is the modern fantasy in full: "science" emerged from Catholicism after a terrible battle but still has the graciousness and magnanimity to offer its help to its benighted and defeated rival. Ugh! Truth be told, the wound caused by the Galileo incident is being constantly picked open, not by the Vatican, but by representatives of secular modernity; the "battle" between religion and science is now pretty much a shadowboxing affair, radical secularism shaking its fists at a phantom.

Watch *Angels and Demons* if you like a thriller or you enjoy computer-generated images of the Vatican, but please don't be taken in by its underlying philosophy.

The Stoning of Soraya M.
and the Figure of Christ

I FIRST BECAME ACQUAINTED with the barbarism of certain aspects of Sharia law through an article published a few years ago in *The New Yorker* magazine. The author detailed how, in many Middle Eastern countries, Muslim men use the prescriptions in the traditional Islamic legal code to terrorize, brutalize, and in extreme cases, kill women who, they claim, have committed sexual offenses. He specified that some of the victims are put to death by their own brothers and fathers! I remember being appalled by this article, but I confess that its impact was short-lived.

It came roaring back to me the other night when I saw the devastatingly powerful film *The Stoning of Soraya M.* The movie is based on the true story of a young woman who lived in a small Iranian village during the years just following the Khomeini revolution of 1979. Soraya was caught in a dreadful situation: her husband, who beat her regularly and cheated on her, wanted to put her away and marry another woman. When Soraya refused to grant him the divorce, her husband conspired with the mullah of the village, the mayor, and several other men to accuse her of adultery, though she was utterly innocent of the charge. When the accusation became public, Soraya raised her voice in protest, but her complaint carried no legal weight, and the council of the village, composed exclusively of men, condemned her, in accordance with Sharia law, to death by stoning. The depiction of Soraya's execution is overwhelming. She is buried to her waist and her hands tied behind her back. The first stones are thrown by her own father and by her two pre-adolescent sons. Next, her husband attacks her and then all of the men of the town rain stones upon her, as they chant *Allahu akhbar* (God is great).

Now I realize how dangerous and delicate it is to raise a matter such as this. It is extremely easy to fall into the trap of tsk-tsk-ing and tut-tutting at the objectionable practices of another religion without admitting to the outrages of one's own. I fully admit that the Judeo-Christian tradition is anything but blameless. The most casual glance at the book of Leviticus discloses that ancient Israel certainly accepted a legal code that sanctioned lethal violence—burning and stoning—for various offenses. And I humbly confess that Christians, over the centuries, have done terrible things in the name of Christ: the burning of witches, the torturing of heretics, the slaughter of non-Christians, etc. Nevertheless, the events described in *The Stoning of Soraya M.* are not from ancient history; they took place a few decades ago. And the imposition of Sharia law is a lively issue in a number of countries today. So what do we do with a movie such as this?

I am convinced that, though Christians rarely have lived up to it, there is an ideal at the heart of the Gospel that represents a permanent challenge to the travesty of justice on display in the story of Soraya. As the film came to its bloody climax, I found myself haunted by the story told in the eighth chapter of John's Gospel of the woman caught in adultery. Many of the dynamics of the Soraya narrative are evident in this account: a woman accused of a sexual offense, the formation of an angry mob, the sanctioning of violence through religious authority, the thrill that comes through scapegoating. But then there is the decisive difference. When the religious leaders of the mob—thirsty for blood and confirmed in their self-righteousness—inquire of Jesus what he would recommend, the young rabbi bends down and writes on the ground. Then he stands up and says, "Let the one among you who is without sin be the first to cast a stone at her" (Jn 8:7). This devastating one-liner causes the elders to drop their stones and prompts the crowd to dissipate like a summer cloud. Jesus doesn't sanction scapegoating violence; he interrupts it. He demonstrates that God stands, not on the side of victimizers, but of victims. And this divine solidarity with victims comes to its richest expression when Jesus becomes himself an innocent victim of a religiously-sanctioned scapegoating mob.

The French philosopher René Girard has argued that all dysfunctional human societies—from coffee klatches to nation states—are predicated upon the scapegoating mechanism, that is to say, the tendency to find someone or some group to blame. In its shared hatred, the group finds a satisfying, though ultimately unstable, unity. One of my colleagues at Mundelein Seminary has summed up Girard's insight as follows: "Wherever two or three are gathered, look for victims." Girard identified the first revelation (*unveiling, revelatio*) of Christianity as precisely this uncovering and de-legitimizing of the scapegoating mechanism, and the second as the manifestation of the God who is friend to the victim.

What particularly gripped me as the movie came to its conclusion was this: Soraya, devout Muslim and innocent victim of mob violence, lying dead in a pool of her own blood, is one of the most powerful Christ figures in recent cinema.

District 9 and the Biblical Attitude Toward the Other

I JUST SAW A REMARKABLE FILM called *District 9*. It's an exciting, science-fiction adventure movie, but it is much more than that. In fact, it explores, with great perceptiveness, a problem that has pre-occupied modern philosophers from Hegel to Levinas, the puzzle of how to relate to "the other."

District 9 sets up the question in the most dramatic way possible, for its plot centers around the relationship between human beings and aliens from outer space who have stumbled their way onto planet earth. As the film gets underway, we learn that in the 1980s a great interstellar spacecraft appeared and hovered over Johannesburg, South Africa. When the craft was boarded, hundreds of thousands of weak and malnourished aliens were discovered. These creatures, resembling a cross between insects and apes, were herded into a great concentration camp near the city, where they were allowed to live in squalor and neglect for twenty some years. In time, the citizens of Johannesburg came to find the aliens annoying and dangerous, and the central narrative of the movie commences with the attempt to shut down the camp and relocate the "prawns" to a site far removed from the city.

Placed in charge of the relocation operation is Wikus van de Merwe, an agreeable, harmless cog in the state machine. While searching for weapons in the hovel of one of the aliens, Wikus comes across a mysterious cylinder. When he examines it, a black fluid sprays out onto his face, and in a matter of hours, he is desperately ill. He is taken to the hospital, and the doctors who examine him are flabbergasted to discover that his forearm has morphed into the appendage of an alien. Almost immediately, the state officials reduce the suffering man to an object, resolving to dissect him and experiment on him. Wikus manages a miraculous escape, but he is ruthlessly hunted down throughout the film. I promise not to give away much more of the plot. I'll add only this: as his transformation progresses, Wikus becomes an ally of the "prawns" and they come to respect him and to protect him from his persecutors.

With this sketch of the story in mind, I should like to return now to the two philosophers I mentioned at the outset. The nineteenth century German philosopher Georg Wilhelm Friedrich Hegel taught that much of human history can be understood as the working out of what he called the "master/slave" relationship. Typically, people in power—politically, culturally, militarily—find a weaker, more vulnerable "other" whom they then proceed to manipulate, dominate, exclude, and scapegoat. Masters need slaves and slaves, Hegel saw, in their own way need masters, each group conditioning the other in a dysfunctional manner. Masters don't try to understand slaves (think of the dominant Greeks who characterized any foreigners as barbarians, since all they said was "bar-bar"); instead, they use them. Furthermore, almost all of history is told from the standpoint of the masters, and mastery is the state to which all sane people aspire.

Emmanuel Levinas, a twentieth-century Jewish philosopher whose family was killed in the Holocaust, reminded us how the Bible consistently undermines this master/slave dynamic, since it recounts history from the standpoint of the other, the outsider, the oppressed. Levinas argued that Biblical ethics commences, not with philosophical abstractions about the good life, but with the challenging face of the suffering "other." The prophets of Israel consistently remind the people that since they too were once slaves in Egypt, they must be compassionate toward the alien, the stranger, the widow, and the orphan. In the faces of those "others," they find the ground for their own moral commitments. They compelled the people not to adopt the attitude of the master, but to move sensitively into the attitude of the slave. This unique Israelite perspective came to embodied expression in Jesus, who "though he was in the form of God, did not deem equality with God a thing to be grasped" and who rather "emptied himself and took the form of a slave." (Phil 2:6-7) In Christ, the God of Israel became himself a slave, the despised other, even to the point of enduring the rejection of the masters and dying the terrible death of the cross. In Jesus, the God of Israel looks out from the face of the other and draws forth compassion from those who gaze upon him.

In *District 9*, we see the master/slave dynamic on clear display: the characterization of the aliens by a derogatory nickname, their sequestration in a squalid ghetto, the violence—direct and indirect—visited on them consistently, etc. These are practices evident from ancient times to the present day. But we see something else as well: an identification of the oppressor with the oppressed, the openness to interpreting the world from the underside, from the perspective of the victim. This, I would submit, is the Biblical difference, though I doubt that most people today would recognize it as such. It is the view that comes from that strange spiritual tradition which culminates in a God who doesn't make slaves but rather becomes one.

The Coen Brothers and the Voice from the Whirlwind

IN THE COURSE OF MY MINISTRY as a teacher, lecturer, and retreat master, I hear, perhaps more than any other question, the following: "How do I know what God wants?" Put in more formal theological language, this is the question concerning the discernment of God's will. Many people who pose it tell me that they envy the Biblical heroes—Moses, Jeremiah, Jacob, David, etc.—who seem to have received direct and unambiguous communication from God. I usually remind them that even those great Scriptural figures wrestled mightily with the same issue. And then typically I draw their attention to Job, the person in the Biblical tradition who anguished most painfully over the matter of discerning what in the world God was doing.

The Coen brothers, among the most gifted and thought-provoking filmmakers on the scene today, have made a movie called *A Serious Man*, which amounts to a contemporary retelling of the story of Job. The hero of their film is Lawrence Gopnik, a mild-mannered Jewish physics professor at a small college in 1960s-era Minnesota. There is nothing particularly impressive about Larry; in fact, he corresponds pretty closely to the stereotype of the *schlemiel*. More to it, he's surrounded by a fairly dispiriting cast of characters, including a henpecking wife, a pair of self-absorbed teenage children, and an unemployed brother who spends his days (and nights) draining a boil on the back of his neck. As the story unfolds, we witness a steady accumulation of woes befalling Larry. First, his wife announces that she is in love with another man and that she wants a divorce; next, the dean of the math department informs our hero that his tenure application is in doubt; then, Larry's brother is arrested for illegal gambling and suspicion of sodomy; finally, the father of one of his students threatens him with a lawsuit. All at once, everything is collapsing around Larry Gopnik, who is a modern Job.

At this point, he turns to his Jewish faith for answers. It's interesting to note that none of the major characters in this film seems to disbelieve in God. As in the book of Job, the question is not whether God exists, but what God is up to. Larry speaks first to a very young rabbi, who seems to be fresh from the Yeshiva and is filled with fairly trite recommendations about changing one's attitude in order to see God in all things. He opens the blinds to reveal the drab parking lot and effervescently comments that God can be found even there. Unsatisfied, Larry moves on to a more mature rabbi, who tells him a strange story. It seems that there was a Jewish dentist who discovered a series of Hebrew letters on the backside of a patient's teeth. They spelled out "help me; save me." This miracle vividly reminded the dentist of God's presence, and sent him on a spiritual quest. Still wondering, still uneasy, Larry comes in desperation to the office of the most respected rabbi in the area, but he is rebuffed by the great man's secretary. "He's busy," she blandly tells him. The three rabbis are meant to represent, it seems clear, the three friends who attempt, unsuccessfully, to comfort Job in the wake of his enormous sufferings.

The answer that Larry seeks comes most unexpectedly. Throughout the film, we see his son Danny preparing, in a fairly desultory way, for his Bar Mitzvah. In the midst of one of his Hebrew classes, the boy is listening on his transistor radio to the Jefferson Airplane song "Somebody to Love." His annoyed instructor confiscates the device and it eventually finds its way to the aged rabbi whom Danny's father had unsuccessfully tried to see. After the Bar Mitzvah ceremony, Danny is ushered into this great man's presence to receive a word of wisdom. To the boy's infinite surprise, the ancient rabbi begins to quote from the Jefferson Airplane song: "When the truth is found to be lies, and all the joy within you dies...wouldn't you want somebody to love? You better find somebody to love."

At the very end of the film, a great tornado is bearing down on the town, and we hear on the soundtrack the powerful voice of Grace Slick intoning those words: "You better find somebody to love." Of course, the book of Job comes to its climax when, in response to Job's questioning, God finally speaks out of a desert whirlwind. "You better find somebody to love" is therefore the Coen brothers' version of this divine word out of the storm; the ultimate answer to the question of what God is up to.

If we look back at the three "answers" given in the film, we find a coherence with the great biblical tradition. The simple word of the young rabbi is, in fact, spiritually rich. God is indeed found in all things, even the most ordinary, and we do need to shift our awareness in order to appreciate his presence. And the story of the mysterious letters is also Biblical: sometimes, on rare occasions, God speaks through miraculous and extraordinary means. But the word of the old rabbi—and the voice that sings out of the whirlwind— is indeed the ultimate communication from the Holy One. If you want to discover God's presence and intention, especially during times of great struggle, "You better find somebody to love." Not bad advice from the rabbis Coen.

The Dangerous Silliness of *Agora*

I RECENTLY SAW THE FILM *AGORA*, which is a retelling of the story of Hypatia, the brilliant woman philosopher from Alexandria who was killed, supposedly by a mob of "Christians," in the year 415. Along with the tales of Galileo and Giordano Bruno, the legend of Hypatia is a favorite of anti-religious ideologues.

I first heard the story from Carl Sagan, the popular scientist whose multi-part program *Cosmos* was widely watched back in the 1970s. *Cosmos*, in fact, comes to its climax with Sagan's melodramatic rehearsal of the narrative. Hypatia, he explained, was a scientist and philosopher who ran afoul of Cyril, the wicked bishop of Alexandria, who then stirred up a mob of his superstitious followers, who subsequently put Hypatia to death. Sagan commented, "The supreme tragedy was that when the Christians came to burn down the great library of Alexandria, there was no one to stop them." And just to rub it in, he said, "and they made Cyril a saint." Sagan's account found its roots in Edward Gibbon's version of the story in his deeply anti-Christian classic *The Decline and Fall of the Roman Empire*. In fact, Gibbon was the first to link the murder of Hypatia with the burning down of the Alexandrian library. Alejandro Amenabar's new *Agora* film stands firmly in the Gibbon/Sagan tradition, presenting Hypatia as a saint of secular rationalism who desperately gathers scrolls from the library before it is invaded by hysterical Christians and who goes nobly to her death, defending reason and science against the avatars of religious superstition.

Well, Hypatia was indeed a philosopher and she was indeed killed by a mob in 415, but practically everything else about the story that Gibbon and Sagan and Amenabar tell is false. For the complete debunking of the myth, take a look at David Hart Bentley's book *Atheist Delusions*, but allow me to share just a few details. The library of Alexandria was burnt to the ground, not by Christian mobs in the fifth century, but by Julius Caesar's troops, some forty years before Jesus was born. A temple to the god Serapis, called the Sarapeon, was built on the site of the ancient library (which might have contained some scrolls in it in the fifth century), and it was this building that was sacked by angry Christians in Hypatia's time, in response to pagan defilements of Christian houses of worship. Now mind you, I'm not excusing any of this for a moment. Whenever Christians respond to such attacks with violence, they are opposing themselves to the one who said "love your enemies" and "turn the other cheek." But I am indeed insisting that the charge that Christians mindlessly and gleefully destroyed the greatest center of learning in the ancient world is pure calumny.

More to it, Hypatia, sadly enough, found herself caught in the middle of a struggle between two powerful figures in Alexandria, namely, Orestes the civil authority and Cyril the bishop. She was most likely killed in retaliation for the murder of some of Cyril's supporters by agents of Orestes. Again, all of this is nasty stuff, and I'm not trying to exculpate anyone, but to pitch this largely political story as a battle between sweet reason and vicious religious superstition is misleading to say the very least.

Finally, though the film portrays her largely as an astronomer (probably to compel comparisons with Galileo), Hypatia was best known as a neo-Platonist philosopher, a devotee of Plato and Plotinus. Not only were there Christians in Hypatia's classes, not only were Christian bishops among her circle of friends, but Christian theologians—Augustine, Ambrose, and Origen, just to name the most prominent—were enthusiastic advocates of neo-Platonism. Therefore, to portray her as the noble champion of reason over and against mouth-breathing Christian primitives is just ridiculous.

But none of this gets to the heart of why I object to *Agora*. In one of the most visually arresting scenes in the film, Amenabar brings his camera up to a very high point of vantage overlooking the Alexandria library while it is being ransacked by the Christian mob. From this perspective, the Christians look for all the world like scurrying cockroaches. In another memorable scene, the director shows a group of Christian thugs carting away the mangled corpses of Jews whom they have just put to death, and he composes the shot in such a way that the piled bodies vividly call to mind the bodies of the dead in photographs of Dachau and Auschwitz. The not-so-subtle implication of all of this is that Christians are dangerous types, threats to civilization, and that they should, like pests, be eliminated. I wonder if it ever occurred to Amenabar that his movie might incite violence against religious people, especially Christians, and that precisely his manner of critique was used by some of the most vicious persecutors of Christianity in the last century? My very real fear is that the meanness, half-truths, and outright slanders in such books as Christopher Hitchens's *God is Not Great* and Richard Dawkins's *The God Delusion* have begun to work their way into the popular culture.

We Christians have to resist—and keep setting the record straight.

Eat, Pray, Love

So many people had urged me to comment on the film *Eat, Pray, Love* that I felt obligated to see it on its opening weekend. The theater in which I viewed the movie was pretty much full, and the gender ratio was approximately 92% female, 8% male. The storyline of *Eat, Pray, Love* adheres fairly closely to the classic spiritual quest trajectory. As the narrative commences, our heroine, Liz Gilbert (played by Julia Roberts), finds herself in a sort of midlife crisis. Her marriage has lost its spark, her job is going nowhere, and her friends don't know how to help her. In one of the most affecting moments in the movie, Liz kneels down and, with tears, simply begs God to show her the way.

She resolves that she will take a year away from her busy life in Manhattan and spend a third of the time in Rome (to enjoy its sensual pleasures), a third of the time at an ashram in India (to commune with her ex-boyfriend's guru), and a third of the time in the Indonesian paradise of Bali (responding to the invitation of a Yoda-like wise man whom she had met the previous year). In Rome, Liz indulges in the beauty of the architecture, revels in the delights of the Italian language, and above all, she eats and eats. As I watched this section of the film, I was put in mind of Pascal's observation that we begin the spiritual journey on the level of the body, which is to say, of the senses and their attendant pleasures. There is nothing in the world wrong with eating, drinking, admiring, listening, and touching. In fact, really attending to these pleasures is of central importance, for one of the ways that spiritual progress is interrupted is to bypass, repress, or look down upon these elemental joys.

After a few months in Rome, Liz makes her way to India (the city is never specified) and participates in the life of a Hindu ashram, where she is schooled in the classic practices of chanting, silence, and meditation. After several months of ascetic exercise, she concludes that "God is in me, as me." This is when I began to suspect there was something seriously wrong with Liz's spiritual itinerary. She was gesturing toward the famous Hindu principle "Atman is Brahman," meaning that the individual soul (Atman) finally becomes transparent to the source of all existence (Brahman), but her formulation seemed to me just a species of narcissism. If God is simply identified with the self (me), including all of its flaws and imperfections (as me), then any real conversion is ruled out and the ego has effectively deified itself.

Liz's godlike self then moves on to Bali, where she promptly falls in with a handsome businessman, played by Javier Bardem. When he proposes that they run off together to a favorite island of his, Liz balks, objecting that he is trying to dominate her. She eventually agrees to accompany him, but only when she is convinced that the journey is being undertaken on her terms. I suppose that this was supposed to count as the "love" part of the program, but again it seemed like self-indulgence to me, the natural consequence of the "God is in me, as me" principle.

Now what especially struck me about *Eat, Pray, Love* is that Liz, presumably a Christian by background and training, never once turned to a Christian spiritual teacher or advisor at any point in her quest. During the Rome part of the movie, we were treated to extraordinary photography featuring the numberless churches of the Eternal City, but never once did Liz darken the door of any of those places of worship. There is a cute scene of Liz sitting on a bench next to a couple of nuns licking ice cream cones, but it never occurs to our spiritual seeker to wonder about the spiritual path those habited women had found.

If she had followed a Christian path, it would have led her to a very different conclusion than "God is in me, as me." Many great Christians—Dante, Augustine, and Ignatius of Loyola come readily to mind—began where Liz Gilbert did: lost, anxious, despairing. But they moved along a very different trajectory. They commenced with detachment, which is to say, a letting go of anything that has taken the place of God—pleasure, money, power, ego. This had nothing to do with Puritanism; it had everything to do with the right ordering of desire. Once they had passed through this purgative and spiritually clarifying process, they discovered the divine center—that God is indeed in them, but certainly not as them. They found God as the power that ordered all of their passions, energies, and talents and that then sent them on mission. The authentically Christian spiritual itinerary never ends with something as bland as "self-discovery." Rather, it ends with the splendid privilege of participating in God's own work of bringing grace into the world.

I very much admired Liz's honest prayer, and I respected her willingness to go on a spiritual journey. I just wish she had asked one of those nuns for advice!

True Grit and
the Everlasting Arms

TRUE GRIT, THE 1969 FILM starring John Wayne, was the first "grown-up" movie I saw as a kid. I was nine years old at the time, and I remember the experience vividly. I also discovered, through that film, that I had a gift for mimicry. For years afterward, at family parties, I was invited to reproduce the Duke's distinctive drawl: "I wouldn't a-asked you to bury him if he wann't dead."

The Coen brothers, the auteurs behind *Fargo*, *No Country for Old Men*, and *A Serious Man*, are among the best and most spiritually alert filmmakers on the scene today. And so it was with great excitement that I learned that the Coens had produced a remake of *True Grit*.

Though their version is far different from the original, I found it compelling, especially in the measure that it brings the religious dimension of the story to the fore.

The leitmotif is set in the opening moments of the movie, as we hear Mattie, the narrator and principal character, say in voice-over, "The only thing in life that's free is the grace of God." The film will unfold as an extended meditation on the play between justice and mercy, between what is owed and what is given as a grace. Fourteen-year-old Mattie, whose father had been killed in cold blood by a man he had befriended, lives in a world of strict justice, of give and take, of contracts and obligations. Bound and determined to see her father's killer hanged, Mattie hires a wizened old law man named Rooster Cogburn (played with characteristic naturalness by Jeff Bridges) and gives him the charge of tracking down the murderer. We get a delicious taste of Mattie's personality as she, with lawyer-ly skill and fierce persistence, wrests from an oily horse trader the money she needs to pay Rooster. And when Cogburn leaves without her, convinced that the teenaged city slicker would only slow him down, she rides her horse right across a raging river to catch up to him—and then reminds him that he is in breach of contract! Mattie is a *mulier fortis*, a woman not to be trifled with.

She moves with Rooster and Le Boeuf—a Texas ranger who is also looking for the murderer—into Indian country, a place of law-lessness, where drifters live outside the constraints of polite society. They corner a couple of members of Ned Pepper's gang, for Rooster is convinced that the killer might have joined forces with these des-perados. After a shoot-out and a violent interrogation, two men are dead and a third is wounded. The next day, by the bank of a river, Mattie encounters her father's killer and manages to wound him be-fore being captured by Ned Pepper and his men. In the most stirring scene in the film, Rooster manages, single-handedly, to take on the entire Pepper gang, holding the reins of his horse in his teeth and firing with both hands. After this encounter, four more men lie dead. Finally, Mattie frees herself and shoots to death her father's murderer, but the recoil on the gun is so strong that she is pushed into a snake pit, where she receives a bite on the hand. I'll get back to the snake pit in a moment, but notice first what this canny fourteen-year-old girl's lust for vengeance has wrought: eight dead men. She wanted only to bring her father's killer to justice, but the single-mindedness of her pursuit conduced toward a disproportionate, even barbaric, result, something far beyond the requirements of justice. Her excessive and one-sided passion for righteousness kicked her into a den of snakes, and no one with a biblical sensibility could miss the symbolic overtone of this kind of fall.

As she lies helpless and desperately injured, Mattie looks up and sees Rooster Cogburn lowering himself by rope to the bottom of the pit. He cuts into her wound and sucks out as much of the poison as he can, then he brings her back up, places her on a horse, and commences a furious ride to the nearest doctor, who is many miles away. When the horse gives way from sheer exhaustion beneath him, Rooster picks up Mattie in his arms and carries her through the night to the doctor's home. Now Cogburn is a man of the law, and like Mattie, he was aiming to bring a killer to justice, but what these heroic actions on behalf of the girl reveal is that he is more than that. His passion for justice is accompanied by, even surpassed by, his mercy, his graciousness, his willingness to give even when that giving was not, strictly speaking, owed.

As the film comes to a close, we have fast-forwarded many years into the future, and a still prim, unmarried, and somewhat cold Mattie has just learned of the death of Rooster Cogburn. We then see that she has but one arm. Though Rooster's graciousness saved Mattie's life, the doctor, evidently, was not able to save her limb. And as the final credits roll, we hear the beautiful old spiritual "Leaning on the Everlasting Arms," which speaks of the "fellowship and joy divine" which comes from "leaning on the everlasting arms" of God. Rooster had carried Mattie in his two arms, evocative of both justice and mercy, attributes that come together supremely in God. Mattie's tragedy is that she had only justice, only one arm.

The same Coen brothers who gave us a powerful image of God in the tornado at the conclusion of *A Serious Man* and in the pregnant police officer in *Fargo* have given us still another in the strong arms of Rooster Cogburn.

Why Exorcism Films
Still Fascinate

THE EXORCISM MOVIE is now something like the gangster film or the cowboy movie or the romantic comedy, which is to say, a genre with fairly predictable characters, plot developments, and dialogue. In recent years, there has been a spate of exorcism films, including *The Exorcism of Emily Rose* and *The Last Exorcist*. More recently we've seen *The Rite*, a movie starring Anthony Hopkins as a grizzled experienced exorcist and Irish newcomer Colin O'Donoghue as his youthful and doubt-plagued apprentice. One interesting feature of this film is that we get to see some of the training program that prospective exorcists pass through in the Vatican. We also get to witness the rather extraordinary theatrical exertions of Hopkins, who leaves not one little piece of scenery unchewed by the end of the film.

But as I suggested, the exorcism genre is a little tired, and the signs of that exhaustion are everywhere in *The Rite*. That is undoubtedly why, throughout the movie, my mind kept drifting back to the *fons et origo* of all such movies, the incomparable *The Exorcist* from 1973. When I first saw *The Exorcist* on TV, some years after its original release, I was terrified and couldn't sleep for several nights thereafter. But when I saw it again, many years later, I was psychologically prepared for Linda Blair's transformation from cute kid into vomit-spewing, head-spinning, cursing-like-a-sailor monster and so was ready to take in some of the deeper themes that were on offer. What became eminently clear to me on that second viewing was that

The Exorcist wasn't primarily about the possessed girl; it was, first and foremost, the story of two priests and ultimately a meditation on the priesthood itself.

You might recall that the younger priest, Fr. Damien Karras, played by Jason Miller, was a trained psychologist, educated at Harvard, and extremely skeptical of the supernatural claims of his Catholic faith. Guilt-ridden over the way he had neglected his aged mother and haunted by nagging doubts about his own priesthood, Fr. Karras is, as the film commences, a very unhappy man. To his attention comes the peculiar case of Regan, this little girl suffering from a malady so bizarre that no physician or psychiatrist had been able to diagnose it, much less treat it. When it is suggested to him that she might be possessed by the devil, he rejects this assessment as so much medieval mumbo jumbo. Some of the more comical scenes in *The Exorcist* show the priest's rather pathetic attempts to deal with a clearly supernatural phenomenon using the hopelessly inadequate theoretical and practical tools he had picked up at Harvard.

At his wit's end, Fr. Karras calls for Fr. Lankester Merrin, played by Max von Sydow, a Jesuit priest and archeologist who specializes in battling the devil. When the old priest arrives at the home of the possessed girl, she emits a harrowing animal scream: "Meeerrriiiin!" The younger priest, still clinging to his psychological training, informs his colleague that the presence seems to manifest a variety of personalities, but Merrin immediately cuts him off: "There is only one." And then he commences to pray, something that the young priest, to that point, had never tried. The most frightening scenes in the movie unfold as the two priests enter Regan's room and begin the rite of exorcism. This, we clearly see, is not an examination or a treatment or a diagnostic exercise; this is a battle—and not with flesh and blood. At the climax of the film, Fr. Merrin, worn out by the rigors of the struggle with the possessed girl, dies of a heart attack, and Fr. Karras invites the demon to leave the girl and take possession of him—at which point, he hurls himself out of the window to his death.

The film is meditating on two great truths. First, it shows how the young priest moved, slowly and painfully, from a cramped rationalism to a keen sense of a dimension that transcends our ordinary experience. It demonstrates how he came to appreciate the properly supernatural and to understand how his priesthood relates him precisely to that realm. I believe, by the way, that the persistent popularity of the genre of the exorcism film is largely a function of this clear communication of the reality of the transcendent realm, especially during our time when an ideological secularism holds sway. In our guts, we know that there is something "more," and stories about demonic possession give that intuition vivid confirmation. Secondly, *The Exorcist* shows that the mission of a priest finds its fullest expression in the willingness to sacrifice one's life for the good of the other. Both priests died in battle, defending a little girl whom they barely knew but who had been entrusted to their care. The very last scene of the film is arresting. As Regan and her mother are pulling away in a car, happily leaving the place where they had endured so much suffering, the girl spots a priest in a Roman collar. She asks the driver to stop, and she runs out, throws her arms around the priest and kisses him. It was her tribute to the men who had saved her.

The Rite comes nowhere near the power and artistry of *The Exorcist*, but it does suggest the reality of the supernatural and even something of the heroic character of the priesthood. At a time when both the supernatural and the priesthood are viewed with a good deal of suspicion, I suppose that this is hardly a bad thing.

The Remarkably Bad Theology
of *The Adjustment Bureau*

THE ADJUSTMENT BUREAU IS ONE of the most explicitly theological films of the last twenty-five years. The only problem is that it proposes an extraordinarily bad theology. It tells the story of David Morris (played convincingly by Matt Damon), an up-and-coming American politician. Morris has just lost a Senate election, but he has met Elise, a woman for whom he feels an immediate and overwhelming attraction. She gives him her phone number and David, despite his electoral defeat, is enthused about pursuing this new relationship.

Then the strangest thing happens. As he arrives at work, David notices that everyone in the office is frozen in place, and mysterious men in fedoras are fussing with the head of one of his co-workers. Horrified, he tries to call 911, but instead he is chased by the invaders and hustled out of the office into a cavernous warehouse, where a number of agents are urgently discussing his "case." It's at this point that he (and we) discover what's going on.

David, like everyone else, is part of a great master plan, managed by a shadowy figure called "the Chairman" (clearly God), and his relationship with Elise runs dramatically counter to the Chairman's intention. The men in fedoras aren't ordinary human beings, but something like angels, and their purpose is to correct glitches in The Plan caused by chance or by stubborn free will. The bizarre invasion of the office and David's kidnapping are part of this "adjustment." Firmly, the agents inform David that they will prevent him from establishing a relationship with Elise and that he must never tell anyone what he knows, lest they be obliged to erase his memory and identity.

So the central conflict of the film is established as a struggle between divinely-imposed fate and individual human freedom. Do we in twenty-first-century America really have any doubt which of these will win? Despite what he knows and despite the herculean efforts of numerous agents, David does manage to run into Elise and to foster a romantic friendship with her. At this point, a particularly powerful agent named Thompson (played by the English character actor Terence Stamp) comes on the scene. He kidnaps David and tells him why he mustn't see Elise. According to The Plan, David is meant to become President of the United States, and Elise a world-famous dancer; but if they stay together, neither of these destinies will be fulfilled.

Enough of the plot. Suffice it to say that both David and Elise in the end decide to resist The Plan, outfox its numerous enforcers, and pursue their relationship with full romantic abandon.

The film presents two things that we human beings desperately want: personal freedom and a Plan. We want, of course, to be free. Liberty is the supreme value in most Western societies. At the same time, most of us want things to make sense. We don't want the world to be simply a jumble of chance occurrences, coincidences, and meaningless pursuits. We savor the idea of a Grand Plan. But the simultaneous realization of these two desires is, it seems, impossible; for Fate and Freedom, we tell ourselves, are mutually exclusive.

This is why *The Adjustment Bureau* is informed by a bad theology. In the modern telling, evident in thinkers from William of Ockham to Jean-Paul Sartre, God's supremacy looms over and against a self-assertive human freedom. The two wills—human and divine—are locked in a desperate zero-sum game, whereby the more the divine will advances, the further the human will has to retreat.

It's The Plan—overwhelming, powerful, strictly enforced—against scrappy, determined human liberty.

But none of this has a thing to do with classical Christian theology. One of the most basic truths that flow from the Incarnation is that divinity and humanity are not competitors. Jesus is not somehow less human because he is also divine. On the contrary, his divinity raises, perfects, and enhances his humanity. Therefore, God's freedom does not suppress human freedom, but rather enables and awakens it. Liberty is not repugnant to The Plan; it is ingredient in it.

Let me try to make this clear through a simple example. A good piano instructor lays out a plan for her charges. In the course of many years, she takes them through a whole series of exercises and practice sessions. She introduces them to relatively simple pieces of music and then, gradually, to Chopin, Mozart, and Beethoven. She invites them to play ragtime and boogie-woogie. She might finally demonstrate the process of composition and encourage them to write their own music. All this time, she is awakening and informing their freedom, pointing it toward the good, giving it purpose. Her ultimate goal—again, if she is a good teacher—is to establish perfect liberty in her students, that is to say, the capacity to play whatever they want. It's not The Plan vs. freedom; it's The Plan undergirding freedom. God, whose glory is that we be fully alive, is something like that piano teacher.

What he is decidedly not like is the shadowy "Chairman" of this film. God is the great Will, which is nothing but love. Hence his Plan doesn't compete with human freedom, but rather guides and fulfills it. Toward the conclusion of his great *Divine Comedy*, Dante wrote a line that is repugnant to the theology of *The Adjustment Bureau* but is perfectly congruent with classical Incarnational theology: "In your will, O Lord, is our peace."

Of Gods and Men

Of Gods and Men, one of the most compelling religious films of the past thirty years, tells the story of the Trappists of Tibhirine, seven brave men who were murdered by Islamist extremists in 1996. Though this fact is not well known, the twentieth century produced more Christian martyrs than all of the preceding nineteen centuries combined. The monks who are the subjects of this film were among the last to die for the faith in that terrible hundred-year period.

These Trappists were transplanted Frenchmen who had established themselves in a very simple monastery nestled in the Atlas Mountains of Algeria. They worked almost exclusively among Muslims, who inhabited the tiny towns and villages nearby. One of their number was a doctor, who provided basic medical care for hundreds of poor, and their abbot was a decent and intelligent man, who in his spare time studied the Qur'an so as better to understand the people whom he served and for whom he prayed. Their prayer life of the monks—which the movie conveys very effectively—was spare and beautiful, grounded in the rhythms of the Psalms.

The drama of the film centers around the growing influence of radical Islam in the vicinity of the monastery. Tales are heard of threats and murders, and then the violence comes close to home as a group of Croatians are found just outside the village with their throats slit. On Christmas Eve, gunmen break into the Trappist monastery and demand to see the abbot. Coolly, he reminds them that no guns are allowed in a place of peace and that the militants are interrupting the celebration of the birth of the prophet Issa (Jesus), who is, of course, reverenced by Muslims. Impressed by the monk's courage, and more than a little embarrassed, the armed men slink away. But the Trappists know that it is only a matter a time before more dangerous extremists will be back.

Accordingly, they commence to debate whether they should stay, return to France, or perhaps relocate to another monastic enclosure in a safer sector of Algeria. From the first, the abbot is adamant that, in accord with their vows of stability and out of love for the people they serve, they should remain. But a few of his brothers sharply disagree, arguing that remaining would be tantamount to suicide. Some of the most affecting scenes in the film are the depictions of the intense, honest, and deeply respectful manner in which these Christian men deliberate this very serious matter. In time, all of the brothers come around to the abbot's point of view and resolve to stay, despite the danger. Luc, the doctor monk played by the wonderful French character actor Michael Lonsdale, beautifully expresses his conviction that he is a free man, since he is willing to endure life or death, ease or hardship, according to God's plan. Just after we hear of the monks' collective resolve, the filmmaker gives us an image, at once weird and spiritually powerful, of Luc tenderly caressing a painting of the crucified Jesus: a free man acknowledging the source of his freedom.

As the Trappists feared, gunmen return. Islamist militants roughly drag the monks from their in beds in the middle of the night and load them onto a truck. They then drive them deep into the wilderness and, on a snowy morning, force-march them into the woods. The final scene of the film is the snowy atmosphere gradually closing around the freezing men as they walk toward the forest. Though this is not depicted in the movie, the Trappists of Tibhirine were put to death, and their headless bodies were later discovered.

Of Gods and Men is a quiet story of great courage and spiritual strength, but it is also a film with an edge—and this becomes clear when we meditate upon its title, taken from Psalm 82: "I said: You are gods, all of you sons of the Most High; Yet like men you shall die, and fall like any prince." This particular psalm represents the sovereign God's judgment of false gods, those who have been mistakenly considered absolute. Yahweh states that these "gods" have failed in their task of assuring justice on the earth, that they have not defended "the lowly and the fatherless" or rendered "justice to the afflicted and the destitute." Who precisely are these "gods"? Within the Biblical framework, they are construed as supernatural beings, but we could also think of them as those political and military "powers and principalities" that make bold to govern the world in any age, usually through threats of violence. Up and down the ages, bully boys with swords or bombs or guns have acted as "gods," exercising their power but doing precious little to ameliorate the human condition. The sovereign God, the true God, passes judgment on these pretenders to ultimacy and announces that they will "fall like any prince."

Though by all appearances the gunmen of Algeria defeated the simple Trappists of Tibhirine, those monks, through their spiritual freedom, became the instruments of God's judgment over all wicked men who act like gods.

Rise of the Planet of the Apes and the Dangers of Consequentialism

THE POPULAR FILM *Rise of the Planet of the Apes* belongs to a genre that goes back at least to Mary Shelley's nineteenth-century masterpiece *Frankenstein*, for it tells the story of a well-intentioned scientist who, through ignoring legitimate moral limits, courts disaster.

James Franco plays a San Franciscan DNA researcher named Will Rodman who is specializing in the treatment of brain disorders, especially Alzheimer's disease. Under the sponsorship of a large pharmaceutical company, he is conducting experiments on apes and chimpanzees in order to see whether he can increase their intelligence through the introduction of a retrovirus. When one of the chimps gives birth, Rodman takes the infant ape home to raise him and monitor his development. From the start, he is stunned by the young chimp's mental acuity and rapid progress. By the time he is three years old, the simian—whom he has named Caesar—has outstripped most of his human counterparts in intelligence, problem-solving, and communication.

As we follow Caesar's progress, we also learn why Will is so interested in Alzheimer's research: his father, Charles, played by John Lithgow, is suffering from the disease. His father's situation becomes so dire that Rodman resolves to steal some of the experimental drug that was used on Caesar's mother and to try it on his own poor father. The results are staggering. The morning after being injected with the substance, Charles springs to life, becomes alert to his surroundings, and even resumes his energetic playing of classical piano. But in short order, Charles's Alzheimer's reasserts itself as his immune system fights off the retrovirus, and his condition rapidly deteriorates. Undaunted, Will begins to experiment on an even more powerful form of the virus, which does indeed dramatically enhance the intelligence of apes but which proves fatal to humans who are exposed to it.

All this time, Caesar, his intelligence deepening and his self-confidence increasing, begins to chafe at being cooped up in the house and treated, more or less, as a pet. When Charles is mistreated by a neighbor, Caesar bursts from the house and brutally attacks the aggressor, compelling Will to remit the clever chimp to a state facility, where Caesar simmers with resentment and manages to organize the other apes into an effective fighting force. I won't go much further into the details of the plot. Suffice it to say that the intelligent apes, led by Caesar, break free from their bondage and commence to wreak havoc in the city of San Francisco, even as the human population begins to succumb to the ill effects of the retrovirus.

Now this film is certainly a well-made sci-fi thriller, but it's more than that, for as I suggested above, it speaks to some hard truths about science and about the all too human tendency to indulge in consequentialist moral reasoning. No serious person doubts that the sciences have proven themselves an enormous boon to the human race, but when they are untethered from moral restrictions, the sciences can indeed become dysfunctional, even disastrously so. For example, despite the protests of many ethicists at the time, and even of some of the scientists involved, the Manhattan Project researchers went ahead with the development of a weapon that they knew would certainly result in the deaths of countless noncombatants—and the world has been haunted ever since by what they produced. Today, many in the scientific community are clamoring for the right to do embryonic stem cell research in order to effect cures to many of the most devastating medical conditions, including Alzheimer's disease. (Here the link to *Rise of the Planet of the Apes* seems far from accidental). In both cases, well-intentioned people tried (and are trying) to address very real evils, but they used (and are attempting to use) means that are morally problematic, namely, the direct killing of the innocent.

The temptation toward consequentialist or "end justifies the means" moral reasoning is always a powerful one—and it is on clear display in *The Rise of the Planet of the Apes*. Will wants desperately to help his father and the millions of others who suffer from a terrible disease, and he opts therefore to use highly questionable means to achieve his end, resulting in chaos. I can't help but think that the scriptwriters were intentional in their naming of the central character in the film, for he is, above all, a man of will, indeed good will, but determined to do whatever it takes to achieve his end.

The Church Fathers read the great permission that God gives to Adam and Eve in the Garden—"eat from all the trees of the Garden"—as the ground of Christian humanism. God wants his human creatures to flourish in every arena: politics, sports, philosophy, culture, science. But they read the great prohibition—"from the tree of the knowledge of good and evil you shall not eat"—as an insistence upon the moral strictures that must surround and condition any human endeavor. When that prohibition was ignored, the Bible teaches, the human project foundered, for no human being can, with impunity, arrogate to himself the prerogative of transgressing moral limits. In its own way, and within the context of its own peculiar story, *The Rise of the Planet of the Apes* is making much the same point.

Moneyball and
Spiritual Leadership

THE MANAGEMENT OF THE 2002 OAKLAND ATHLETICS found itself in a bind. The team had performed very well the previous year, making it to the playoffs, but in the offseason, three of its best players were lured away by lucrative contracts offered by East coast powerhouses. In a relatively small market and with a very limited budget, the A's had to find a way to compete. Their general manager, former big-leaguer Billy Beane, stumbled upon a revolutionary strategy to make the Athletics winners while remaining within their means. It doesn't sound exactly like the kind of storyline that Hollywood would embrace with enthusiasm, but it provides the foundation for a terrific film called *Moneyball*, starring Brad Pitt as the visionary general manager. *Moneyball* is not only a great baseball film; it is also a compelling exploration of the dynamics of leadership and the psychology of success. And as such, it is a movie that teaches a great deal about the spiritual life.

Beane's breakthrough occurred through the ministrations of a young, untested, Yale-trained junior executive named Peter Brand (played by Jonah Hill). Setting aside the assumptions that had, for decades, determined the way baseball talent was assessed, Brand asked a pair of elemental questions: what wins games? Answer: scoring runs. And what makes scoring runs possible? Answer: getting on base. Therefore, he concluded, if you want to win games, you have to acquire players who have a knack for getting on base, through hits, walks, getting struck with the ball, etc. He had developed a metric for determining precisely who had that ability—and found that, more often than not, baseball executives and scouts overlooked or undervalued those very players.

Inspired by Brand's vision, and armed with his statistics, Beane assembled his scouts for a meeting regarding the acquisition of players for the upcoming year. Over and again, the grizzled and experienced baseball men spoke of the "look" or the "body" of a player, the way the ball "jumped off the bat" of one prospect, the "confidence" of another. Exasperated, Beane shouted, "But do they get on base?!" He was implying that a great-looking, athletic, skillful player might not actually be the kind of player that wins games. He wanted his scouts, who were beguiled by the romance of the game, to share his own clarity of vision in regard to their ultimate purpose. Needless to say, the old veterans didn't jump right on board. Neither did the manager; neither did the sports writers; neither did the fans. And when Beane's team, assembled according to Brand's calculations, started the season slowly, the critics came out in force, accusing the general manager of arrogantly standing athwart years of baseball common sense. But Beane stuck to his guns, and the team of "misfit toys" began to gel, and then to excel, and finally to produce the longest winning streak in American League history.

The single most important quality of a leader is clarity of vision, and his second most important quality is a willingness to do what he has to do in order to realize that vision. Abraham Lincoln, for instance, was no great economist. He did not have extensive experience in government, nor was he a particularly skilled legislator. But at the most dire moment in American history, he saw with crystal clarity what the country needed, and he had the intestinal fortitude to make it happen. "If I can save the Union by freeing some of the slaves, I will do it; if I can save the Union by freeing none of the slaves, I will do it; if I can save the Union by freeing all of the slaves, I will do it," he famously said. Then, in the course of the war, despite choruses of criticism, he fired and hired a whole bevy of generals until he found the man he needed. When people complained about the drunken General Ulysses Grant, Lincoln said, "I can't spare this man; he fights," and then, playfully, "Send a case of Grant's whiskey to all my other commanders." The President knew that he had to win the Civil War and that in order to win the Civil War he needed a general who would bring the battle to the enemy.

In the Gospel of John, Jesus turns on two young men who are following him and asks, "What do you want?" It's an indispensably important question. Many people go through life not really knowing what they most fundamentally want, and accordingly, they drift. The correct answer to Jesus' question is "eternal life" or "friendship with God" or "holiness." This corresponds to Billy Beane's "scoring runs" or Lincoln's "winning the Civil War," for it is the simple, clear, unambiguous articulation of The Goal that any believer should have as he endeavors to "lead his life." Now other people may know, more or less, what they want spiritually, but they lack the courage and attention to pursue that end in the face of distractions and opposition. They know that they should be growing in holiness, but the secular culture proposes sex, pleasure, power, and honor so attractively that they lose their way. Or perhaps they receive withering criticism from those who are stuck in the old, standard way of life, and they give in.

What is true at the personal level obtains at the institutional level as well. How many Catholic dioceses can clearly state their objective, what it is, precisely, that they are trying to accomplish through all of their programs and activities? How many bishops can see past old patterns and tired strategies that are no longer serving the purpose of making people holy? How many can resist (or dismantle) bureaucracies whose *raison d'etre* is self-preservation rather than the proclamation of the Gospel?

Moneyball is a portrait of leadership in the world of baseball. But its lessons apply to any seeker on the spiritual path.

The Ides of March and
the Danger of Idolatry

GEORGE CLOONEY'S TAUT POLITICAL THRILLER *The Ides of March* commences with a beautiful depiction of the act of idolatry, and everything else in the film flows, by a strict logic, from that act. At the prompting of his gifted and hyper-focused press aid Stephen Myers (played by Ryan Gosling), Governor Mike Morris (played by Clooney himself), a Democratic candidate for President, responds at a televised debate to a question dealing with his religion. "I was raised a Catholic," he calmly explains, "but I'm no longer a practicing Catholic. I'm not a Protestant, a Jew, a Muslim, or an atheist. My religion, what I believe in, is the Constitution of the United States." At this point, his audience enthusiastically applauds. Now one can love the Constitution; one can defend it and admire it. But to believe in it is to commit what the Bible calls idolatry, for it is to make something less than God into God, which is to say, into one's ultimate concern, one's central preoccupation. The wager of the Scriptures is that right worship, which is to say, the worship of God alone, conduces toward the right ordering of the worshipper. Once a person's central focus is clear, then all of the secondary desires and longings of his soul will find their proper orientation and integration. Concomitantly, when a person's worship is misguided, when it is centered on anything other than the true God, that person falls apart; he disintegrates, his secondary desires devolving into a jumble of warring impulses.

More to the point, the Bible shows over and again that a community marked by idolatry crumbles apart and tumbles into violence.

The Ides of March is a brilliant depiction of the effects of idolatry at both the personal and collective levels. All of the major figures in the film center around Mike Morris and hence are marked by his false worship—and not one of them is happy. All of them are driven, many of them are smart, most are politically canny and energetic, but they never seem to find any joy in what they're doing. And their relations to one another are nothing but cold, brutal, and calculating. The plot of the film is driven by the machinations of Tom Duffy (played by the wonderful character actor Paul Giamatti), the manager of the rival Presidential campaign, who, it appears, is trying to lure Stephen into his camp. In fact, he is trying simply to take a gifted opponent out of the game. In the wake of their meeting, Duffy leaks the news of their encounter to the always-hungry press, which leads Stephen to lose his job due to disloyalty. When the younger man comes back to Duffy, expecting to be welcomed with open arms, he is tossed aside—just one more victim of hardball politics.

In the meantime, Stephen has been consorting with a young intern on Morris's staff (played by Evan Rachel Wood), a girl eager to get what she wants both sexually and professionally. After one of their late-night encounters, the girl's cell phone rings and Stephen picks it up and realizes, to his dismay, that the caller on the other end is Morris himself. His jealousy is eclipsed by his concern that the governor has put himself in a precarious position politically. And his concern develops into panic when he learns that the young intern is pregnant with Morris's child. Oblivious to the woman's feelings and never even bothering to tell the governor, Stephen spirits her off to an abortion clinic and instructs her to take care of the mess as quickly as possible. Afterward, ashamed of what she had done and frightened that the story will leak out, the intern commits suicide. When Stephen learns that he has been fired, he turns on Morris with a vengeance, threatening to reveal the sordid details of his affair with an underage girl. Realizing he is cornered, the governor fires his devoted campaign manager and replaces him with Stephen.

What we witness, in short, is a sordid series of betrayals and manipulations, all in service of political success. It is no accident that the film is entitled *The Ides of March*, recalling the day when Caesar was stabbed to death by his erstwhile colleagues, for practically every major character stabs every other major character in the back at some point in the course of this movie. What I would urge you to see is that this is not simply a depiction of political corruption and moral turpitude; it is a story of the spiritual corruption that sets in when something less than God is put in the place of God. When people believe in the Constitution or in success or in a political personality, they necessarily lose their spiritual and ethical center, and this means that, at the end of the day, any kind of morally outrageous behavior becomes possible. Notice how relentless the Bible is on this score. When people are tempted to idolize kings or the Israelite empire, the Bible gives us David the adulterer and murderer, Solomon the apostate, and a whole line of hopelessly corrupt leaders. When people are tempted to idolize their families, Jesus says, "Unless you love me more than your mother and father, more than your very life, you are not worthy of me." (Lk 14:26) The Old Testament authors have nothing against kings in themselves, and Jesus has nothing against the family in itself, but when kings or families become one's ultimate concern, trouble will follow as night follows day. *The Ides of March* tells that truth with extraordinary clarity and power.

The Hunger Games: A Prophecy?

WHEN I WAS A JUNIOR IN HIGH SCHOOL, I read Shirley Jackson's great short story "The Lottery," and I will confess that her narrative still haunts me. You might remember the plot. The townspeople of a village in the American heartland are gathering on a beautiful summer day in late June for a festival. There is good food, lively conversation, and upbeat music. It becomes clear that the focus for this celebration is the annual lottery, and the reader naturally assumes that the winner of the lottery will receive a prize of some kind. But when the choice is made, the "winner" shrinks away in fear, protesting the injustice of it all, while her fellow citizens close in on her, rocks and stones in hand. As the story ends, they are upon her.

In ancient Mexico, the Aztecs would choose a particularly handsome and brave warrior from a rival tribe. For a year, they would wine and dine him, provide entertainment for him, and treat him like a celebrity. Then, at the close of the year, they would lead him to the top of a tall pyramid and rip his still-beating heart from his chest, and offer it to the gods.

In the arenas of ancient Rome—most famously in the Colosseum—young gladiators would engage in mortal combat for the entertainment of bloodthirsty mobs, and emperors would use these spectacles for cynical political purposes.

In the mythological story of Theseus and the Minotaur, we hear that the king of Crete obligated the king of Athens every year to send seven young men and seven young women to battle the

Minotaur, who was hidden in a devilishly complex maze. No one survived the ordeal, until Theseus managed to outwit the monster and escape from the maze.

All of these examples—both fictional and non-fictional—of human sacrifice swirled through my head as I watched the much-anticipated film *The Hunger Games*, based on the wildly popular series of novels. As in Jackson's story, a lottery results in the choice of sacrificial victims from each "district" of a post-apocalyptic North American nation state. These teenagers are then taken to the capital city and, like the Aztec prisoners, they are pampered, made up, and treated as celebrities for an extended period. Next, they are compelled to engage in mortal combat, so that, of the twenty-four participants, only one will survive. Like the Roman crowds of old, the people of the nation watch this process unfold and find it deeply entertaining, while the leadership manipulates the games (and the people's feelings) for their own political ends. Finally, two of the participants in the Hunger Games (after the rules are adjusted) play the role of Theseus and manage to survive their ordeal, promptly calling into question the games themselves.

The really interesting question is: why has this motif of the sacrificial victim played such a large role in the human imagination for so long? Why do we keep acting out this scenario, both in reality and in our literature? The contemporary literary theorist René Girard has speculated that practically every human community is grounded in what he calls "the scapegoating mechanism." This is the process by which we discharge our societal tensions onto a victim whom we have decided, collectively, to punish. In this, we effectively (at least for a time) manage to bring some peace and stability to our always volatile communities—which goes a long way toward explaining why the scapegoating dynamic is so popular with governments and why it is usually given a quasi-religious sanction. If you doubt Girard on this score, I would invite you to take a good, long look at what Hitler accomplished through his scapegoating of Jews—and at what most of us accomplish through gossip and backstabbing. As the Mundelein colleague I quoted earlier put it: "Wherever two or three are gathered, look for victims."

Girard discovered something else, which, despite his Catholic upbringing, took him quite by surprise. He found that Christianity was the one religion, philosophy, or ideology that both unmasked this scapegoating mechanism and showed a way out. For at the heart of Christian revelation is God's utter identification, not with the perpetrators of violence, but with the scapegoated victim. The crucified Jesus is hence the undermining of the dynamic that has undergirded most civilizations and that continues to beguile the human imagination to this day. If we find stories like "The Lottery" and *The Hunger Games* disturbing, it is due to our at least implicit Christian formation. Human sacrifice flourished in the midst of some of the most sophisticated and intellectually advanced civilizations in history. It is demonstrably the case, and not just a matter of speculation, that what brought these sacrifices to an end in both the Roman and Aztec contexts was nothing other than the influence of Christianity, the religion centered on a crucified Lord.

What haunted me as I watched *The Hunger Games* was that the instinct for human sacrifice is never far from the surface and that it could easily exist alongside of tremendous cultural and technological sophistication. That makes this film disturbingly prophetic. We might comfort ourselves with the thought that such things could never happen here, but as we in the West enter increasingly into a secular, post-Christian cultural space, we place ourselves in danger of reverting to wicked forms of behavior and social organization.

Viva El Cristo Rey!

THE FEATURE FILM *FOR GREATER GLORY* tells the story of the Mexican Cristero war, which broke out in the 1920s when the secularist government, under the leadership of President Plutarco Elias Calles, decided to enforce the strict anti-clerical laws embedded in the Mexican constitution of 1917. All religious ceremonies—Masses, baptisms, confirmations, weddings, etc.—were banned; bishops were forced to leave the country, and priests were forbidden to wear clerical garb in public. Priests who resisted were imprisoned, tortured, and, in some cases, killed outright. One of the most affecting scenes in the film is the execution of Padre Christopher, an old priest played by the great Peter O'Toole. As the *federales* arrived in his small town, the priest refused to hide or flee. Instead, he sat quietly in his church, robed in Mass vestments, and accepted his fate as an act of witness. Others also resolved to resist through nonviolent means, most notably Anacleto Gonzalez Flores (played by Eduardo Verastegui), a magazine editor and activist, who rallied Mexican youth through his speeches and writings.

But given the intensity and violence of the attack on Catholicism—which Graham Greene called the most thorough persecution of a religion since the time of Elizabeth I—it was practically inevitable that an armed resistance would emerge. The bulk of *For Greater Glory* concerns this Cristero rebellion, which began with small and disorganized bands of guerrilla fighters, but grew, under the leadership of General Enrique Gorostieta (Andy Garcia), into an efficient military operation. The emotional heart of the film is the relationship between the general and a twelve-year-old boy named José, who had been a friend of Padre Christopher and witnessed the priest's murder. Despite his youth, José joined the Cristero army, serving as standard-bearer and aide-de-camp to Gorostieta. In the course of a particularly brutal battle, José was captured by the *federales*, who then tortured him mercilessly, hoping to compel him to renounce the ideals of the Cristeros and accept the decisions of the government. Even in the face of this horrendous attack, José refused to give in, stubbornly repeating the motto of the resistance: *Viva el Cristo Rey!* (Long live Christ the King!).

I won't give away any more of the story, but I would like to reflect on that motto, which is heard throughout the film on the lips of dozens of characters. *Viva el Cristo Rey!* is the hinge on which this entire Cristero episode turns and is, indeed, the central teaching of the New Testament. The great Scripture scholar N.T. Wright has argued that the four Gospels are fundamentally the story of how Yahweh, the God of Israel, through the life, death, and resurrection of Jesus of Nazareth, established himself as king. On the Biblical reading, the world had long been governed by various "kings" who ruled through violence and cruelty: Pharaoh, the Amalekites, the Philistines, the Assyrians, the Babylonians, the Greeks, and the Romans. But Yahweh had promised that one day, through his anointed servant, he would deal with these tyrants, and would himself come to shepherd and to reign. It is of enormous significance that when Jesus first appeared as a preacher in the hills of Galilee, his theme was "the kingdom of God is at hand!" In other words, in his own person an entirely new way of ordering things is on offer. Then—in his love and nonviolence, in his open-table fellowship, in his outreach to prostitutes and tax collectors, in his mocking of the Pharisees and religious establishment, in his healing and teaching—Jesus was demonstrating precisely what the reign of the God of Israel looks like.

This way of life inevitably awakened the opposition of the powers that be. At the climax of his ministry, Jesus faced down the resistance of "the world," to use the typical New Testament term, meaning that whole congeries of cruelty, betrayal, denial, violence, corruption, and hatred by which human affairs are typically ordered. He permitted all of that darkness to wash over him, to crush him, to snuff him out. But then, on the third day, he rose again from the dead in the power of the Holy Spirit, and thereby outflanked, outmaneuvered, and swallowed up the darkness. In a delicious irony, it was Pontius Pilate who anticipated the significance of this victory: over the cross of Jesus, the Roman governor had placed a sign, written in the three great languages of that time and place, which read "Jesus of Nazareth, King of the Jews."

In the light of the Resurrection, the first Christians knew that, in Jesus, the God of Israel had become king, and that the world was now under new management. They saw their mission as the declaration of that kingship to everyone. This did not imply at all that they were advocating "theocracy" in the crude sense. (Indeed, both Peter and Paul urge their readers to show deference to the properly instituted Roman authority.) But they were insisting that Jesus is the one to whom final allegiance is due, and that he is more powerful than any of the "kings"—political, economic, military, or cultural— who tend to dominate human affairs. They reveled in the fact that Jesus' kingly power was exercised, not through violence and domination, but through the nonviolence of the cross. They gladly announced to anyone who would listen that the true king wore a crown of thorns, and reigned from a throne that was a Roman instrument of torture.

At the very close of *For Greater Glory*, we see a listing of those figures from the film that the Catholic Church beatified or canonized as saints. Without exception, they were those who chose the path of nonviolent resistance. As I said, I certainly understand why an armed rebellion sprang up in the Mexico of that time, and I wouldn't dream of questioning the motives of those who participated in it. But I would indeed say that those who advocate the kingship of Jesus should fight the way he did: invading the darkness by light, swallowing up hatred through love.

Viva el Cristo Rey!

Spider-Man, Iron Man, Superman, and the God-Man

THIS PAST DECADE HAS SEEN A PLETHORA of movies dealing with superheroes: the Batman films, *The Green Lantern, Iron Man, The Incredible Hulk, Thor*, etc. But the most popular—at least judging by box office receipts—has been the Spider-Man franchise. Since 2002, there have been five major movie adaptations of the Marvel Comics story of a kid who gets bitten by a spider, undergoes a stunning metamorphosis, and then "catches thieves just like flies."

What is it about these stories—and the Spider-Man tale in particular—that fascinate us? I suggest that it has something to do with Christianity, more precisely, with the strange hybrid figure around which all of the Christian religion revolves.

St. Athanasius's most significant contribution to the Christological debates of the early centuries of the Church's life was a soteriological argument for the dual nature of Jesus. In the saint's pithy formula: only a human being could save us; and only God could save us. If Jesus were only divine—as the Monophysites argued—then his saving power wouldn't be truly applied to us. If he were only human—as the Arians and Nestorians argued—then he could not really lift us out of the morass of sin and guilt in which we find ourselves mired. In a word, salvation was possible only through a God-man, someone in the world but not of it, someone like us in all things but sin, and at the same time utterly unlike us.

I can't help but hear an echo of the ancient Christological doctrine in the latest films featuring Batman, Superman, and Spider-Man. All three of these superheroes are hybrids—combinations of the extraordinary and the ordinary. In all three cases we have someone who, in his lowliness, is able completely to identify and sympathize with our suffering and, in his transcendence, is able to do something about it. A particular charm of *The Amazing Spider-Man* is that Andrew Garfield, the actor who plays Peter Parker, is quite obviously an ordinary and even geeky kid who at decisive moments gracefully demonstrates godlike powers.

Another obliquely Christological feature of the new Spider-Man film—and in some of the other superhero movies as well—is the motif of mission and vocation. Once aware that he is in full possession of stunning physical capabilities, Peter mercilessly taunts an obnoxious classmate, who had, sometime before, humiliated him. His Uncle Ben, skillfully underplayed by the always-watchable Martin Sheen, quickly upbraids the young man for indulging a crude desire for revenge. Precisely how he should use the gifts he has discovered emerges as perhaps the central theme of the movie. Should he use them as the means to aggrandize his ego and settle old scores? Or should he make them ingredient in a program of protection and service—a program of love?

Both Matthew and Luke portray Jesus, at the beginning of his public career, wrestling with a similar question, namely the meaning and implication of his Messiahship. He indeed knew himself to be the beloved son of his heavenly Father, but what did this identity entail? The classical interpretation of these accounts of Jesus' time in the desert is that the Lord confronted and finally resisted the temptation to use his Messianic authority for the acquisition of sensual pleasure, for the puffing up of his ego, and for power. It is the conviction of the Church that every baptized and confirmed person has been equipped with gifts from the Holy Spirit, which are participations in the identity of Christ Jesus. The whole drama of an individual's life hinges on the decision concerning the use of those gifts. As Peter Parker's literature professor puts it toward the end of the film, "There is finally only one plot line to every story ever written, namely, who am I?"

A third theological theme in *The Amazing Spider-Man*—and in the Batman movies, *Iron Man*, and *The Avengers* as well—is that of knowledge and the abuse of knowledge. When the Spider-Man comics were written in the 1950s, during the Cold War, there was a great deal of concern in the general culture about the way science was being used for less than constructive purposes. In the current film, Peter Parker's father, as well as his colleague, Dr. Connors, are endeavoring through biological research to perfect the technique of mixing species in order to address a variety of human ailments and deformities. Their motives might have been laudable, but their hubris was unconstrained, and the results of their overreaching proved a disaster.

The biblical story of original sin centers on an act of grasping at knowledge. This is not tantamount to a disavowal of knowledge as such, but it is indeed a warning that the use of knowledge as a means of achieving godlike control over nature is nefarious. The conceit that we can eliminate all suffering—physical, political, psychological—through the exercise of reason has invariably resulted in an increase in suffering, as the secularist ideologies of the last century amply prove. Though Jesus certainly cured some people, the heart of his salvific work was not the total eradication of human pain but precisely his own embrace of it. This indispensable Christ move, I would argue, is present in almost all of the superhero movies to which I alluded above.

The Amazing Spider-Man and its cinematic cousins might appear to be just summer popcorn movies, but upon closer examination it appears that they carry a considerable amount of theological weight.

Still Another Cinematic Christ

IN ONE WAY OR ANOTHER, all religions deal with the problem of evil; both how to explain it and how to solve it. Buddhism, for example, teaches that all life is suffering and that the only way out is through the extinction of egotistic desire, that "blowing out of the candle" designated by the Sanskrit word *nirvana*. All of Buddhist practice, theory and doctrine are devoted to the attainment of this blissful state. Manichaeism and Gnosticism—ancient theories still very much alive today—teach that evil is a powerful force that does battle with good down through the ages. Usually, but not always, Gnostics tend to identify the good principle with the spiritual and the evil principle with matter. A variant on the Manichaean philosophy is represented in the Star Wars films, which feature an ongoing struggle between the dark and light sides of the Force. Judaism understands evil as the result of a departure from God's command and tends to see the solution, therefore, as a more faithful following of the divine law.

All four of these approaches are operative in our culture, though often in disguised form. But the most dominant is still, despite the increasing secularism of our time, the Christian proposal, namely, that the problem of evil is solved only through an act of self-emptying love on the part of a savior. The Gospels are certainly interested in the teachings of Jesus, but they are primarily concerned with the strange act that took place at the end of his life; a sacrifice by which the sins of the world were taken away. Throughout his public career, Jesus provoked opposition, for his words and deeds put him at odds with the standard manner of thinking and acting. This opposition came to a climax when Jesus, around the year 30, entered the Holy City of Jerusalem for the Passover celebration. Betrayal, denial, stupidity, violence, cruelty, institutional injustice, and just plain hatred massively came at him. Read the still compelling Passion Narratives in any of the Gospels for the details. The culmination of this assault was his execution at the hands of the Roman occupying power. They nailed him to a cross, employing a peculiarly brutal method of torture that the Romans had perfected. In the face of all of this punishing darkness, Jesus said, "Father, forgive them, for they know not what they do." Like an animal offered in the Temple, Jesus took upon himself the sins and dysfunction of others, and by his self-emptying love, took them away. The efficacy of this move was ratified three days later when the now-risen Jesus, still bearing his wounds, said to his frightened and guilt-ridden disciples, "Shalom" (Peace). What the first Christians felt—and you can sense it on practically every page of the New Testament—is that Jesus, through that terrible cross, had deflected evil from them, suffered so that they wouldn't have to suffer.

I went into this in some detail in order to make explicit what is so often implicit in the popular culture, especially in the West. Consciously or not, the archetype of Christ the Savior still haunts the imaginations of our writers, critics, philosophers, and especially our filmmakers. One instance of this is the Batman movie *The Dark Knight Rises*.

As this third film in the Batman trilogy opens, we find Bruce Wayne a broken man, both physically and psychologically, still bearing the terrible wounds of his struggle with evil some eight years before. After initial hesitation, he resolves to don his Batsuit and re-enter the lists, since a new and especially menacing figure, Bane, has emerged to threaten Wayne's beloved Gotham City. A graduate of the same quasi-monastic school of fighters that had shaped the Dark Knight, Bane is not only physically overpowering but also morally bankrupt, and he will stop at nothing to achieve his destructive ends. Having been facially disfigured as a young man, he also sports a mechanized mouthpiece that makes him sound like a combination of Darth Vader and Sean Connery. In a word, he is a particularly effective symbol of the evil that darkens the human heart. As the culmination of his assault on Gotham City, Bane has arranged for the detonation of a neutron bomb. Much of the drama of the second half of the film is generated by Batman's race against time to deal with both Bane and his bomb.

At this juncture, I have to issue a spoiler alert. To make my point, I have to give away the end of the movie. Things are so desperate that the only way for the city to be saved is for Batman to use his specialized plane to tow the nuclear device out to sea. Since there is no autopilot on the vehicle, Batman will have to sacrifice himself in order to protect Gotham. Only an act of love, even love unto death, will avert cataclysmic suffering, and Batman is willing to perform that act.

The solution to suffering proposed by this film is not a shift in consciousness, not the extinction of desire, not the correct following of the law, and not a direct confrontation with evil. It is, instead, a heroic act of love on the part of a savior willing to take upon himself the dysfunction that he fights. And this makes Batman, unavoidably, an icon of Christ.

Woody Allen, Moralist

WHO WOULD HAVE THOUGHT THAT WOODY ALLEN, who not long ago was separating from his longtime girlfriend to notoriously marry her adopted daughter, would emerge as a defender of what can only be called traditional morality? And yet, I find that conclusion unavoidable after viewing the writer-director's offering *To Rome with Love*. This film, one in a series of Woody Allen movies that includes *Match Point*, *Vicky Christina Barcelona*, and *Midnight in Paris*, each celebrating great European cities, shares with the last of those three a certain whimsical surrealism.

To Rome with Love presents a number of storylines, none of which interweave at the narrative level, but all of which share a thematic motif, namely, the need to resist those things that would tempt us away from real love. The funniest and most bizarre of Allen's tales has to do with a very ordinary man, Leopoldo, played by the wonderful Italian character actor Roberto Benigni, who one day inexplicably finds himself the center of intense media attention. As he makes his way to his car, Leopoldo is mobbed by photographers and reporters peppering him with questions about his breakfast preferences and his favorite shaving cream. Everywhere he goes, he is recognized and lionized. Women suddenly appear, offering themselves for his sexual gratification. When he asks one of his colleagues why this is happening, the answer comes, "You're famous for being famous." Now at one level, of course, this is a parody of our "breaking news," celebrity-obsessed, Kardashian culture. But Allen uses this little fantasy to make another, deeper observation. Though put off by many aspects of his "fame," Leopoldo also becomes addicted to it. When another very ordinary figure suddenly attracts the media spotlight, Leopoldo, lamenting his lost fame, dances on one foot in the middle of a busy intersection just to get people to notice him once more. At this point, the poor man's wife intervenes, and Leopoldo realizes that his notoriety, superficial and evanescent, is no match for the affection of his wife and children.

Another farcical tale has to do with Milly and Antonio, a newlywed couple from the Italian countryside who have ventured into Rome for their honeymoon. Looking for a hairdresser, Milly gets hopelessly lost and finds herself on the set of a movie starring one of her favorite actors. In short order, the leading man charms her, romances her, and leads her back to his hotel room. But before he can complete his seduction, they are held up at gunpoint by a thief who manages to chase the frightened actor away. Dazzled by his looks and by the "excitement" he represents, Milly then gives in and makes love to the thief. Meanwhile, in a case of mistaken identity, the abandoned Antonio meets Anna, a voluptuous prostitute played by Allen favorite Penelope Cruz. Despite his embarrassment and protestations, Antonio gives in to Anna's charms and allows himself to be seduced. Covered in shame, Milly and Antonio eventually make their way back to their honeymoon hotel suite and admit to one another that they would like to return to their home in the country and raise a family.

In some ways the most conventional of the stories is the one that features Woody Allen himself as a retired opera producer who has come with his wife to Rome to meet the parents of the young man to whom their daughter is engaged. Allen's character is utterly bored by his future son-in-law's parents until he hears the father,

Giancarlo, singing—like a combination of Caruso and Pavarotti—in the shower. When he presses the man to share his gift with the wider world, he is met with complete resistance. When Giancarlo gives in and agrees to audition, he fails to impress. Finally, it dawns on the opera impresario that the man can sing well only in the shower. That light bulb having gone off, Allen's character arranges for him to sing publicly, but in a makeshift shower! Giancarlo gives a triumphant performance in Pagliacci, and it appears as though fame and fortune await. But upon reading the reviews with pleasure, the man refuses to tour and eagerly returns to his ordinary employment (he's an undertaker) and the embrace of his family.

These various characters confront, in all of their vivid and seductive power, fame, sex, pleasure, and material success. In each case, moreover, the embrace of these things would involve the compromising of some unglamorous but stable and life-giving relationship.

Thomas Aquinas said that the happy life is the one that remains centered on love, for love is what God is. Furthermore, he argued that the unhappy life is one that becomes centered on the great substitutes for love, which are wealth, pleasure, power, and honor. What I found utterly remarkable about *To Rome with Love* is how its writer and director consistently and energetically insisted that simple love should triumph over glitz, glamour, and ephemeral pleasure. I'm entirely aware that Woody Allen's private life leaves quite a bit to be desired from a moral standpoint, but in regard to the fundamental message of *To Rome with Love*, Aquinas couldn't have said it better.

Victor Hugo's Retelling
of the Gospel

IN RECENT YEARS WE'VE SEEN FILM VERSIONS of J.R.R. Tolkien's *The Hobbit* and its more substantive successor *The Lord of the Rings*, both of which are replete with Catholic themes. But I recently saw another film adaptation of a well-known book, namely, Victor Hugo's *Les Misérables*. Though Hugo had a less than perfectly benign view of the Catholic Church, his masterpiece is, from beginning to end, conditioned by a profoundly Christian worldview. It is most important that the spiritual heart of Hugo's narrative not be lost.

The story revolves around the figure of Jean Valjean, a man who, in his youth, had been convicted of the crime of robbing a loaf of bread to feed his starving child. For this eminently excusable offense, he had been imprisoned and sentenced to hard labor for nineteen years. The experience made him, understandably enough, embittered and deeply distrustful of both individuals and societal institutions. Having escaped from prison and fallen into desperate straits, he was taken in by a kindly bishop, who fed him and gave him a place to sleep. But Valjean answered this kindness by stealing two silver candlesticks from his benefactor. Apprehended by the police, he was brought back to the bishop. Instead of accusing and condemning Valjean, the prelate blithely told the constables that the candlesticks were a gift and even gave the thief more valuables. To the uncomprehending criminal, the bishop then explained that this grace was meant to awaken a similar graciousness in Valjean.

In this simple and deeply affecting episode, one of the most fundamental principles of the spiritual life is displayed. God is love. God is nothing but gracious self-gift. And what God wants, first and last, is that his human creatures participate in the love that he is, thereby becoming conduits of the divine grace to the world. What Jean Valjean received through the bishop was precisely this divine life and the mission that accompanies and flows from it. If the bishop's gesture had been, in any sense, self-interested, it would not have conveyed God's manner of being. But in its utter gratuity, it became a sacrament and instrument of uncreated grace.

The bulk of *Les Misérables* then unfolds as the story of Valjean's sharing of this divine life with others. He becomes the mayor of a town, and in that capacity proves a benefactor to the poor and destitute. Most notably, he reaches out to Fantine, a woman who had been forced into a life of prostitution in order to feed her child. (Anne Hathaway's performance of Fantine's desperate song "I Dreamed a Dream" is one of the most moving moments in the film). Upon Fantine's death, Valjean takes in her daughter, Cosette, and becomes a father to her. At the climactic moment of the film, when Valjean has the opportunity to kill the chief constable Javert, a man who had been mercilessly pursuing Valjean for decades, he relents and lets his persecutor go. Time and again, we see that unmerited love (the bishop's forgiveness many years before) gives rise to unmerited love.

Let me say a further word about the relentless Javert, portrayed in the film by Russell Crowe. The constable seems to appear at every key moment of Valjean's life, judging exactly how and whether Valjean lives up to the demands of the law. Even the slightest offense fills him with righteous indignation. Victor Hugo seems to have been using this tortured and torturing character as the embodiment of law in the absolute sense, law unchecked by mercy. Whereas

Valjean had been touched by grace, Javert remained locked in by legality and moral demand. Throughout the film, Crowe's expression is as severe and unchanging as his uniform. After the moment I described above, Javert repairs to a height overlooking the Seine and, after singing a final lament, hurls himself to his death. What became clear in his swan song is that Javert simply could not fathom what Valjean had done. There was no room for grace in his uncompromisingly legalistic worldview, and therefore the breakthrough of mercy broke him. I can't think of a better image, by the way, for what the Church means by damnation and the suffering of the damned.

The tension between Valjean and Javert should not be overstated in a dualistic way, as though mercy simply eliminates justice. Pope Benedict XVI argued that no society could survive, even in the most rudimentary way, without justice, that is to say, without law, structure, order, moral demand, legitimate punishment, etc. But at the same time, the Pope insists that a society characterized simply by justice will become, in the long run, dysfunctional—as frozen, resentful, and lifeless as Javert.

At the close of the film, as Valjean nears death, he is visited by two heavenly figures: the bishop who had shown him such kindness and Fantine, the mother of the child that he raised. The appearance of these long-dead figures speaks the important truth that grace is properly eternal, precisely because it is identical to the divine life. Since God is love, love is more powerful even than death.

Isn't it curious that at a time when an aggressive secularism is, with increasing vehemence, announcing the death of religion, a popular film like *Les Misérables* is filled with the Gospel spirit?

The Preachings of
F. Scott Fitzgerald

THE APPEARANCE OF YET ANOTHER FILM VERSION of F. Scott Fitzgerald's *The Great Gatsby* provides the occasion for reflecting on what many consider the great American novel. Those who are looking for a thorough review of the movie itself will have to look elsewhere, I'm afraid. I will say only this about the movie: I think that Baz Luhrmann's version is better than the sleepy 1974 incarnation, and I would say that Leonardo DiCaprio makes a more convincing Gatsby than Robert Redford. But I want to focus, not so much on the techniques of the filmmaker, as on the genius of the writer who gave us the story.

F. Scott Fitzgerald belonged to that famously "lost" generation of artists and writers that included Ernest Hemingway, John Dos Passos, Ford Madox Ford, and others. Having come of age during the First World War, these figures saw, in some cases at close quarters, the worst that human beings can do to one another, and they witnessed as well the complete ineffectuality of the political and religious institutions of the time to deal with the horrific crisis into which the world had stumbled. Consequently, they felt themselves adrift, without a clear moral compass, lost. Hemingway's novels— and his own personal choices—showed one way to deal with this problem, namely, to place oneself purposely in dangerous situations so as to stir up a sense of being alive. This explains Hemingway's interests in deep-sea fishing, big game hunting, battling Nazis, and above all, bullfighting. Fitzgerald explored another way that people coped with the spiritual emptiness of his time, and his deftest act of reportage was *The Great Gatsby*.

As the novel commences, we meet Tom and Daisy Buchanan, two denizens of East Egg, a town on Long Island where "old money" resides. Ensconced in a glorious mansion, wearing the most fashionable clothes, surrounded by servants, and in the company of the most "beautiful" people, Tom and Daisy are, nevertheless, utterly bored, both with themselves and their relationship. While Daisy languishes and frets, Tom is carrying on a number of illicit love affairs with women from both the upper and lower echelons of the social order. One of the more affecting scenes in the Baz Luhrmann film depicts Tom and a gaggle of his hangers-on whiling away an afternoon and evening in a rented Manhattan apartment. In the aftermath, they are all drunk, sexually sated, and obviously miserable.

Meanwhile, across the bay from the Buchanans, in West Egg, is the hero of the story, ensconced in his even more glorious mansion. Gatsby wears pink suits, drives a yellow roadster, and associates with the leading politicians, culture mavens, and gangsters of the time. But the most intriguing thing about him is that, week after week, every Saturday night, he opens his spacious home for a wild party, attended by all of the glitterati of New York. Fitzgerald's description of these parties—all wild dancing, jazz music, cloche hats, sexual innuendo, and flapper dresses—is certainly one of the highlights of the book. We discover that the sole purpose of these astronomically expensive parties is to lure Daisy, with whom Gatsby had had a romantic relationship some years before. Though Daisy is a married woman, Gatsby wants to steal her from her husband. When Nick Carraway, the narrator, chides Gatsby that no one can repeat the past, the hero of the novel responds curtly, "What do you mean you can't repeat the past? Of course you can." Without going into any more plot details, I will simply say that this set of circumstances leads to disappointment, hatred, betrayal, and finally, Gatsby's death at the hand of a gunman.

Fitzgerald saw that, given the breakdown of traditional morality and the marginalization of God, many people in the postwar West simply surrendered themselves to wealth and pleasure. Commitment, marriage, sexual responsibility, and the cultivation of a spiritual life were seen as, at best, holdovers from the Victorian age, and at worst, the enemies of progress and pleasure. Gatsby's parties were, we might say, the liturgies of the new religion of sensuality and materiality; frenzied dances around the golden calf. And despite his reputation as a hard-drinking sensualist, Fitzgerald, in *The Great Gatsby*, was as uncompromising and morally clear-eyed as an evangelical preacher. He tells us that the displacement of God by wealth and pleasure leads, by a short route, to the corroding of the soul.

There is a burnt-out and economically depressed city that lies on Long Island in between West Egg and Manhattan, and the main characters of *The Great Gatsby* pass through it frequently. In fact, one of Tom Buchanan's mistresses lives there. Fitzgerald is undoubtedly using it to symbolize the dark underbelly of the Roaring Twenties, the economic detritus of all of that conspicuous consumption. But he also uses it to make a religious point. For just off the main road, there are the remains of a billboard advertising a local ophthalmologist. All we can see are two bespectacled eyes, but they hover over the comings and goings of all the lost souls in the story. Like all symbols in great literary works, this one is multivalent, but I think it's fairly clear that Fitzgerald wanted it, at least in part, to stand for the providential gaze of God. Though he has been pushed to the side and treated with disrespect, God still watches, and his moral judgment is still operative.

It's a sermon still worth hearing.

Superman, General Zod, and God

I DIDN'T REALLY CARE FOR the latest cinematic iteration of the Superman myth. Like way too many movies today, it was made for the generation that came of age with video games and MTV and their constant, irritatingly frenetic action. When the CGI whiz-bang stuff kicks in, I just check out, and *Man of Steel* is about three-quarters whiz-bang.

However, there is a theme in this film that is worthy of some reflection, namely, the tension between individual autonomy and a state-controlled society. *Man of Steel* commences with a lengthy segment dealing with the closing days of the planet Krypton. We learn that a fiercely totalitarian regime, led by a General Zod, is seeking the arrest of a scientist called Jor-El. It becomes clear that Jor-El has attempted to undermine the regime's policy of strictly controlling the genetics of Kryptonite newborns. Very much in the manner of Plato's *Republic*, Kryptonite children are rigidly pre-programmed to be a member of one of three social groups. Jor-El and his wife have conceived a child in the traditional manner and are seeking to send their son, born in freedom, away from their dying planet.

I won't bore you with many more plot details, but suffice it to say that the child (the future Superman) does indeed get away to planet Earth and that General Zod manages to survive the destruction of his world. The movie then unfolds as the story of a great battle between the representative of freedom and the avatar of genetic manipulation and political tyranny.

Lest you think that the link to Plato is a bit forced, the director at one point shows the teenaged Superman reading *The Republic*. In his classic *The Open Society and Its Enemies*, Karl Popper, a survivor of Nazi tyranny, presented Plato's *Republic* as the forerunner of all totalitarianisms that have sprung up in the West. Very often, Popper saw, these tyrannies begin with the best of intentions. Good-hearted leaders believe that they have hit upon some form of life that will benefit the greatest number and thus they endeavor to implement their vision through binding legal prescription. Plato himself thought that the guardians of his ideal republic should have all property—including wives and children—in common and hence called for a strictly enforced communism among social elites. Further, he felt that the soldiers who protect his perfect city should have their emotions trained in a very precise manner and therefore decreed that tight censorship should obtain in regard to their reading and entertainment. On Popper's interpretation, post-revolutionary French society, Hitler's Germany, Stalin's Soviet Union, and the Iran of the Ayatollahs would become imitations of the Platonic original: idealistic visions that quickly devolved into totalitarian oppression.

In answer to these totalizing systems, Popper proposed the open society, which is to say, a political arrangement that places stress on the prerogatives and freedom of the individual. Thomas Jefferson's insistence that government exists primarily for the purpose of guaranteeing the liberty of individuals to determine their own destinies, to seek happiness as they see fit, is deeply congruent with Popper's ideal. Much of the political history of the past three hundred years might be characterized as a battle between these two visions, these contrasting ideologies. At its limit, the Platonic system results in the apotheosizing of the state and/or the divinization of the ruler. And this is why General Zod (so close to "God") is aptly named. At its limit, the open society conduces toward the apotheosizing of the individual will, so that personal freedom becomes absolute. Many times before, I have pilloried the US Supreme Court statement in the matter of Casey v. Planned Parenthood, whereby individual freedom is entitled to define even the meaning of the universe! If Plato is the philosopher who best articulates the nature of the totalitarian society, Friedrich Nietzsche is the philosopher who best expresses the limit case of the apotheosized ego. Beyond good and evil, he said, lies the will of the *Ubermensch*, literally the superman. We might read the battle between General Zod and Superman, therefore, as a symbol of the struggle between two falsely deified realities, the nation-state and the ego.

Happily, there is a state of affairs that lies beyond this clash. Biblical religion is eminently clear that there is one God and that any attempt to deify the state, the king, or the self-asserting ego results in spiritual calamity. If you're curious about particular references, I might urge you to read the account of the fall in Genesis 3, the story of the Tower of Babel in Genesis 11, Samuel's critique of kingship in 1 Samuel 8, and the story of David and Bathsheba in 2 Samuel 11. The Bible recommends neither the heteronomy of the oppressive state nor the autonomy of the individual will, but rather, if I can borrow a term from Paul Tillich, "theonomy," which means allowing God to become the inner law of one's life. Both the state and the will are under God's judgment and hence neither General Zod nor Superman is the answer.

I'm sure that you will forgive my revealing the none-too-surprising ending to *Man of Steel*: Superman's victory over the wicked general. In a biblical telling of the story, the hero of individualism, having conquered General Zod, would kneel to God.

World War Z and the Council of Trent

THERE WERE A NUMBER OF REASONS why I liked *World War Z*, the film based on Max Brooks's book of the same name. First, it was a competently made thriller and not simply a stringing together of whiz-bang CGI effects. Secondly, it presented a positive image of a father. In a time when Homer Simpson and Peter Griffin are the norm for fatherhood in the popular culture, Brad Pitt's character, Gerry Lane, is actually a man of intelligence, deep compassion, and self-sacrificing courage. But what intrigued me the most about *World War Z* is how it provides a template for thinking seriously about sin and salvation.

As the movie opens, an ordinary American family is alarmed by news of a mysterious contagion that is spreading quickly across the globe. In a matter of days, the disease has reached their hometown of Philadelphia, and they are forced to flee. It becomes clear that a virus is turning people into the walking dead who are hungry for human flesh. What is particularly frightening about this iteration of the zombie myth is that the undead of *World War Z* are not the lumbering oafs that we've come to expect, but rather are fast-moving, teeth-grinding, extremely focused killing machines.

After a series of close calls, Gerry and his family manage to escape and make their way to a ship off the eastern seaboard. We learn that Gerry had been a special operative for the United Nations, skilled in fighting his way in and out of hot spots around the world.

His superiors draft him back into service, charging him with the task of finding out how to contain the virus. Accompanied only by a small team of scientists and military personnel, Gerry wings his way first to Korea and then to Jerusalem, where, at least for the moment, the Israeli government has managed to keep the zombies at bay behind a high and thick wall. Now when Jerusalem came into focus, I realized that the filmmakers perhaps had some ambitions beyond simply another ringing of the changes on the zombie story.

One of the more thought-provoking assertions of the sixteenth century Council of Trent is this: original sin is passed on from generation to generation, *propagatione et non imitatione* (by propagation and not by imitation). What the fathers of Trent meant is that sin is not so much a bad habit that we pick up by watching other people behave; rather, it is like a disease that we inherit or a contagion that we catch. A newborn inheriting a crack addiction from his mother would be an apt trope for the process. If it were simply a matter of imitation, then the problem of sin could be solved through psychological adjustment or mental conditioning or just by trying harder. But if it is more like a disease, then sin can be fully addressed only through the intervention of some medicine or antidote that comes from the outside. Moreover, if sin were just a bad habit, then it wouldn't reach very deeply into the structure of the self; but were it more like a contagion, it would insinuate itself into all the interrelated systems that make up the person. The fathers of Trent specify that sin causes a falling-apart of the self, a disintegration of mind, will, emotions, and the body, so that the sinner consistently operates at cross-purposes to himself. Do you see now why the zombie—a human being so compromised by the effects of a contagion that he is really only a simulacrum of a human—is such an apt symbol for a person under the influence of sin? And do you see, further, why the erection of a mighty wall would be an utterly unsuccessful strategy against such a threat? Indeed, one of the most memorable scenes in *World War Z* is of the zombies swarming over the walls of Jerusalem.

A bad habit might be solved by a teacher, but a disease requires more radical treatment. I won't burden you with all of the plot details, but Brad Pitt's character figures out that the zombies are dissuaded from attacking if they sense a deadly disease in someone. Accordingly, he enters a lab, protected by a veritable army of zombies, in order to inject himself with a noxious contagion. Having done so, he is able to walk among the undead unmolested, and from his blood, an antidote can be produced for the world. Now one would have to be inattentive in the extreme not to notice the rather clear Christ symbolism at play here. Gerry does not fight the zombies on their own terms; rather, he enters courageously into their environment, takes on a deadly disease and then, through his blood, offers a cure to suffering humanity.

St. Paul said that, on the cross, Jesus became sin so that "in him we might become the righteousness of God" (2 Cor. 5:21); and "in him we have redemption through his blood" (Eph. 1:7). Jesus becomes the healer (*Soter* in Greek, *Salvator* in Latin), precisely in the measure that he enters the world of sin, even to the point of shedding his blood, and explodes it from within.

The great story of salvation is still in the intellectual DNA of the West, and that is why it pops up so regularly in the popular culture. And perhaps this is happening precisely because the Christian churches have become so inept at relating the narrative. To those who don't know this fundamental story well, I might recommend a thoughtful viewing of *World War Z*.

Noah: A Postmodern Midrash

DARREN ARONOFSKY'S CINEMATIC RETELLING of the story of Noah has certainly stirred people up. While quite a few reviewers, both religious and non-religious, have given the film high marks, many Christians, both Evangelical and Catholic, have registered a far less than enthusiastic reaction. One prominent Catholic blogger and movie reviewer opined that *Noah* is "embarrassingly awful" and "the stupidest film in years." Most of the religious critics have complained that the film plays fast and loose with the Genesis account, adding all sorts of distracting and fantastic elements to the well-known story. In the midst of all of this—and no doubt in part because of it—*Noah* took in $44 million on its opening weekend.

Noah is best interpreted, I think, as a modern cinematic *midrash* on the Biblical tale. The *midrashim*—extremely popular in ancient Israel—were imaginative elaborations of the often spare Scriptural narratives. They typically explored the psychological motivations of the major players in the stories and added creative plot lines, new characters, etc. In the *midrashic* manner, Aronofsky's film presents any number of extra-biblical elements, including a conversation between Noah and his grandfather Methuselah, an army of angry men eager to force their way onto the ark, a kind of incense that lulls the animals to sleep on the ship, and most famously (or infamously), a race of fallen angels who have become incarnate as stone monsters. These latter characters are not really as fantastic or arbitrary as they might seem at first blush. Genesis tells us that the Noah story unfolds during the time of the Nephilim, a term that literally means "the fallen" and that is usually rendered as "giants." Moreover, in the extra-biblical book of Enoch, the Nephilim are called "the watchers," a usage reflected in the great hymn "Ye Watchers and Ye Holy Ones." In Aronofsky's *Noah*, the stone giants are referred to by the same name.

What is most important is that this contemporary *midrash* successfully articulates the characteristically biblical logic of the story of Noah. First, it speaks unambiguously of God: every major character refers to "the Creator." Second, this Creator God is not presented as a distant force, nor is he blandly identified with Nature. Rather, he is personal, active, provident, and intimately involved in the affairs of the world that he has made. Third, human beings are portrayed as fallen, with their sin producing much of the suffering in the world. Some of the religious critics of *Noah* have sniffed out a secularist and environmentalist ideology behind this supposed demonization of humanity, but Genesis itself remains pretty down on the way human beings operate—read the stories of Cain and Abel and the Tower of Babel for the details. And *Noah's* portrayal of the rape of nature caused by industrialization is nowhere near as vivid as Tolkien's portrayal of the same theme in *The Lord of the Rings*. Fourth, the hero of the film consistently eschews his own comfort and personal inclination and seeks to know and follow the will of God. At the emotional climax of the movie (spoiler alert), Noah moves to kill his own granddaughters, convinced that it is God's will that the human race be obliterated, but he relents when it becomes clear to him that God in fact wills for humanity to be renewed. What is significant is that Noah remains utterly focused throughout, not on his own freedom, but on the desire and purpose of God. God, creation, providence, sin, obedience, salvation: not bad for a major Hollywood movie!

There is a minor scene in the film which depicts some members of Noah's family administering the sleep-inducing smoke to the animals. They look, for all the world, like priests swinging thuribles of incense around a cathedral. I'm quite sure that this was far from the mind of the filmmakers, but it suggested to me the strong patristic theme that Noah's Ark is symbolic of the Church. During a time of moral and spiritual chaos, when the primal watery chaos out of which God created the world returned with a vengeance, the Creator sent a rescue operation, a great boat on which a microcosm of God's good order would be preserved. For the Church Fathers, this is precisely the purpose and meaning of the Church: to be a safe haven where, in the midst of a sinful world, God's word is proclaimed, where God is properly worshipped, and where a rightly ordered humanity lives in justice and nonviolence. Just as Noah's Ark carried the seeds of a new creation, so the Church is meant to let out the life that it preserves for the renewal of the world.

If Aronofsky's *Noah* can, even subliminally, suggest this truth, it is well worth the watching.

The Fault in Our Stars and
the Sacred Heart of Jesus

JOHN GREEN'S NOVEL *THE FAULT IN OUR STARS* has proven to be wildly popular among young adults in the English-speaking world, and the film adaptation of the book has garnered both impressive reviews and a massive audience. A one-time divinity school student and Christian minister, Green is not reluctant to explore the "big" questions, though he doesn't claim to provide anything like definitive answers. In this, he both reflects and helps to shape the inchoate, eclectic spirituality that holds sway in the teen and twentysomething set today. After watching the film however, I began to wonder whether his Christian sensibility doesn't assert itself perhaps even more clearly and strongly than he realizes.

The story is narrated by Hazel Grace Lancaster, a teenager suffering from a debilitating and most likely terminal form of cancer. At her mother's prompting, Hazel attends a support group for young cancer patients that takes place at the local Episcopal Church. The group is presided over by a well-meaning but nerdy youth minister who commences each meeting by rolling out a tapestry of Jesus displaying his Sacred Heart. "We are gathering, literally, in the heart of Jesus," he eagerly tells the skeptical and desultory gaggle of teens. At one of these sessions, Hazel rises to share her utterly bleak, even nihilistic philosophy of life: "There will come a time when all of us are dead. All of us. There will come a time when there are no human beings remaining to remember that anyone ever existed or that our species ever did anything. [...] There was time before organisms experienced consciousness, and there will be time after. And if the inevitability of human oblivion worries you, I encourage you to ignore it. God knows that's what everyone else does." The only response that the hapless leader can muster to that outburst is, "Good advice for everyone." It would be hard to imagine a more damning commentary on the state of much of so-called Christian ministry today!

At one of these meetings, Hazel meets a handsome, charming cancer survivor named Augustus Waters, and the two fall almost immediately in love. Though they both consider the support group fairly lame, there is no denying that they were brought together over the heart of Christ. Kind, encouraging, funny, and utterly devoted, Augustus (Gus) draws Hazel out of herself and lures her into a more active engagement with life. They both love a novel called *An Imperial Affliction*, written by a reclusive author named Peter Van Houten. After establishing e-mail contact with Van Houten, they arrange, through a kind of "Make-A-Wish" foundation, to fly to Amsterdam to commune with their literary hero. Just before the encounter, Gus and Hazel engage in some serious conversation about God and the afterlife. Gus says that he believes in God and in some sort of life after death; otherwise, he argues, "What is the point?" Still clinging to her bleak materialism, Hazel retorts, "What if there is no point?"

The next day, the young couple, filled with enthusiasm, comes to Van Houten's home only to find that their hero is a depressed alcoholic who has no interest in talking to them. When they press him for answers about mysteries in his novel, he comments on the meaninglessness of life, effectively mirroring Hazel's nihilism back to her. Just after this awful conversation, the two teenagers make their way to the Anne Frank house, where Hazel manages, despite her cumbersome oxygen tank and her weakened lungs, to climb to the attic where Anne Frank hid from the Nazis. In that room, evocative of both horrific, meaningless violence and real spiritual hope, Hazel and Gus passionately kiss for the first time. It is as though their love, which began in the heart of Jesus, asserted itself strongly even in the face of darkness.

But we are not allowed to dwell on this hopeful moment, for Gus reveals, just before they return home, that his cancer has reasserted itself and that his condition is terminal. Not long after they return, Gus dies, at the age of eighteen, and Hazel sinks into profound sadness: "Each minute," she says, "is worse than the previous one." At the funeral, even as Christian prayers are uttered, Hazel just goes through the motions, pretending to find comfort, precisely for the sake of her family and friends. But some days after the funeral, she discovers that Augustus had written a note to her just before his death. It closes with the words, "Okay, Hazel Grace?" To which the young woman responds, while gazing up into the sky, "Okay." With that word, the film ends.

Pretty grim stuff? Yes...but. Does nihilism have the last word? I don't know. The question that haunts the entire movie is how can there be meaning in the universe when two wonderful young kids are dying of cancer? As any Philosophy 101 student knows, our attempts to justify the existence of evil through abstract argumentation are a fairly useless exercise. However, a kind of answer can be found precisely where Hazel and Gus met, that is to say, in the Sacred Heart of Jesus. The central claim of Christianity is that God became one of us and that he shared our condition utterly, accepting even death, death on a cross. God entered into our suffering and thereby transformed it into a place of springs, a place of grace. I don't think it is the least bit accidental that Waters (Gus's last name) and Grace (Hazel's middle name) met in the Sacred Heart of Christ and thereby, despite their shared suffering, managed to give life to one another. And is this why I think Hazel effectively repudiates her nihilism and materialism as she responds across the barrier of death to Gus's "Okay." I'm convinced that Hazel senses, by the end of the story, the central truth of Christian faith that real love is more powerful than death.

Is this film a satisfying presentation of Christianity? Hardly. But for those who are struggling to find their way to meaning and faith, it's not an entirely bad place to start.

Hercules, N.T. Wright, and the Modern Meta-Narrative

On the first day of my vacation last week, I perused N.T. Wright's latest book, a collection of essays on contemporary issues in light of the Bible. A point that Wright makes in a number of the articles is that modernity and Christianity propose fundamentally different meta-narratives in regard to the meaning and trajectory of history. Modernity—at least in its Western form—is predicated on the assumption that history came to its climax in the mid- to late-eighteenth century, with the definitive victory of empirical science in the epistemological arena and liberal democracy in the political arena.

Basic to this telling of the story is that modernity emerged victorious only after a long twilight struggle against the forces of obscurantism and tyranny and that the matrix for both of these negative states of affairs was none other than the Christian religion, which enforced a blind dogmatism on the one hand and an oppressive political arrangement on the other. For an extreme but very clear expression of this point of view, consider Diderot's famous remark, "Men will not be free until the last king is strangled on the entrails of the last priest."

For a more benign expression of the modern myth of origins, Wright suggests, take a dollar bill out of your wallet and turn it over. You will see a pyramid topped by a single human eye, and at the base of that structure, you will notice the motto *novus ordo seclorum* (the new order of the ages). This represents the founders' extraordinary conviction that they were launching, not simply a new political arrangement, but an entirely new way of seeing the world.

Now Christianity proposes a completely different account of how history comes to a climax and what precisely constitutes the new order of the ages—which helps to explain why so many of modernity's avatars, from Diderot to Christopher Hitchens, have specially targeted Christianity. On the Christian reading, history reached its highpoint when a young first century Jewish rabbi, having been put to death on a brutal Roman instrument of torture, was raised from the dead through the power of the God of Israel. The state-sponsored murder of Jesus, who had dared to speak and act in the name of Israel's God, represented the world's resistance to the Creator. It was the moment when cruelty, hatred, violence, and corruption—symbolized in the Bible as the watery chaos—spent itself on Jesus. The Resurrection, therefore, showed forth the victory of the divine love over those dark powers. St. Paul can say, "I am certain that neither death nor life, neither angels nor principalities, nor any other creature can separate us from the love of God," precisely because he lived on the far side of the Resurrection.

This is also why Paul and so many of his Christian colleagues can speak of "new creation" and "a new heavens and a new earth." For all of Paul's spiritual descendants, therefore, the eighteenth century might indeed signify a leap forward in science and political arrangements, but it can by no stretch of the imagination be construed as the climax of history. I believe that N.T. Wright is correct when he maintains that this "battle of narratives" is far more crucial for the Church today than any of our particular arguments about sex and authority, but that's an article for another day.

All of this was swimming in my mind when, on the evening of the first day of my vacation, I went to see the new cinematic iteration of the Hercules story, starring Dwayne Johnson (aka The Rock).

Now don't get me wrong: I don't think that this summer popcorn entertainment is trading in grand ideas. However, it does represent in its own surprising way a telling of the modern metanarrative. In classical mythology, of course, Hercules is the son of Zeus, and his grand exploits are a function of his supernatural status. But in the current film, Hercules is an ordinary man around whom a legend has been cynically built, and his "mythic" opponents are frauds and deceptions. Hence Cerberus the three-headed dog is just three rather fierce wolves that have been leashed together; the many-headed Hydra is just a group of soldiers with a clever disguise; the centaurs are ordinary mounted warriors who have been misperceived, etc. At the climax of the film, a "seer" tells Hercules that, though he is not divine, he will find sufficient strength to save the day if only he "believes in himself." Moreover, as he utters his last "prediction," the seer mutters with a shrug, "but what do I know?" In a word, everything has been flattened out, rendered mundane, any reference to the properly supernatural expunged or explained away. And the political part of the modern myth is not forgotten, for the kings over whom Hercules triumphs are tyrants, who have been using religion to cover up their own criminal machinations.

Again, I don't think that makers of *Hercules* have particularly high intellectual ambitions, but their film joins a long line of recent movies—*300*, *Agora*, the various reboots of Star Trek and Clash of the Titans—which tell the story of the triumph of "reason" over "mysticism" and the natural over the supernatural. If N.T. Wright is correct about the battle of narratives, we Christians should be sensitive to the many and very effective ways that the popular culture tends to out-narrate us.

The Giver and the Fading Memory
of Christianity

LOIS LOWRY'S 1993 NOVEL *THE GIVER* has garnered a very wide audience over the past two decades, since it has become a standard text in middle schools and high schools across the English-speaking world. With the enormous success of *Harry Potter, Twilight*, and *Hunger Games*, Hollywood has been busy adapting books written for the young adult audience. A recent example is the movie version of *The Giver*, which was produced by Jeff Bridges and which stars Bridges and Meryl Streep. Having never even heard of the novel, I came at the film with no expectations, and I confess I was quite surprised both by the power of its societal critique and by its implicit Christian themes.

The story is set in the near future, in a seemingly utopian city, where there is no conflict, no inequality, and no stress. The streets are laid out in a perfectly symmetrical grid, the domiciles and public buildings are clean, even antiseptic, and the people dress in matching outfits and ride bicycles so as not to pollute the environment. The "elders," the leadership of the community, artificially arrange families and carefully assign vocations, all for the sake of the common good. In order to eliminate any volatile emotions that might stir up resentment or compromise the perfect equilibrium of the society, each citizen is obligated to take a daily injection of a kind of sedative. If someone's speech veers even mildly in the direction of suggesting self-assertion or individuality, he is corrected with a gentle but firm admonition: "precision of language, please." Most chillingly, the elderly and unacceptable children are eliminated, though the people have been conditioned not to think of this as killing but only as a peaceful transition to "Elsewhere." The calm "sameness" of the city is maintained, above all, through the erasing of memory: no one is permitted to remember the colorful but conflictual world that preceded the present utopia. No one, that is, except the Giver, an elder who retains memories of the previous world for the sole purpose of consulting them in case an emergency arises and specialized knowledge is called for.

Utopian societies, maintained through totalitarian control, have been dreamed about at least since the time of Plato, and, to be sure, many attempts have been made over the centuries to realize the dream. The twentieth century witnessed quite a few of them: Mao's China, Stalin's Soviet Union, Hitler's Third Reich, Pol Pot's Cambodia. Indeed, there are echoes of all of these social arrangements in *The Giver*'s version of utopia, but I think what *The Giver*'s city most readily calls to mind is modern liberalism, especially in its European incarnation. We find the fierce enforcement of politically correct speech, the manic attempt to control the environment, coldly modernist architecture, the prizing of equality as the supreme value, the rampant use of drugs, the denial of death, and the wanton exercise of both euthanasia and abortion. Will all of this produce a balanced and peaceful society? Well, it might bring about a kind of equilibrium, but at a terrible cost.

The plot of *The Giver* centers on a young man named Jonas who was chosen by the elders to become the sole recipient of the suppressed memory of the previous world. Through a sort of telepathy, the Giver communicates to Jonas all of the richness, color, drama, and joy of the pre-Utopian society. The most beguiling image he receives is of himself sledding down a snowy hill and coming upon a cottage from which he hears emerging the strains of a song he had never heard before (in fact, both snow and music had been excluded from his world). In time, the Giver fills out the picture, communicating to the young man the pain and conflict of the previous world as well. Though at first he is horrified by that experience, Jonas realizes that the colorful world, even with its suffering, would be preferable to the bloodless and inhuman dystopia in which he had been raised. As the story moves to its climax, Jonas escapes from the city and ventures out into the forbidden wilderness. The weather turns fiercely cold and he wanders through the snow until he comes to a clearing where he spies the sled that he had previously seen in memory. Following the prompts of the recollection, he rides the sled down a snowy hill, comes to the quaint cottage, and listens to the song. It is only then that we hear that they are singing the best-known and best-loved Christmas hymn, "Silent Night."

And now we see that what makes the society in *The Giver* most like contemporary Europe is precisely the forgetfulness of Christianity. What the story suggests, quite rightly, is that suppression of the good news of the Incarnation is in fact what conduces to dysfunctional and dangerous totalitarianism. The source of the greatest suffering throughout human history is the attempt to deal with original sin on our own, through our political, economic, military, or cultural efforts. When we try to eliminate conflict and sin through social reform, we inevitably make matters worse. As Pascal said long ago, "He who would turn himself into an angel, turns himself into a beast." The key to joy at the personal level and justice at the societal level is in fact the conviction that God has dealt with original sin by taking it on himself and suffering with us and for us. This belief allows us to embrace the world in both its beauty and its tragedy, for we see salvation as God's project, not our own. It is the Incarnation—the event celebrated by the singing of "Silent Night"—that frees us from our self-importance and gives the lie to our programs of perfectibility.

I can't help but think that the recovery of this lost memory—so key to the authentic renewal of contemporary society—is what *The Giver* is finally about.

TAKE AND READ:
GOD IN BOOKS

The Pathos of Liberal Catholicism

KERRY KENNEDY, A DAUGHTER of Robert and Ethel Kennedy, has written a bestseller called *Being Catholic Now: Prominent Americans Talk About Change in the Church and the Quest for Meaning*. It features brief reflections from thirty-seven men and women, largely, though not exclusively, drawn from the left side of the Catholic spectrum. Though it's always difficult to generalize when dealing with such a variety of contributors, I would like to draw attention to two themes that come up with great, and, I must say, disturbing regularity in this book. The first is the favoring of "the faith" or "spirituality" over the institutional Church, and the second is the reduction of Catholicism to the works of social justice.

In her preface to the text, Kennedy evokes, movingly enough, her intensely Catholic childhood, which involved frequent prayers, personal devotions, Bible reading, immersion in the lives of the saints, celebrations of the liturgical seasons, and regular attendance at Mass. But then she recounts the process by which she became gradually disillusioned with pompous bishops and out-of-touch priests. She tells us how her mother, if offended by an insensitive or long-winded homily, would simply get up and lead her brood of children out of church. The conclusion she drew is starkly stated: "I learned from her to distinguish between my faith and the Institutional Church." Now, I know all about priests and bishops who sometimes say stupid things, and worse, sometimes do harmful things. I agree with Kennedy and many of her collaborators in the book that the clergy sex abuse scandal, in all of its ramifications, represented the prime example of this distortion of speech and abuse of power.

But this acknowledgment should never lead one to conclude that the faith is divorceable from the hierarchical structure of the Church, as though the Catholic faith could float free of the pesky interference of priests and bishops. The Church is neither a philosophical debating society nor a political party, but rather a mystical body, hierarchically ordered in such a way that authentic teaching and sacraments come through the ministrations of the ordained.

What I saw in the image of Ethel Kennedy walking out of church in response to an offensive sermon was the Donatism of the left. In the fourth century, St. Augustine battled the Donatist heresy which held that only morally praiseworthy priests could legitimately administer the sacraments and preach. The great saint insisted that the power of word and sacrament does not come (thank God) from the personal worthiness of the minister but from Christ who works through them. So even today, the "faith" cannot be severed from the "institution," even when that institution is represented, as it always is, by deeply flawed people.

The second theme that disturbed me could be found in almost every essay in the book. In reflection after reflection, we hear that Catholicism amounts to a passion for service to the poor and the marginalized. Again and again, the contributors said that what they prized the most in their Catholic formation was the inculcation of the principles of inclusivity, equality, and social justice. The Church's social teaching comes in for a great deal of praise throughout the book. But in the vast majority of the pieces, no mention is made of distinctively Catholic doctrines such as the Trinity, the Incarnation, redemption, original sin, creation, or grace. For the most part, it would be very difficult to distinguish the social commitments of the contributors from those of a dedicated humanist of any or no religious affiliation. The problem here is that the social teaching of the Church flows necessarily from and is subordinated to the doctrinal convictions of classical Christianity. We care for the poor precisely because we are all connected to one another through the acts of creation and redemption. More to it, we worry about the marginalized precisely because all of us are cells, molecules, and organs in a mystical body whose head is Christ risen from the dead. And our work on behalf of social justice is nourished by the Eucharist, which fully realizes and expresses the living dynamics of the mystical communion.

The great Catholic advocates of social justice in the twentieth century—Dorothy Day, Peter Maurin, Romano Guardini, Reynold Hillenbrand, Thomas Merton—were all deeply immersed in the doctrinal and liturgical traditions. No one would have mistaken any of them for a blandly secular humanist. My fear is that a Catholicism reduced to social justice will, in short order, perhaps a generation or two, wither away.

Being Catholic, now as at any other time, must always involve a living relationship with both the hierarchical Church, made up as it is of flawed individuals, and with the doctrines and sacramental practices that flow from and refer to Christ Jesus. Without these connections, it loses its soul.

What Should Catholics Make of Eckhart Tolle?

OPRAH WINFREY RECOMMENDED to her world-wide audience a book written by the German-born spiritual teacher Eckhart Tolle entitled *A New Earth: Awakening to Your Life's Purpose.* As expected, the book became a runaway bestseller, and an Internet program featuring Oprah and Tolle has attracted millions of participants. But then something happened that wasn't expected: Oprah's advocacy of *A New Earth* prompted a vigorous reaction from evangelical Christians who claimed that the book represented an attack on classical Christianity. A Christian-sponsored YouTube video critical of Tolle and Winfrey has received over seven million hits.

What can we Catholics make of this controversy?

Part of the genius of Catholicism is its capaciousness, its ability to take in and assimilate to itself whatever is true in other religions, spiritualities, and philosophies. And there is much in Tolle's teaching that is compatible with a robust Christianity. He speaks, for example, of the need to overcome the ego-driven self, the "I" predicated upon the assertion of superiority and independence. Well, any number of Catholic mystics and spiritual masters over the centuries have spoken of the "false self," with its tendencies toward attachment, violence, and pride. And they have urged, as Tolle does, the discovery of the true self, grounded in love, connection to others, and the transcendence of egotistic preoccupations. More to it, Tolle defends the existence of what he calls "the pain-body," a semiautonomous psychological structure taking its rise from the suffering and injustice that a person has endured. Frequently, Tolle claims, the psyche is, as it were, possessed by this highly-charged negative force, compelling one toward actions one would not otherwise perform. St. Paul, in his letter to the Romans, speaks of sin as just such a darkly compelling force: "I do not do the good that I want, but I do the evil that I don't want...but I see in my members another principle at war with the law of my mind...the law of sin." The reason for these correspondences—and there are others as well—is that Tolle's spirituality represents what scholars have called the *philosophia perennis* (the perennial philosophy); a distillate of elemental truths discoverable in most of the philosophical and religious traditions of the world. The Church has never despised the *philosophia perennis*, but at the same time it has regarded it with caution.

As I read Tolle's book, I was reminded frequently of St. Irenaeus and his struggle against Gnosticism, an ancient form of the *philosophia perennis* which Tolle enthusiastically embraces. Like the Gnostics, Tolle sees Jesus primarily as a teacher and interprets salvation as a transformation of consciousness, a kind of waking up to a new awareness. The Church certainly affirms that Jesus is a teacher, but it emphatically states that he is infinitely more than a spiritual guru or a wise and enlightened philosopher. Jesus is God, and that makes all the difference. He is not simply one teacher among many who has found a way to God—he, in person, is the Way. He is not simply one enlightened figure among many who has come upon the truth—he, in person, is the Truth. What he brings, therefore, is not one teaching, however moving and transformative; what he brings is the divine life, a participation in God. And thus salvation is much more than the clearing up of a false consciousness. It is a transfiguration of the entire self through the grace of God, made available through a mystical participation in Jesus.

But my fundamental problem with Tolle is the same as Irenaeus's fundamental problem with the Gnostics: an impersonal view of God. Tolle will speak of getting in touch with Life or with Being or with the Universe considered as a totality, and he characterizes these breakthroughs as self-divinization. But this places his program thoroughly outside the ambit of the Bible. For the biblical authors, God is neither an impersonal force, nor the universe as such, nor the energy that flows through and connects all things, but rather the personal creator of the world, Someone who stands utterly outside the world even as he sustains and governs it, and Someone who has entered history personally and directly. C.S. Lewis commented that much of modern mysticism thinks of God as a kind of pleasant background music to which one can turn for inspiration, whereas the Bible thinks of God as a Person, powerful, overwhelming, and unpredictable—a Person who seizes us and calls us to himself. Tolle's "Universe" has little to do with the God of the Bible.

A last point: toward the beginning of his text, Tolle excoriates the classical religions—especially Catholicism—for contributing to the violence and dysfunction of the world by making exclusive truth claims. I could only smile at this. Does Tolle think that he's not making truth claims and that he, therefore, holds alternative views to be wrong and worthy of critique? God knows that far too many religious people across the ages have backed up their assertions with violence, but this regrettable fact cannot prevent Catholics from saying that, in essential matters, we are right. Despite his protestations, Eckhart Tolle does the same.

Ends and Means and
The Audacity to Hope

SOMEHOW DURING THE LONG 2008 CAMPAIGN SEASON, I never got around to reading Barack Obama's *The Audacity of Hope*. Finally, two very bright friends of mine—and not political supporters of the president—rather warmly recommended the book to me. So in preparation for a long plane trip, I bought *The Audacity of Hope* at the airport and read it en route. I saw clearly why my friends thought highly of the book, for there is much to admire in it. It is gracefully and persuasively written, revealing on practically every page the considerably charming, reflective, and intelligent character of its author. Obama has many insightful things to say about polarization in government, the dangers of our money-driven political culture, the evolution of the Democrat-Republican debate in the years following the roiled sixties, the similarities between Reagan and Clinton—and much else. And his tone throughout the book is optimistic, uplifting, and inspiring.

One of the chapters of *The Audacity of Hope* is concerned with the Constitution, and I confess that I turned to it with special interest, given the fact that Obama had been for some years a professor of constitutional law at the University of Chicago. The President shows that the peculiar genius of Madison, Jay, and the other framers of the Constitution lay in their establishment of a system of checks and balances, a deliberate pitting of conflicting interests and factions against one another so as to produce, through a lengthy process of debate and argument, a rough practical consensus. Precisely in this, they saw that violent domination by any one party or set of interests be precluded. Obama sings the praises of this rough-and-tumble, pragmatic process, identifying it as a uniquely American contribution to political philosophy and praxis. So far, so good. But then comes this rather startling line: "Implicit...in the very idea of ordered liberty was a rejection of absolute truth, the infallibility of any idea or ideology or theology..." And a page later, this: "The rejection of absolutism...has encouraged the very process...that allows us to make better, if not perfect, choices, not only about the means to our ends, but also about the ends themselves." This pragmatism even about ultimate ends allows us, Obama continues, to escape "the cruelties of the Inquisition, the pogrom, the gulag, or the jihad." I'm afraid that this is where I felt obliged to get off the train.

I completely share the President's enthusiasm for deliberative pragmatism and creative checking and balancing in regard to the nuts and bolts of practical governance. But when he allows what is legitimate at that level to hold sway at the level of the moral structure of a political system, he points the country down a short road to chaos. Both St. John Paul II and Pope Benedict XVI vigorously defended the democratic form of government, but both popes also reminded us that a representative democracy must be grounded in certain definite ethical principles, lest it devolve into license, disordered freedom. Members of a democracy can debate all they want about the best means of achieving their moral ends, but if the ends themselves become the subject of debate, the system implodes. Indeed, one of the surest signs that one has fudged this distinction is the tendency to characterize those who hold to moral absolutes as "jihadists" or purveyors of "inquisitions."

Now here's what's really puzzling: I think Obama agrees with me! As the chapter on the Constitution unfolds, we can, as it were, see into the worried workings of his lawyerly mind. Having made his vigorous argument for deliberative pragmatism at all levels, he draws back, recalling the examples of William Lloyd Garrison, Frederick Douglass, Harriet Tubman, and John Brown during the period just prior to the Civil War. Those impassioned abolitionists did not think that the deep immorality of slavery was a matter for debate or pragmatic compromise. They were, for want of a better word, absolutists on the subject, and yet they all participated, in different ways and to varying degrees, in the democratic system. And it was their principled, uncompromising convictions that led to changes in our country without which Barack Obama's emergence on the public stage would have been unthinkable. It leads him to this conclusion: "I am robbed even of the certainty of uncertainty—for sometimes absolute truths may well be absolute." Quite so, Mr. President, but you can't have it both ways.

All of which conduces to the issue which oddly haunts *The Audacity of Hope*: abortion. Obama addresses the question of abortion directly in his chapter on faith, but it is surprising just how frequently he mentions it, obliquely and tangentially, throughout his book. If I might risk a bit of armchair psychologizing, it is a subject that clearly preoccupies him, bugs him. And it does so, I would argue, precisely because it lies on the fault line in his thinking that I've just identified. The direct killing of the innocent is, like slavery or racial discrimination, one of those absolute intrinsic evils, the avoidance of which constitutes the moral framework of any decent human society. One ought no more to deliberate about the rectitude of killing the innocent than to debate the legitimacy of holding other human beings as property.

It is only when we have real moral clarity about ends and means that we might have the audacity to hope for a just society.

The Apocalypse of
Robert Hugh Benson

I'VE JUST FINISHED READING a most extraordinary novel, one that sheds considerable light on the spiritual predicaments of our own time. The odd thing is that it was written just over a hundred years ago. It's called *The Lord of the World*, and it was authored by Robert Hugh Benson. Benson was the son of the Archbishop of Canterbury, and to the shock and chagrin of much of British society, he left the Anglican Church and became a Catholic priest. Benson died young, at 41, just after finishing this book.

The Lord of the World is an apocalypse. It tells the story of the cataclysmic struggle between a radically secularist society and the one credible alternative to it, namely, the Catholic Church. In Benson's imagined future, Europe and America are dominated by a rationalist regime bent on making life as technologically convenient and politically harmonious as possible. The leaders of this government see the Catholic Church, with its stress on the supernatural, on divisive dogma, and on the enduring power of sin, as the principle obstacle to progress. A great messianic figure—Julian Felsenburg—emerges from the heart of the secularist political structure, and he prosecutes a progressively brutal persecution of the Church, culminating in the elimination of the Church, the curia, and most of the bishops of the world. He then establishes an alternative liturgy, predicated upon the worship of an idealized humanity and the rhythms of nature. (In a delicious touch, Benson imagines a former Catholic priest as the master of ceremonies of the new secular liturgy). In the meantime, one surviving cardinal—an Englishman who bears a striking physical resemblance to Felsenburg—becomes the pope and takes up his administration of the Church in simple quarters in Jesus' home town of Nazareth. The novel concludes with the climactic struggle between Felsenburg's secular power and the spiritual power of the Church.

Now like any apocalypse, this one is a bit exaggerated and melodramatic; nevertheless, there are a lot of lessons for us in it. It is truly impressive that, in 1907, Benson saw, as clearly as he did, the dangerous potential of the secularist ideology. By this I mean the view that this world, perfected and rendered convenient by technology, would ultimately satisfy the deepest longing of the human heart. One of the most elemental truths that the Catholic Church preserves is that human beings have been created by and for God and that they will therefore be permanently dissatisfied with anything less than God.

In his monumental study of modern society, *The Secular Age*, the philosopher Charles Taylor speaks of the "disenchanted universe" that has come as a result of the eclipse of religion. This means a world without ultimate meaning or a transcendent reference; a world that speaks only of itself. Benson's book paints a distressing but realistic picture of people moving about in a disenchanted universe, oscillating between the poles of boredom and fear. One of the most pathetic characters in the novel is Mabel Brand, the wife of a leader of the English political establishment and a woman who once believed in the new secular religion with all her heart. When she saw through its façade to its underlying brutality and inhumanity, she cracked and saw no way out. Like many in her exhausted society, she opted for self-induced and state-sponsored euthanasia. One doesn't have to be terribly perceptive to appreciate how prophetic all of this has proven to be.

The other truth that Benson grasped was that the Catholic Church, with its firm teaching on the reality of the supernatural, is, finally, the single great opponent to this worldview. There is a high paradox here. Catholics know that what makes this world fascinating and enticing is precisely the conviction that it is not ultimate; that there is a denser and more permanent world that transcends it. In the light of faith, the things of this ordinary universe, which in themselves would never be enough to satisfy us, become sacraments of an eternal reality.

Someone who caught this same paradox was Benson's contemporary G.K. Chesterton. Chesterton said that when he was an agnostic and expected to find joy in this world, he was always listless and depressed but that when he found faith, and realized that he was not meant to be fulfilled in this world, he actually became happy and took delight in ordinary things. A younger contemporary of both Chesterton and Benson, Evelyn Waugh, expressed much the same thing when he observed, "for Catholics, the supernatural is the real."

What Robert Hugh Benson saw with extraordinary clarity is that all political fights or cultural battles are all relatively superficial struggles. The final—and finally interesting—battle is metaphysical and religious. It comes down to this question: Do we live in an enchanted universe or not? Everything hinges on the way that question is answered.

A Catholic Reads *The Shack*

PERHAPS YOU'VE HEARD of the publishing phenomenon called *The Shack*. The book, written by William P. Young, was brought out in 2007 and has become an international sensation, riding atop the *New York Times* paperback bestseller list for years and remaining a fixture on the Amazon bestseller lists. What makes *The Shack* an extremely unusual bestseller is that it's a modern retelling of the book of Job, an exploration of the problem of God in relation to human suffering.

The book's protagonist is Mackenzie Phillips, a decent family man whose youngest daughter, Missy, we learn, had been kidnapped and brutally murdered by a twisted serial killer. The last trace of his daughter, a blood-stained dress, had been found on the floor of a dilapidated shack set deep in the woods. In the wake of the murder, a crushing depression settled on Mackenzie, and he began to question his belief in God. As the novel opens, Mack receives a mysterious invitation to come to the shack. The note, without return address or any other identifying marker, is signed, "Papa," the name that Mack's wife typically uses for God. Fully aware of the dangers (the note could have been penned by the killer), but desperate for answers, Mack goes to the shack and there he meets, to his infinite surprise, the three-personed God.

The second half of the novel unfolds as a series of conversations that the grieving man has, together and separately, with the Father, Jesus, and the Holy Spirit. What I found immediately attractive—and theologically right—about *The Shack* is that God is portrayed as love right through. The Father, Son, and Spirit relate to one another as friends and insist, over and again, that they want to draw Mack, and the whole human race, into a share in their fellowship. Thomas Aquinas referred to this as *deificatio* (deification), a participation in the dynamics of the Trinitarian love.

Further, the three persons of God are depicted by William Young as both infinitely and intimately knowledgeable: God knows Mack through and through; he knows every detail of his painful story; he knows the quality and depth of Mack's resistance to grace. I do think that many in our culture are haunted by a deism that places God at a great distance from our ordinary concerns. The God of *The Shack* is decidedly not the deist God, but rather the God of Psalm 139: "Lord, you search me and you know me. You know my resting and my rising; you discern my purpose from afar." And this means, in turn, that God is someone to whom we can speak, and not just in the sometimes stilted and abstract language of formal prayer. Mack goes on long walks with Jesus; he gardens with the Holy Spirit; he helps to prepare meals with the Father. I realize how strange this can sound, but then we recall that, in the Genesis story, Adam walked with God in the cool of the evening and conversed with him friend to friend, and that Jesus ate and drank with his disciples, even preparing a meal for them by the Sea of Galilee.

The central issue of the novel—Mack's anger over God's seeming refusal to protect Missy—is also handled creatively and in the biblical spirit. God explains that the original sin involved the establishment of the limited human mind as the criterion of what is ultimately good and evil. What this led to was a loss of trust in the God whose purposes are always good, even when that goodness lies beyond the human capacity to see.

Now many critics of *The Shack* have emerged (which is inevitable when the topic is God!), and I can't possibly explore all of the objections. I will focus only on what bothered me the most. Toward the end of the novel, Mack's conversations with the Trinity turn to the issues of law and "religion," and I was somewhat disquieted when God began to sound like Martin Luther! We hear that God gave us the Ten Commandments only to convince us how incapable we are of ever living up to them and that the law involves an interruption in the grace of relationship and that those who are in Jesus are free from the demands of "rules and obligations." As I say, all of this is out of the standard Reformation handbook, and Catholics have legitimately balked at it for five hundred years. We appreciate the law, not as a reminder of our incapacity, but as the structuring logic of love, the rules that govern our lives within the household of God. Luther and his disciples (including William Young) tend to set up a dialectic of opposition between law and grace, but Catholics see the two as analogically related, law fulfilled by grace and grace leading to a deeper embrace of the heart of the law.

Would I recommend *The Shack*? Yes, absolutely, especially to those who have suffered a great loss. But, if I can borrow a metaphor, reading it is a bit like eating a watermelon: lots of good sweet stuff to eat, but you've got to spit out a few seeds!

A Tale of Two Hitchenses

I'VE WRITTEN OFTEN ABOUT CHRISTOPHER HITCHENS, the world's most prominent atheist. I wrote a piece on the CNN blog urging Christians to pray for Hitchens as he battled a very serious form of cancer—and to my astonishment, this benign recommendation was met with an extraordinarily negative reaction from atheists. But that's a story for another day. On vacation, I took two books with me, Christopher Hitchens's memoir *Hitch-22*, which I had begun and wanted to finish, and his brother Peter Hitchens's *The Rage Against God: How Atheism Led Me to Faith*, a stunning account of the younger Hitchens's journey through militant Trotskyite atheism to a robust Christianity. It was a fascinating, and I must admit rather unnerving, experience to overhear, as it were, the brothers Hitchens debating with one another in my own head. Things got so intense that Christopher Hitchens actually appeared in one of my dreams during the vacation!

Whereas Christopher has a rather baroque literary style, his brother writes soberly and directly. His fundamental theme is this: though the atheists claim just the contrary, the collapse of Christianity carries in its wake dire consequences for civilization itself. Peter Hitchens was a foreign correspondent in Moscow during the waning years of the Soviet Union, and he experienced a culture in deep crisis. There was political corruption of every type on every level of the system; there was widespread drunkenness; abortions far outnumbered live births; and a suspension of common courtesies—exchanging common signs, holding doors, etc.—was everywhere in evidence. How does one begin to explain this almost total ethical collapse? Hitchens argues that it followed ineluctably from a conscious and brutally enforced Soviet policy in regard to religion. From the earliest days of the regime, that is to say, even before the rise of Stalin, the Soviet government launched a systematic attack on religion, especially Russian Orthodoxy. Priests and nuns were, in great numbers, put to death or arrested, and the few that were allowed to live were consistently harassed, mocked, and humiliated. Furthermore, religion was constantly pilloried as "unscientific" and "backward"; considered the stuff of crude superstition and pre-modern mythology. And religious instruction was strictly disallowed in the educational system. In fact, it was routinely characterized as a form of child abuse, a poisoning of the minds of the young.

Peter Hitchens suggests that there is a clear causal relationship between this brutal anti-religious strategy and the civilizational breakdown that was universally on display in the Soviet Union by the early 1990s. This is precisely because the moral matrix that one tends to take for granted is in fact a consequence of certain very basic religious convictions, including and especially the belief in God as a guarantor of moral absolutes. Once God has been jettisoned, or at the very least marginalized, morality becomes relative. And once morality is relativized, it devolves, finally, into a function of oppression, the behavioral system instituted by and for the powerful.

Now what Peter Hitchens sees in the work of his brother and the other popular atheist writers—Sam Harris, Richard Dawkins, Daniel Dennett, etc.—is a tragic repeat of the Soviet program. All of the "new" atheists call for the elimination of religion as something poisonous; they all characterize it as "pre-scientific" and "superstitious", and in perhaps the most damning parallel, they, to a person, describe religious education as a species of child abuse. Peter's conclusion is that this sort of aggression, though often presented as an enlightened strategy, would result in precisely the same kind of moral collapse that he witnessed in the Gorbachev-era Soviet Union. The "new" atheists, he thinks, don't realize that the very ethical principles that they point to with such vigor (Christopher, for example, is in a constant state of high dudgeon over any number of moral outrages around the world) are mortally threatened by an attack on God. Without a transcendent referent, morality becomes as vacillating and capricious as the human will itself. Christopher Hitchens and his colleagues, Peter argues, don't see that, in making ethical appeals, they are implicitly accepting the very cultural matrix that they are explicitly trying to undermine.

Peter Hitchens sees, in point of fact, some disturbing signs in our own Western societies that the breakdown of religion is having just this ethically destabilizing effect. In a culture where an absolute and transcendentally grounded moral code has been jettisoned, "nursing has become less dedicated, wives more inclined to leave their babbling husbands in care homes to be looked after impersonally by paid strangers...and soldiers readier to save themselves while their comrades lie in pain within reach of the enemy." Traditional morality, grounded in a keen sense of the divine command, called people consistently beyond themselves and their own desires, even when that call involved the total sacrifice of the self. Atheist morality devolves, almost inevitably, into a species of might makes right, the will of the stronger becoming the criterion of good and evil.

We've all had ample opportunity over the years to hear the reflections of Christopher Hitchens. I think it would be a fine idea indeed to listen now to his eloquent brother.

The Last Acceptable Prejudice
Rides Again

ANTI-CATHOLICISM HAS LONG BEEN A FEATURE of both the high and the low culture in America. From the nineteenth century to the middle of the twentieth century, it was out in the open. Many editorialists, cartoonists, politicians, and other shapers of popular opinion in that era were crudely explicit in their opposition to the Catholic Church. But then, in the latter half of the twentieth century, anti-Catholicism went relatively underground. It still existed, to be sure, but it was considered bad form to be too obvious about it. However, in the last decade or two, the old demon has resurfaced. There are many reasons for this, including the animosity to religion in general prompted by the events of September 11th and, of course, the clerical sex abuse scandal that has, legitimately enough, besmirched the reputation of the Catholic Church. I'm not interested here so much in exploring the precipitating causes of this negative attitude as I am in showing the crudity and unintelligence of its latest manifestations. Permit me to share two examples.

I recently finished James Miller's *Examined Lives*, a biographical study of twelve great philosophers, from Socrates to Nietzsche. I found Miller's treatment of St. Augustine to be extraordinary, not because it shed any particularly new light on the saint's work, but because it was so unapologetically anti-Catholic. Miller comments approvingly on the young Augustine, the intellectual seeker who moved from Manichaeism to neo-Platonism in the open-minded

SEEDS OF THE WORD: FINDING GOD IN THE CULTURE

quest for the always elusive truth. But on Miller's reading, the seeker's fall from grace was his embrace of the "closed system" of Christianity, which led Augustine to become a coldly oppressive sectarian. Here is how Miller brings his analysis of Augustine to a close: "He lay the conceptual grounds for creating perhaps the most powerful community of closed belief in world history—the Catholic Church that ruled over medieval Western Europe as an all-encompassing, if not quite totalitarian theocracy, unrivaled before or since by any other religious or secular one party state, be it Muslim or Communist." The not so subtle implication (despite that little "not quite" in front of "totalitarian") is that the Catholic Church has proven more oppressive than the Taliban and the states fronted by Lenin, Stalin, Mao, and Pol Pot!

But Miller's excursions into anti-Catholicism seem as nothing when compared to the exertions of Mark Warren, the executive editor of *Esquire* magazine. In a piece on his blog, Warren drew attention to an exposé of the Church of Scientology that appeared in the pages of *The New Yorker* magazine. He praised the author for revealing the ridiculous beliefs of Scientology, which are based upon the wild science-fictionesque musings of L. Ron Hubbard. But then Warren commented that these claims are no wilder, no more irrational, than those of any other of the "great" religions, including and especially Christianity. What follows is one of the most ludicrous "summaries" of Christian belief I've ever read. Here are some highlights: "I grew up believing that every breath I drew sent a god-made-man named Jesus Christ writhing on the cross to which he had been nailed—an execution for which he had been sent to earth by his heavenly father." And "yet I was born not innocent but complicit in this lynching, incomprehensibly having to apologize and atone for this barbarism for all my days and feel terrible about myself and all mankind." And "his [Jesus'] spirit had risen on a cloud into heaven to rejoin the same god in the sky who had sent him on this errand in the first place."

One notices here something that is also on display in the anti-Christian polemics of Bill Maher and Christopher Hitchens, namely, a presentation of Christianity that is informed by a painfully childish "theology," something out of a half-understood grade-school catechism. For example, Maher, Hitchens, Warren, and many other critics speak of the Christian belief in a "sky god," betraying absolutely no sensitivity to the dynamics of symbolic language in a religious context. The "heavenly" Father of whom biblically minded people speak is not a being who dwells in the clouds, but rather a reality that radically transcends the categories of ordinary experience. And I can only smile at the sheer weirdness of Warren's characterization of the purpose and meaning of Christ's death on the cross.

The correct doctrine is that God, in Christ, entered, out of love, into the depth of human misery, sin, and failure in order to bring the divine light even to those darkest places. It is in this sense that he took away the sins of the world and brought us life from the Father. In John's Gospel, Jesus said, simply, "I have come that you might have life and have it to the full," and St. Irenaeus, the great second-century theological master, said, "The glory of God is a human being fully alive." I don't know where Mark Warren received his education in Catholic theology, but I can assure him that not one of his breaths is causing Jesus to suffer, and that he has no need to "atone" or "apologize" for what the Lord did on the cross. To address all of the issues that he raises, I'd have to offer Mr. Warren a course in basic theology and invite him to move beyond his elementary school understanding of Christian doctrine.

Convinced that Christian teaching is as much "mumbo-jumbo" as L. Ron Hubbard's silliness, Warren urges his fellow journalists to let small-fry Scientology off the hook and go after some bigger fish, especially the cult into which he was initiated as a child—the Catholic Church. He wants them (and here the anti-Catholicism is blatant) to target the pope in his "palace in the Vatican" who protects "criminals and child-molesters...with the ruthless demeanor of the CEO of a massive corporation lawyering up against the barrage of lawsuits to come." Well. The sex-abuse crisis is real and devastating, but no one in the world has done more to address it over the past twenty years than Joseph Ratzinger, Pope Benedict XVI. No one has taken more concrete steps to deal with abusive priests and dysfunctional institutional patterns than him. To identify him as one of the "creeps" (Warren's word) that journalists should investigate is not only mean-spirited but stupid.

Again, what is most remarkable in all of this is not the unintelligence of the explicit claims being made but rather the blatancy of the contempt for the Church. When this hoary old prejudice shows itself, Catholics have to stand up to it, lest it be allowed to evolve into something even more dangerous.

One More Swing at the Catholic Straw-Man

IN 2005, Harvard scholar Stephen Greenblatt published a wonderful book on Shakespeare called *Will in the World*. Witty, insightful, and surprising, it caused thousands of people, including your humble scribe, to look at the Bard with new eyes. Thus it was with great anticipation that I opened my copy of Greenblatt's next book, *The Swerve: How the World Became Modern*. Like its forebear, this book is indeed lively, intelligent, and fun to read, but as I moved through it, I grew increasingly irritated and finally exasperated by its steady insistence upon one of the most tired myths of the contemporary academy, namely, that the modern world, in all of its wonder and promise, emerged out of a long and desperate struggle with (wait for it) Roman Catholicism.

The unlikely hero of Greenblatt's story is one Poggio Bracciolini, a humanist of the early fifteenth century who labored as a scribe at the papal court and who, in his spare time, searched for ancient texts that were neglected and moldering in monastic libraries across Europe. On a hunting expedition, most likely to the great monastery at Fulda, Poggio liberated a text that, Greenblatt holds, decisively shaped the evolution of the modern mind: *De rerum natura* (On the Nature of Things), composed by the first century BC Roman writer Lucretius. In this philosophical poem Lucretius argued that the universe is made up exclusively of atoms—tiny, invisible particles—that, across infinite time and through infinite space, randomly arrange themselves into patterns and then fall apart. Furthermore, he taught that there is no divine mind governing the process; the soul is as mortal and dissoluble as the body; there is no afterlife; humans are not unique in the cosmos but rather are animals somewhat more evolved than others; religion is fear-based and cruel; and the whole point of life is to maximize pleasure and avoid pain. Greenblatt takes the rather cold and grim vision of the universe laid out in *De rerum natura* as a harbinger of the "modern" view that happily holds sway today—at least in Ivy League faculty lounges.

To make his story more dramatic, Greenblatt had to portray Poggio as a culture warrior, battling against a retrenched and oppressive Catholicism—and this is where his book really goes off the rails. I will give just a few examples of the egregious caricature of medieval Christianity that he feels compelled to present. Whereas Lucretius, Poggio, and their modern intellectual successors were marked by a restless curiosity and an adventurous desire to explore the physical universe, Catholics, Greenblatt maintains, were dogmatic, repressive, and exclusively otherworldly. As evidence for this claim, he cites the medieval conviction, cultivated especially in the monasteries, that *curiositas* is a sin. Well, it might have helped if he had searched out what medieval Christians meant by that term. He would have discovered that *curiositas* names, not intellectual curiosity, but what we might characterize as gossip or minding other people's business, seeking to know that which you have no business knowing. In point of fact, the virtue that answers the vice of *curiositas* is *studiositas* (studiousness), the serious pursuit of knowledge. And as anyone even mildly familiar with medieval Christianity knows, this virtue was exemplified by some of the greatest spirits that western civilization has produced. St. Albert the Great assiduously studied Aristotelianism, which was the leading science of his time and which was concerned, above all, with searching out the causes of things. St. Thomas Aquinas's soaring intellectualism is on vivid display on every page of his voluminous work, which runs the gamut from God and the angels to planets, plants, human societies, economics, politics, animals, etc. Bonaventure, Duns Scotus, William of Ockham, Alexander of Hales, Henry of Ghent, Roger Bacon—to name just some of the most prominent figures—pursued scientific, practical, and metaphysical questions with an intensity and, yes, a curiosity rarely rivaled. I readily grant that an intellectual paradigm shift occurred in the sixteenth century, but to claim that the sciences emerged out of rank and uncurious superstition is simply a calumny.

A second feature of Greenblatt's caricature is that medieval Christianity was dualistic, morose, deeply opposed to the pleasures of the body, and masochistic in its asceticism. As evidence he brings forward the many accounts of self-flagellation and use of the "discipline" that took place in medieval monasteries and among penitential societies. No one can deny that such practices were a feature of medieval religious life, but to take them as somehow paradigmatic of the medieval attitude toward the body is simply ridiculous. Nowhere in the literature of the world do we see more boisterous and even bawdy celebrations of the body, sensual pleasure, and sexuality than in Dante's *Divine Comedy*, Chaucer's *Canterbury Tales*, and Boccaccio's *Decameron* and even a casual glance at the figures in the colored glass windows of Chartres Cathedral or the Sainte Chapelle reveals an extraordinary celebration of the energy and color of ordinary life. That the dominant Christian attitude in the Middle Ages was a life-denying asceticism is quite absurd.

Despite Greenblatt's assertions, the Catholic Middle Ages did not require Lucretius's *De rerum natura* to learn the importance of either intellectual curiosity or the joys of this life. And in point of fact, the cultural world of modernity that emerged through the exertions of Descartes, Pascal, Galileo, Newton, Jefferson and company actually owed a great deal, intellectually and artistically, to the medieval period. The story of modernity's rise is much more complex and finally much more interesting than the one told by Stephen Greenblatt, and it is altogether possible to celebrate the legitimate achievements of modern culture without knocking down a strawman version of Catholicism.

The Gospel According to *The Hobbit*

LIKE *STAR WARS*, *The Divine Comedy*, and *Moby Dick*, J.R.R. Tolkien's *The Hobbit* is the story of a hero's journey. This helps to explain, of course, why, like those other narratives, it has proved so perennially compelling.

The hero's tale follows a classical, almost stereotyped, pattern: a person is wrenched out of complacency and self-absorption and called to a great adventure, during which he (or she), through struggle, comes to maturity and vision. In *Moby Dick*, the young Ishmael quits the narrow space of his depressed mind ("whenever it is a damp drizzly November in my soul") and goes on a long and dangerous voyage of discovery; in *The Divine Comedy*, the middle-aged Dante leaves the dark wood where he had become lost and goes on a pilgrimage through Hell, Purgatory, and Heaven, until he comes at last to salvation; and in *Star Wars*, the teenage Luke Skywalker (who is modeled in many ways after Dante) is forced out of the quietude of his aunt and uncle's home and summoned to an intergalactic struggle against dark powers, which results in his coming of age.

The Hobbit begins, humbly enough, with this line: "In a hole in the ground there lived a hobbit." Tolkien is quick to clarify that this is not a nasty or unkempt hole, like the lair of a mouse, but rather a cozy place, filled with fine furniture, doilies, and a well-stocked kitchen. This is the homey, all-too-comfortable space from which Bilbo Baggins (the hobbit in question) will be summoned to adventure.

To the door of Bilbo's residence comes Gandalf the wizard, a figure evocative of the in-breaking of grace. This association between the wizard and supernatural grace is not an arbitrary one, for Tolkien was a devout Catholic, and Christian themes abound in this particular hero's story. Though he ardently resists it at first, Bilbo eventually accepts Gandalf's invitation to join a cadre of dwarves on their mission to recover a horde of treasure that had been absconded by a dragon named Smaug. He will come to maturity precisely in the measure that he leaves his "comfort zone" and finds the path of self-sacrificing love.

The mission is marked, at every turn, by danger. Bilbo and the dwarves confront hungry trolls, fierce orcs, wicked goblins, ferocious wolves, giant spiders, and eventually the mighty fire-breathing dragon himself. These fanciful characters signal the fact of serious evil at work in the world. Tolkien was a participant in the trench warfare of the First World War, and thus experienced firsthand cruelty, violence, injustice, depravity, and mind-numbing fear. His Christian faith gave him the conviction that all of this evil was the result of sin, at both the human and super-human level. It also helped him to see that the whole point of life was to enter into the fights against evil; to find one's unique calling to battle wickedness and hence bring the world more into conformity with the reign of God.

What is particularly instructive in *The Hobbit* is the manner in which a Christian knight properly engages in the battle. At a key moment in the story, Gandalf suggests that while many think darkness is best opposed through exercises of great worldly power, in point of fact, it is most effectively countered through simple acts of kindness. This is, of course, nothing but Jesus' still deeply challenging teaching in the Sermon on the Mount that evil is properly resisted through love, nonviolence, and forgiveness. The most striking example of this principle in action is Bilbo's refusal to kill the loathsome and dangerous Gollum when he has the chance. As readers of *The Lord of the Rings* know, Gollum would, despite himself, play a decisive role in the destruction of the ring. Had Bilbo indulged his violent instincts and put Gollum to death, the day would not have been saved. That evil is best engaged through pity is a deeply Christian and profoundly counterintuitive insight.

At the climax of *The Hobbit*, the adventurers come face-to-face with Smaug, the dragon who, deep in the bowels of a great mountain, guards a pile of treasure absconded from the dwarves many years before. The beast knows every little bit of his horde: each coin, each goblet, each jewel and precious stone. To be sure, he cannot possibly use or benefit from any of it, but he wallows in it and protects it with his life. Tolkien refers to this weird obsession as "the dragon sickness," and he implies that it bedevils many people in contemporary society, those who know the value of everything and the worth of nothing.

Nurtured by Catholic social teaching, Tolkien was no defender of laissez-faire capitalism or modern industrialism. In fact, he saw both as soul-killing, for the spirit thrives, not on gaining possessions, but on emptying out the self in love. This is why the killing of the dragon is such a moment of liberation. However, it is most important to observe how the sudden freeing up of the treasure awakens the dragon-sickness in hundreds of other creatures in Tolkien's Middle Earth, who stream toward the mountain to claim Smaug's trove. The battle of these rival claimants is held off (and I won't give too much of the story away here) by an unexpected act of letting-go on Bilbo's part, not unlike the letting-go of the ring at the conclusion of *The Lord of the Rings*. Once more, maturity comes, not from getting, but from giving.

A coming-of-age story, a rollicking adventure tale, a delicious fantasy, and a droll commentary on human foibles—*The Hobbit* is all that. But finally, it is a narrative spun by a serious Catholic who wants to communicate the still-surprising ethics of the Gospel.

The City Upon a Hill and an Almost Chosen People

In 2012, when Ross Douthat published *Bad Religion: How We Became a Nation of Heretics*, it certainly became the most talked-about religion book of the year. The *New York Times* op-ed columnist discussed his work everywhere: CNN, the 700 Club, Andrew Sullivan's *Daily Beast* video blog, and even *Real Time with Bill Maher*. His central thesis can be rather simply stated: institutional religion is in disarray and decline in America, yet an overwhelming majority of Americans are religious. And this means, Douthat argues, that they have succumbed, for the most part, to heretical versions of classical Christianity; forms of thought that draw a good deal of inspiration from orthodox Christianity but manage to depart from, even pervert, the substance upon which they are parasitic.

He names and explores a number of these modern-day Christian heresies, including the "Prosperity Gospel," which more or less identifies the goal of the spiritual life as material success, as well as the "God-Within" religion, which turns the God of the Bible into a greater Self—something like the Oversoul in Ralph Waldo Emerson's mysticism. This latter heresy is on vivid display, Douthat argues, in much of Oprah Winfrey's spiritual teaching, in the feel-good ruminations of Deepak Chopra, and in novels such as *Eat, Pray, Love*, which extols the God "who is in you as you." Both of these spiritualities borrow extensively from classical Christianity. Thus Joel Osteen, the most popular advocate of the Prosperity

Gospel, is the son of an evangelical preacher; and Winfrey, Chopra, and their innumerable disciples cite the New Testament and the teachings of Jesus frequently. This blending of Christianity with decidedly unchristian ideas makes these contemporary ideologies—like the Gnosticism of the second century or the Manichaeism of the fourth century—Christian heresies.

Since I've written quite a bit about the two heresies mentioned above, I would like to draw attention to a third corruption of Christianity upon which Douthat rather deftly puts his finger. This is the tendency to identify the Kingdom of God, as described in the Bible, with American ideals and the American cultural system. Douthat draws attention to an extraordinary rally, organized and led by the conservative political commentator Glenn Beck, during which Beck seamlessly blended his vision of a dominant America with the spiritual aspirations of the prophets of Israel toward the realization of God's reign. And he observes the affinity between this Beckian perspective and the triumphant affirmation, made most memorably by President George W. Bush in his second inaugural address, of American democracy as a world-saving, God-inspired ideology. That Bush's claims were much more than abstract became unmistakably clear when the President sent planes, tanks, and troops in order to impose democracy on an Iraq that was utterly unprepared, politically and culturally, for such an imposition.

Douthat insists that this identification of the American system with divine purpose is by no means the exclusive preserve of conservatives. In fact, in the course of the twentieth century, liberal statesmen have been some of its most devoted advocates. At the close of the First World War, Woodrow Wilson shared his vision that an American-style democracy, including the rule of law and respect for the rights of ethnic peoples to self-determination, would usher in a world free of war. That Wilson could not even get his own Congress to agree to his pet idea of a League of Nations, and that Europe, within two decades of the end of the First World War, plunged into a second and even more devastating conflagration were rather clear indications of the utopian character of this dream. Moreover, in the middle of the last century, both John F. Kennedy and Lyndon B. Johnson offered new versions of the Wilsonian project: the New Frontier and the Great Society, both attempts to realize the Kingdom through political change. Much of the American politics of the last four decades can be read as a response—by turns angry, nostalgic, and skeptical—to that earlier utopianism.

Douthat concludes, quite correctly, that the Kingdom of God, as the Bible envisions it, ought never to be identified with any political or cultural status quo. That Kingdom represents the accomplishment of God's grace. Hence, every political or cultural system—even one as relatively benign as the American—falls under judgment. And indeed the best of our political and religious figures have clearly understood this. Many American statesmen—Ronald Reagan most recently—have drawn inspiration from John Winthrop's 1630 sermon "A Model of Christian Charity," in which the colonial leader spoke of the society he and his fellows were about to found as "a city upon a hill," which is to say, a visible place of great interest to the rest of the world. If one reads the whole of Winthrop's homily, it becomes clear that he is not one-sidedly extolling the virtues of the new colony, but just the contrary. He is warning his people that since their experiment in ordered liberty would be carefully watched, they must be vigilant lest sin get the better of them.

President-elect Abraham Lincoln, in a February 1861 address to the New Jersey General Assembly, said, "I shall be most happy indeed if I shall be a humble instrument in the hands of the Almighty, and of this his almost chosen people..." How wonderful that

Lincoln, who certainly read American history in light of his belief in Divine Providence, was careful not simply to identify America with the chosen people of Israel, but to imply that an "almost chosen" people would always stand in need of correction.

Why Faith is Indeed a Light

IN "NEW" ATHEIST AND SECULARIST CIRCLES today, faith is regularly ridiculed. It is presented as pre-scientific mumbo jumbo, Bronze Age credulity, the surrender of the intellect, unwarranted submission to authority, etc. Time and again, the late Christopher Hitchens, echoing Immanuel Kant, called on people to be intellectually responsible, to think for themselves, to dare to know. This coming of age would be impossible, he insisted, without the abandonment of religious faith. And in standard accounts of cultural history, the "age of faith" is presented as a retrograde and regressive dark age, out of which emerged, only after a long twilight struggle, the modern physical sciences and their attendant technologies. In accord with this cynical reading, the contemporary media almost invariably present people of "faith" as hopelessly unenlightened yahoos or dangerous fanatics. If you want the very best example of this, watch Bill Maher's film *Religulous*.

It was to counter this deeply distorted understanding of faith that Pope Benedict XVI composed an encyclical letter, which appeared under the name of his papal successor and bears the title *Lumen Fidei* (The Light of Faith). The text—smart, allusive, ruminative, informed by a profound grasp of cultural trends—is, though signed by Pope Francis, unmistakably Ratzingerian. Though it is impossible in the context of this brief article to do justice to its rich content, I should like to gesture, however briefly, to a few of its principal motifs.

The holy father's move is to confront directly the sort of rationalistic dismissal of faith that I just outlined. Moderns, in love with the illuminating power of technological reason, have, as we have seen, tended to view faith, not as light, but as obscurity. But the pope insists that faith is the proper, indeed reasonable, response to the experience of the living God, who is not an object in the world, but rather the Creator of the world. Precisely because he is the source of all finite existence, God is not one being among many, and hence cannot be pinned down on an examining table and lit up with the harsh light of technological reason. The prophet Isaiah expressed this point with admirable economy: "Truly you are God who hides himself, O God of Israel, Savior" (Isa 45:15). Isaiah does not mean that God is a worldly reality that is, for the moment, hidden away, like the dark side of the moon; rather, he means that God is a reality which cannot, even in principle, be seen in the ordinary way. Further, the hidden God is not an abstract force or a distant first cause. He is, instead, a living person, and this means that he cannot be manipulated, controlled, or analyzed in an intrusive manner. Therefore, faith, or trusting acceptance, is the only legitimate response to an experience of such a reality.

The encyclical's second move is to show how the darkness of faith, once embraced, actually turns into light. By accepting God's overture, the faith-filled person finds the supreme value, which unifies and gives direction to the whole of his life; he basks in the light, which illumines every aspect of his existence. In the absence of faith in the one God, a person necessarily drifts from idol to idol, that is to say, from one fleeting value to another. One of the Pope's most brilliant observations is that idolatry, therefore, is always a type of polytheism, a chase after a multiplicity of gods, none of which can satisfy: "Idolatry does not offer a journey but rather a plethora of paths leading nowhere and forming a vast labyrinth." What an apt description of the spiritual state of so many in our postmodern condition. And how deeply congruent with the biblical notion that the rejection of God conduces automatically to a disintegration of the self. Notice that biblical demons speak typically in the plural.

The pope's third major move is to show that authentic faith is liberating, and he does this by returning to St. Paul's classic texts on justification. Famously, the apostle argued in his letter to the Romans and elsewhere that salvation comes, not through works of the law, but through faith in what Jesus has accomplished. The Holy Father reads this, not in the Lutheran manner, as a demonization of "good works," but rather as a reminder that real salvation comes by way of surrendering to God's purposes. When we are convinced that our fundamental well-being depends on our efforts and the accomplishment of our plans, we lock ourselves into the cramped quarters of the sovereign Self. But when we acknowledge through faith the primacy of grace, we move in the infinite and exciting space of God's intentions for us. As all of the great spiritual masters have acknowledged, our lives are not, finally, about us, and in that realization we find peace and joy. Dante expressed the idea splendidly: "In your will, O Lord, is our peace."

I think that this encyclical could best be interpreted as Pope Benedict's and Pope Francis's challenge to the secularist ideology that has already enveloped Western Europe and that is now threatening our country. It is a reminder that faith alone can deliver us from the tyranny and sadness of the closed-in self.

Debunking the Debunker

WHEN I SAW THAT REZA ASLAN'S PORTRAIT of Jesus, *Zealot: The Life and Times of Jesus of Nazareth*, had risen to number one on the *New York Times* bestseller list, I must confess, I was both disappointed and puzzled. For the reductionist and debunking approach that Aslan employs has been tried by dozens of commentators for at least the past three hundred years, and the debunkers have been themselves debunked over and over again by serious scholars of the historical Jesus.

Here is how the method works: a scholar focuses on one aspect of Jesus' life, finds all of the Gospel passages that emphasize that aspect and declares them historically reliable, and then casually characterizes the rest of the Gospels as the non-historical musings of the evangelists and their communities. So in the course of the last three centuries, Jesus has been presented as, exclusively, an eschatological prophet, an itinerant preacher of the kingdom, a wonder-worker, a magician, a social revolutionary, an avatar of enlightened ethics, a cynic philosopher, etc. To be sure, evidence can be culled from the Gospels for all of these identities, but the problem is that these portraits invariably fail to present "Jesus in full," the strange, beguiling, elusive, and richly complex figure that emerges from a thorough reading of the New Testament.

The Jesus that Aslan wants to present is the "zealot," which is to say, the Jewish insurrectionist intent upon challenging the Temple establishment in Jerusalem and, above all, the Roman military power that dominated the land of Israel. His principle justification for this reading is that religiously motivated revolutionaries were indeed thick on the ground in the Palestine of Jesus' time; that Jesus claimed to be ushering in a new Kingdom of God; and that he ended up dying the death typically meted out to rabble-rousers who posed a threat to Roman authority. Jesus, he argues, fits neatly into the pattern set by Menahem, the heroic defender of Masada, Judas the Galilean, Simon son of Giora, Simon bar Kochba, and any number of other revolutionaries who claimed messianic identity and who, in the end, were ground under by the Romans. On this reading, Jesus indeed died on a Roman cross, but he didn't rise from the dead; instead, his body was probably left on the cross to be devoured by dogs or the birds of the air.

Now questions immediately crowd the mind. What about Jesus' extraordinary stress on nonviolence and love of enemies (hardly the stern stuff we would expect from a zealot)? Oh, it was made up by the later Christian community that was trying to curry favor with Roman society. What about Jesus' explicit claim that his kingdom was "not of this world"? Oh, those were words placed in his mouth by John the evangelist. What about his practically constant references to prayer, the spiritual life, and trust in divine providence? Oh, that was pious invention. What about the stories of his outreach to the woman at the well, the man born blind, and Zacchaeus? What about the healing of Bartimaeus, the raising of Lazarus, and the raising of the daughter of Jairus, actions having precious little to do with anti-Roman activism? By now, you can guess the answer, and I trust you see the problem: huge swaths of the Gospel and the early Christian witness have to be cut away in order to accommodate the portrait that Aslan paints.

The most massive difficulty with Aslan's interpretation is that it cannot begin to account for the stubborn fact that no one except specialist historians remembers Judas the Galilean, Menahem, or Simon bar Kochba—but everyone remembers Jesus of Nazareth. The clearest indication possible that someone was not the Messiah of Israel would have been his death at the hands of Israel's enemies, for the Messiah was supposed to be a liberator and conqueror. And this is precisely why those failed revolutionaries were so quickly forgotten. But Christianity emerged as none other than a messianic movement. Paul said, over and over again, *Iesous Christos*, simply his Greek rendering of *Ieshouah Maschiach* (Jesus the Messiah). How could he and the other early evangelists have declared the messianic identity of a crucified criminal unless they knew that, despite his ignominious death, he had indeed conquered the enemies of Israel? And how could they have come to that conclusion apart from the resurrection of that crucified criminal from the dead? It turns out that the most convincing explanation, on historical grounds, of the emergence and endurance of the Christian movement is the very thing that Aslan and like-minded interpreters write off as a later concoction of the community.

I would like to say just a bit more about this last point. As I've indicated, the favorite strategy of the Jesus reductionists is to claim that much of the Gospel material was invented, made up out of whole cloth by the developing Christian communities. Time and again, they insist that, since the earliest Gospel was written forty years after the time of Jesus, it couldn't possibly contain more than a smattering of historically reliable material. But this is so much nonsense. Would we automatically reject as non-historical a book published in 2003 about the Kennedy assassination? Wouldn't we naturally assume that the author had consulted historical records as well as numerous eyewitnesses to the events of November 22, 1963?

Those who knew Jesus, who listened to his words and saw his great deeds, who witnessed his death and resurrection didn't disappear en masse in 30 AD, leaving the Gospel writers with nothing to work with but their theologically informed imaginations. To give just one example: tradition holds (and there is no serious reason to doubt it) that Mark, the first evangelist, was a friend and companion of St. Peter, during the time of the great apostle's sojourn in Rome. His Gospel was therefore grounded in the reminiscences of someone who knew Jesus intimately and who saw the Lord after his resurrection. There is absolutely no reason to doubt that the Gospel of Mark, though it was written forty years after the time of Jesus, is filled with reliable history.

There are far, far better accounts of the historical Jesus than the book under consideration. I would recommend studies by E.P. Sanders, James Dunn, Richard Bauckham, Ben Witherington III, or N.T. Wright. What they will show you is that the real Jesus remains far more interesting and compelling than the superficial caricature offered by Reza Aslan.

Why Jesus is God: A Response to Bart Ehrman

I'm writing this essay at Easter time, and that means that the mainstream media and publishing houses can be counted upon to issue debunking attacks on orthodox Christianity. The best-publicized of these is Bart Ehrman's latest book *How Jesus Became God: The Exaltation of a Jewish Preacher from Galilee*. Many by now know at least the outlines of Ehrman's biography: once a devout Bible-believing evangelical Christian, trained at Wheaton College, the alma mater of Billy Graham, he saw the light and became an agnostic scholar and is now on a mission to undermine the fundamental assumptions of Christianity. In this tome, Ehrman lays out what is actually a very old thesis, going back at least to the eighteenth century and repeated ad nauseam in skeptical circles ever since, namely, that Jesus was a simple itinerant preacher who never claimed to be divine and whose "resurrection" was in fact an invention of his disciples, who experienced hallucinations of their master after his death. Of course Ehrman, like so many of his skeptical colleagues across the centuries, breathlessly presents this thesis as though he has made a brilliant discovery. But basically, it's the same old story. When I was a teenager, I read British biblical scholar Hugh Schonfield's *Passover Plot*, which lays out the same narrative, and just a few months ago I read Reza Aslan's *Zealot*, which pursues a very similar line, and I'm sure next Christmas or Easter I will read still another iteration of the theory.

And so, once more into the breach. Ehrman's major argument for the thesis that Jesus did not consider himself divine is that explicit statements of Jesus' divine identity can be found only in the later fourth Gospel of John, whereas the three Synoptic Gospels, earlier and thus presumably more historically reliable, do not feature such statements from Jesus himself or the Gospel writers. This is so much nonsense. It is indeed the case that the most direct affirmations of divinity are found in John—"I and the Father are one"; "before Abraham was I am"; "He who sees me sees the Father" etc. But equally clear statements of divinity are on clear display in the Synoptic Gospels, provided we know how to decipher a different semiotic system.

For example, in Mark's Gospel, we hear that as the apostolic band is making its way toward Jerusalem with Jesus, "they were amazed, and those who followed were afraid" (Mark 10:32). Awe and terror are the typical reactions to the presence of Yahweh in the Old Testament. Similarly, when Matthew reports that Jesus, at the beginning of the last week of his earthly life, approached Jerusalem from the east, by way of Bethpage and Bethany and the Mount of Olives, he is implicitly affirming Ezekiel's prophecy that the glory of the Lord, which had departed from his temple, would return from the east, by way of the Mount of Olives. In Mark's Gospel, Jesus addresses the crippled man who had been lowered through the roof of Peter's house, saying, "My son, your sins are forgiven," to which the bystanders respond, "Who does this man think he is? Only God can forgive sins." What is implied there is a Christology as high as anything in John's Gospel.

And affirmations of divinity on the lips of Jesus himself positively abound in the Synoptics. When he says, in Matthew's Gospel, "He who does not love me more than his mother or father is not worthy of me," he is implying that he himself is the greatest possible good. When in Luke's Gospel he says, "Heaven and earth will pass away, but my words will never pass away," he is identifying himself with the very Word of God. When he says in Matthew's Gospel, in reference to himself, "But I tell you, something greater than the Temple is here," he is affirming unambiguously that he is divine, since for first-century Jews, only Yahweh himself would be greater than the Jerusalem Temple. Perhaps most remarkably, when he says, almost as a tossed-off aside at the commencement of the Sermon on the Mount, "You have heard it said, but I say…" he is claiming superiority to the Torah, which was the highest possible authority for first-century Jews. But the only one superior to the Torah would be the author of the Torah, namely, God himself. Examples such as these from the Synoptic authors could be multiplied indefinitely. The point is that the sharp demarcation between the supposedly "high" Christology of John and the "low" Christology of the Synoptics, upon which the Ehrman thesis depends, is simply wrong-headed.

And now to the "hallucinations." Most of the skeptical critics of Christianity subscribe to some version of Scottish philosopher David Hume's account of the miraculous. Hume said that since no reasonable person could possibly believe in miracles, those who claimed to have experienced a miracle must be unreasonable. They must, then, be delusional or naïve or superstitious. Hume's logic was circular and unconvincing in the eighteenth century, and it hasn't improved with age. Yes, if we assume that miracles are impossible, then those who report them are, to some degree, insane, but what if we don't make things easy for ourselves and assume the very proposition we are trying to prove? What if we keep an open mind and assume that miracles are, though rare, possible? Then we don't have to presume without argument that those who claim to have experienced them are delusional, and we can look at their reports with unjaundiced eyes.

What in fact do we find when we turn to the resurrection appearance accounts in the New Testament? We find reports of many different people who experienced Jesus alive after his death and burial: Peter, John, Mary Magdalene, the twelve, "five hundred brothers at once," and Paul. Does it strike you as reasonable that all of these people, on different occasions, were having hallucinations of the same person?

The case of Paul is especially instructive. Ehrman argued that the visions of the risen Jesus were created in the anxious brains of his grief-stricken disciples, eager to commune once more with their dead Master. But Paul wasn't grieving for Jesus at all; in fact, he was actively persecuting Jesus' followers. He didn't crave communion with a dead Master; he was trying to stamp out the memory of someone he took to be a pernicious betrayer of Judaism. And yet, his experience of the risen Jesus was so powerful that it utterly transformed his life, and he went to his death defending the objectivity of it.

Debunkers of orthodox Christianity have been around for a long time. In some ways, it is a testimony to the enduring power of the Christian faith that the naysayers feel obliged to repeat their tired arguments over and over. Faithful believers have simply to declare their Christianity with confidence and, patiently but firmly, tell the critics that they're wrong.

CITY ON A HILL:
GOD IN POLITICS

Tolerance, Choice, Argument, and Religion

THE RESULTS OF THE PEW FORUM STUDY on religion in America were released not long ago. In accord with many surveys over the past fifty years, this poll showed that the vast majority (92%) of Americans believe in God, but that an increasing number of our countrymen prefer their own spiritual experience to the dogmas and doctrines of traditional Christianity. Also there is among Americans, a general acceptance of positive, life-affirming beliefs but a deep suspicion of negative ideas such as divine judgment and hell. The director of the Pew Forum summed up the findings as follows: Americans are wary of dogmas precisely because we live in such an ethnically, culturally, and religiously diverse society. To place a stress on doctrine, it seems, would lead to conflict and, at the limit, violence in such a pluralistic context. Another commentator observed that the embrace of positive beliefs is a concomitant of the premium that we place on choice and the right to choose. After all, who would ever opt for belief in hell and judgment? I would like to say a word about each of these points.

The reticence about making religious truth claims in the public forum is, of course, a consequence of the Enlightenment. Almost all of the philosophers and social theorists of the modern period—from Descartes and Spinoza to Kant and Thomas Jefferson—were mortified by the wars of religion that followed the Reformation, and they accordingly wanted to find a means of controlling religious violence. Their solution, adopted in most of the modern political constitutions, was to tolerate religion as long as it remained essentially a private matter, something confined to the hearts of individual believers. The result of this "peace treaty" was what Richard John Neuhaus characterized as "the naked public square," that is to say, a political forum stripped of properly religious assertions and convictions. The events of September 11, 2001 simply confirmed for many in the West the wisdom of this arrangement. Since religious people cannot defend their claims rationally, the argument goes, the public appearance of religion will always be accompanied by some form of direct or indirect violence.

I have always found the either/or quality of this analysis tiresome: either religious antagonism or privatization; either September 11th or bland toleration. Our problem is, as theologian Stanley Hauerwas put it, that we have forgotten how to have a good argument about religion in public. The most dramatic indication that rational discourse has broken down is, of course, warfare between the disputants. Once conversants have resorted to fisticuffs, we know that the careful process of marshaling evidence, presenting argument and counter-argument, responding to objections, and avoiding contradictions, has been abandoned. But there is another sure sign that rationality has been left behind, and that is the slide into an anything-goes, your-opinion-is-just-as-good-as mine sort of toleration. Truth claims, by their very nature, are public because truth, by its very nature, is universal. It would be ludicrous to say that 2+2=4 for me but not for you or that adultery is wrong for me but not for you. Therefore, if I were to tolerate your view that 2+2 just might be equal to 6, or that adultery is, depending on the circumstances, acceptable, then I have stepped out of the arena of rationality and public argument, and I've essentially given up on you. It's glaringly obvious that the perpetrator of violence is a disrespector of persons, but the perpetrator of "tolerance" is just as disrespectful, since he's despaired of reason. We have to recover—yes, especially in our pluralistic society—John Henry Newman's sense that religious claims are rational and thus can and should be the subject of vigorous argument. This is the religious reason that lies beyond the tired options of warfare or bland tolerance.

And now just a brief observation about our unwillingness to accept the tougher, more "negative" features of the religious traditions. In a thousand different ways, we reverence choice in our culture. We choose our political leaders, the products we purchase at the store, the kind of films that we watch, the sort of people with whom we associate. And we revel in the wide variety of choices available to us. But there are certain realities that are so basic in their goodness, beauty, and importance that they are not so much chosen as given. Beethoven's 9th symphony, the Swiss Alps, Dante's *Divine Comedy*, the French language, moral absolutes, and the saints are goods that give themselves to us in all of their complexity and compelling power. We don't choose them; they choose us. We don't make demands of them; they impose a demand upon us. We wouldn't presume to excise those sections of Beethoven that are "unpleasant" or those features of French that are too difficult or those dimensions of morality that are hard to live up to. The Word of God, preserved in the Church, is a supreme value of this type. We shouldn't therefore speak of choosing sections of it that we like and leaving behind those that bother us. Rather, we should let it, in all of its multivalence and complexity, claim us.

Challenging ideas, I know, for us Americans. But we cannot allow our Americanism, as much as we reverence it, to compromise or position our Catholicism.

Seeing Political Corruption
with Biblical Eyes

PEOPLE ALL OVER THE COUNTRY—but especially here in Illinois—are reeling from the revelations concerning Governor Rod Blagojevich's alleged attempt to sell a Senate seat to the highest bidder. The tapes of a foul-mouthed governor carrying on like a character from the Sopranos have been, to say the least, disquieting. But how do biblically-minded people in particular assess this phenomenon of gross political corruption? They do so, I would argue, with a sort of clear-eyed realism. Anyone even vaguely acquainted with the biblical world knows that the scriptural authors are far from naïve when it comes to the abuse of power by unscrupulous politicos.

Consider just a few representative passages. In the first book of Samuel, we hear that the people of Israel petitioned the prophet Samuel to anoint for them a king "as the other nations have." Displeased with this request, Samuel laid out for them exactly what a king would do: "he will take your sons and assign them to his chariots and horses, and they will run before his chariot...he will set them to do his plowing and his harvesting...he will use your daughters as cooks and bakers. He will take the best of your fields and give them to his officials..." In short, he will abuse his power and oppress the people for his own benefit. Despite this warning, the people persist in demanding a king, and so God tells Samuel ruefully, "Grant their request and appoint a king to rule them." What follows, over the course of many centuries, is one of the most corrupt, incompetent, and abusive lines of monarchs in human history. It's as though God were saying, "I told you about these kings."

In the second book of Samuel, we read of a particularly grievous sin of King David, one that went beyond personal evil and involved the conscious and wicked abuse of political authority. David wanted to marry Bathsheba, whom he had impregnated, but he faced the inconvenient fact that Bathsheba was already married to Uriah the Hittite, an officer in the Israelite army. Undeterred, David arranged for Uriah to be placed in the thick of the battle where the unfortunate man was killed. Once he had Uriah out of the way, David married Bathsheba, but we hear that the Lord was deeply displeased with what David had done. God sent his prophet Nathan to the King who confronted him bluntly with his crime and detailed for him the Lord's punishment.

In the Gospel of Matthew, we find the account of Jesus' confrontation with the devil in the desert. After tempting Christ with sensual pleasure ("turn these stones into bread") and with glory ("throw yourself down and the angels will hold you up"), the devil entices him with the allurement of power: "all these kingdoms I will give you if you but fall down and worship me." What is most interesting about this final temptation is that the devil couldn't offer all of the kingdoms of the world to Jesus unless he, the devil, owned them. Indeed, in Luke's account, this is made explicit. Satan says, "I shall give to you all this power...for it has been handed over to me, and I may give it to whomever I wish." I don't know a passage in any of the literature of the world that is as critical of political power as that one! All the kingdoms of the world belong to a fallen spiritual force.

Whereas many (if not most) cultures both ancient and modern tend to apotheosize their political leaders, the Bible sees right through politics and politicians. One of the most important contributions of the Scriptures to contemporary politics, at least in the

West, is this deep suspicion that power tends to corrupt. The institutionalization of this suspicion in complex systems of checks and balances is a healthy outgrowth of the biblical view.

To be sure, scripturally-minded people should not allow their suspicion to give way to a complete cynicism regarding politics. Since God is powerful, power in itself cannot be construed as something evil, and indeed the Bible frequently states that legitimate political authority participates in God's own governance of the cosmos. But given the general human tendency toward self-absorption and violence—about which the Bible is remarkably clear-eyed—one should never put one's total trust in political systems, leaders, or programs. And one should ever be aware of the fact that human legal arrangements are under the judgment and authority of God. When a politician abuses his office and uses his power for his own aggrandizement, biblical people should rise up and protest with all of the insistence, courage and eloquence of Nathan in the court of David.

The Fetishism of Dialogue

I'VE WAS CONCERNED ABOUT the 2009 Notre Dame commencement ceremony, which featured President Barack Obama, who received an honorary law degree. But as I listened to the commencement speeches given by Fr. John Jenkins, the President of the University, and Barack Obama, the President of the United States, I was even more dismayed. Both are decent men and both are eloquent speakers, but both, I'm afraid to say, are confused in regard to some fundamental matters. Fr. Jenkins wrapped himself in the mantle of humility and open-mindedness, protesting that he was standing in the great Catholic intellectual tradition of dialogue and conversation, and President Obama cast himself in the role of reconciler and peacemaker, discoverer of "common ground" between people who radically disagree with one another. When protestors shouted out during his speech and Notre Dame students began to chant the Obama campaign slogan, "Yes we can," in order to drown out the offending voices, the President calmly passed his hand over the crowd and said, "We're alright; we're alright." He seemed to embody the very principle that he was articulating. So why was I dismayed at such humility and equanimity?

It comes down to that slippery little word "dialogue." I realize that to say that one is against dialogue is akin to saying that one is impatient with motherhood, patriotism, and sunny days. But the point is this: one should, in certain circumstances, be suspicious of dialogue. The great Canadian Jesuit philosopher Bernard Lonergan laid out the four basic moves that characterize the action of a healthy mind. First, he said, a properly functioning mind ought to be attentive, that is to say, able to take in the facts, to see what is there to be seen. Second, it ought to be intelligent, by which he meant, able to see forms and patterns of meaning. In the scientific context, this corresponds to the formulation of hypotheses or likely theories. In more ordinary cognitional contexts, it means conversation, the sharing of ideas, dialogue. It is at this stage that open-mindedness is a great virtue, because sometimes the most outrageous theory turns out to be right. But the healthy mind cannot stop at this stage. It must move next to what Lonergan called reasonability. This stage of judgment, the moment when the mind, having surveyed a variety of possibilities and scenarios, having listened to a range of perspectives, finally decides what the truth is. Many people balk at judgment, precisely because it is painful. The word "decide" comes from the Latin term *scisere*, which means "to cut." The same word stands at the root of "scissors" and "incision." All judgments, all decisions, are bloody, because they cut off a whole range of rival points of view. Then finally, having judged, Lonergan says, the mind must move to responsibility; it must accept the implications, both intellectual and behavioral, of the judgment that it has made.

What I sensed in both Jenkins's and Obama's speeches was a sort of fetishism of dialogue; an excessive valorization of the second stage of the cognitional process. The conversation, they seemed to imply, should remain always open-ended, the dialogue ongoing, decision or judgment permanently delayed. But dialogue is a means to an end; it is valuable in the measure that it conduces toward judgment. G.K. Chesterton said that the mind should remain open, but only so that it might, in time, chomp down on something nourishing. The Church has come to the considered judgment that abortion is morally objectionable and that *Roe v. Wade* is terrible law, as bad as the laws that once protected the practices of slavery and segregation in our country. To suggest, therefore, that a Catholic university is a place where dialogue on this matter is still a *desideratum* is as ludicrous as suggesting that a Catholic university should be the setting for a discussion of the merits of slavery and Jim Crow laws.

I would like, actually, to stay with these last examples. Fr. Theodore Hesburgh, the legendary retired President of Notre Dame, was mentioned several times in President Obama's speech as a model of the dialogue and openness to conversation that he was extolling. Does anyone think for a moment that Fr. Hesburgh, at the height of the civil rights movement, would have invited, say, George Wallace to be the commencement speaker and recipient of an honorary degree at Notre Dame? Does anyone think that Fr. Hesburgh would have been open to a dialogue with Wallace about the merits of his unambiguously racist policies? For that matter, does anyone think that Dr. Martin Luther King would have sought out common ground with Wallace or Bull Connor in the hopes of hammering out a compromise on this pesky question of civil rights for blacks? The questions answer themselves.

Then why in the world does anyone think that we should be less resolute in regard to the heinous practice of abortion which, since 1973, has taken the lives of 43 million children? Why does anyone think that further dialogue and conversation on this score is a good idea? I think those questions answer themselves, too.

In Whom Do We Place Our Trust?

THE RENAMING OF THE SEARS TOWER in Chicago speaks volumes about modern cities and their culture. Joseph Campbell, the historian of religion, commented that we can discern the dominant values of a society by looking at its buildings—more precisely, at which kind of buildings are most prominent. For instance, consider medieval Europe. It is easy to see that spiritual values were supreme because the towns and cities were, almost invariably, dominated by churches. Think of Thomas Merton's lyrical description, in *The Seven Storey Mountain*, of the little medieval town of St. Antonin in southern France. Merton recalls prowling through the narrow streets of this village when he was a boy, and remarking that all of the roads and alleys and avenues pointed, like spokes, to a central point where the little cathedral was situated. The symbolism was clear: every aspect of the daily life of that provincial village revolved around the liturgical rhythms of the church. Go to the city of Chartres, and you'll see the same thing on a larger scale. As you approach the town, you'll see the famous Cathedral rising like a mountain out of the wheat fields, and once you're in Chartres itself, you'll appreciate how the Cathedral broods over the place, determining the whole of its life.

Campbell points out that, in the Renaissance period, a cultural change occurred and became visible in architecture. In many European cities, the church was still prominent but was rivaled by political buildings and the great palaces of the wealthy and powerful. Just think of the Farnese and Barberini palazzos in Rome which, in their sumptuousness and grandiosity, practically rise to the level of St. Peter's basilica. What we see is a psychological and cultural struggle between the values of the spirit and values of a this-worldly political order. In the modern era, Campbell observes, the shift in cultural consciousness became more obvious and was, again, reflected in architectural priorities. In most modern cities in America, Europe, and Asia, the dominant buildings are clearly those of the great commercial enterprises. A visitor to Chicago, for instance, can't miss the headquarters of major commercial and economic enterprises that tower over the city. But he would have to dig a bit to find the mayor's office, and he would need a very special guide in order to find the cathedral of the archbishop.

Thus we come to the announcement that the tallest building in Chicago would no longer be referred to as the Sears Tower, but rather as the Willis Tower. The Willis company, it turns out, is a venerable, Britain-based insurance firm, and this means that the three tallest structures in Chicago—the Willis Tower, the Aon Building, and the John Hancock Building—are all named after insurance corporations. And thereupon hangs a tale, spiritually speaking.

Let me clarify, before I go any further. I have absolutely nothing against insurance companies in general or these firms in particular. Within the overall context of a democratic polity and capitalist economy, they surely have a respectable place. However, I just can't resist exploring the symbolic power of this trifecta of insurance buildings dominating the skyline of Chicago.

If Joseph Campbell is right, then what is most important to us is finding the kind of security that insurance can provide: enough money to stave off the dangers of unemployment, illness, and natural disaster. Keeping ourselves physically safe and economically secure are the highest values in our culture. I'm sure many religious people would protest, assuring me that their relationship to God is of paramount value, but I might ask them to look at the actual patterns of their lives: how do they spend their time, where do they spend their money, how do they behave when threatened with danger? I would suspect that the "skylines" of the inner psychological cities even of most religious people would resemble the skyline of Chicago!

In the sixth chapter of the Gospel of Matthew, we find these unforgettable and confounding words of Jesus from the Sermon on the Mount: "Look at the birds in the sky; they do not sow or reap, they gather nothing into barns, yet your heavenly Father feeds them. Are not you more important than they?...Do not worry and say, 'what are we to eat? and what are we to drink? and what are we to wear?' Your heavenly Father knows that you need them all...But seek first the Kingdom of God and all these things will be given to you besides." Notice how Jesus does not dismiss the reality and importance of concrete concerns, but at the same time notice how radically he relativizes them in relation to the Kingdom of God. What must always come first is our radical trust in the Lord, our surrender to his will and providential purpose. Within that context, we can indeed seek after the goods of the world, but spiritual sickness comes when we invert the relationship.

The fullest exemplification of this teaching is Jesus, nailed to his cross, stripped of every possible worldly security, saying to his Father, "Into your hands I commend my spirit." Could you even imagine that symbol of total insecurity, abandonment, and trust in God looming over the skyline of Chicago or the inner skyline of your soul?

Why It Matters That
Our Democracy Trusts in God

I WAS PLEASED TO SEE THAT the United States Supreme Court dismissed a suit brought by Michael Newdow, a Sacramento man who wanted to remove the phrase "In God We Trust" from the nation's coins and paper currency, as well as from the fronts of our public buildings. The tired argument that the gentleman brought forward was that this custom somehow violates the First Amendment guarantee that the government shall make no law either establishing an official religion or prohibiting the free exercise of religion in the United States. As many have pointed out over the years, the invocation of God or the presence of religious symbols in the public space have nothing to do with what the Founders meant by the establishment of an official religion—a practice whose dangerous consequences they knew only too well from relatively recent English history. The affirmation that there should be no governmentally sanctioned religion in the United States by no means carries as an implication the elimination of religious language and values from the public square.

I will argue, in point of fact, that the aggressive eradication of religion from the public forum does serious damage to our democracy. In order to see the truth of this, it might be wise to journey in imagination to a stuffy boarding house in Philadelphia in the summer of 1776, where a young Virginian lawyer is laboring over the opening lines to a rather significant document. Providing the widest possible context for his argument that the American colonies

148   SEEDS OF THE WORD: FINDING GOD IN THE CULTURE

ought to be free of British tyranny, Thomas Jefferson writes, "We hold these truths to be self-evident: that all men are created equal and that they are endowed by their Creator with certain inalienable rights. Among these are life, liberty, and the pursuit of happiness." Now if one peruses the history of political philosophy prior to the emergence of Christianity—consulting, say, the works of Plato, Aristotle, and Cicero—one would be hard-pressed indeed to find any ringing affirmations of equality and human rights. In fact, for the classical thinkers, the deep and undeniable inequalities that obtain among us—differences in intelligence, courage, physical beauty, virtue, etc.—must be fully acknowledged if a just society is to emerge. The suggestion that the equality of all people is the foundation of the political order would have struck Plato as the height of folly and, practically speaking, a formula for chaos.

How do we possibly explain the transition from the classical idea that equality is self-evidently false to Jefferson's notion that it is self-evidently true? The best clue is in the very language of Jefferson's prologue, more precisely, in a word that we usually rush past without noticing: "All men are created equal." Jefferson knew as surely as Aristotle that human beings are radically unequal in practically every category of existence, but he also knew something from his Christian heritage that Aristotle couldn't possibly have known, namely, that all people are indeed equally the children of God. Take God and creation out of the calculus, and Jefferson's claim becomes anything but self-evident.

Another of Jefferson's axioms is that all people, equal before God, have been endowed by that same God ("their Creator") with certain rights which are inalienable, that is to say, which can be neither granted nor rescinded by any human institution or contrivance. Once again, if we consult the classical political theorists, we find none of this. For Plato, Aristotle, Cicero, and their colleagues, special privileges belonged to those who had earned them or had inherited them from aristocratic forebears. That every person in the political order is the subject of rights to life and liberty would have struck them as a ridiculous and counterintuitive proposition.

So we are compelled to ask what made the difference, and the answer, once again, is God. Take out of consideration the Creator, who made every person in love and destined each for eternal life, and properly inalienable rights promptly disappear. And individuals become, in very short order, the objects of political manipulation and domination. To see the truth of this, all we have to do is look at the totalitarianisms of the last century, governments that were grounded in an explicit denial of God. The negation of equality and the suppression of fundamental human rights in Hitler's Germany, Stalin's Russia, Mao's China, Pol Pot's Cambodia, and Castro's Cuba followed directly from the systematic denial of the Creator God.

Democracies appropriately involve the debating of public policy, the electing of officials, the existence of a free press, and the rule of law, but those practices and customs are rooted in certain conditions that are not themselves the object of deliberation. They are founded in moral absolutes—among which are liberty, equality, the inviolability of life, and the right to pursue happiness. These non-negotiable truths are in turn logically correlative to belief in a Creator God. This is why I would hold, precisely as an American, that it is supremely dangerous to our democracy to eradicate references to God from our public space. Therefore, as an adept of both Thomas Aquinas and Thomas Jefferson, I say "Bravo" to the Supreme Court for this decision.

A Nation Under God, a Nation That Keeps the Sabbath

In 2011, the US Open was won by Northern Irishman Rory McIlroy in convincing fashion indeed. Wielding one of the most impressive swings in golf, McIlroy absolutely dominated the field, winning by eight strokes over his nearest competitor and posting the lowest score ever in the 111-year history of that storied tournament.

But an interesting controversy distracted some attention from McIlroy's big day. NBC commenced its coverage of the final round with a patriotic montage of flags, soldiers, and salutes (the tournament was played at the Congressional Country Club just north of Washington, DC). The voiceover was of a group of school kids reciting the Pledge of Allegiance. We heard "I pledge allegiance to the Flag of the United States of America, and to the Republic for which it stands, one Nation…indivisible, with liberty and justice for all." Strangely, inexplicably, the phrase "under God" was excised. NBC was flooded, almost immediately, with protests from around the country, and Dan Hicks, the anchor for the golf coverage, was compelled to issue an apology, even if it was one of those less than convincing "We apologize to anyone who might have been so small-minded as to have been offended…"

One wonders whom the producers of the broadcast were trying to impress or not to offend. I guess it must have been atheist and agnostic golf fans, for I can't imagine people of any religious denomination who would have been outraged at the mention of God.

Of course, by not offending that rather small community, they manage to offend everyone else—and to do violence to the words of the Pledge.

And though it might not be immediately apparent, this is no small thing. The claim that we are a nation "under God" is an affirmation that we stand opposed to tyrannies of all stripes. What creates a tyrant is the assumption that he and his policies are beyond criticism, because his will is the criterion of truth. Political rulers are, in fact, under God, because God is the ultimate criterion of truth and justice; and there is, therefore, a limit to what any political figure can, with moral rectitude, legislate or command. When God is denied, political power knows no limit—even if that power rests in a legislature or in the will of "the people"—and therefore tyranny becomes almost inevitable. If you doubt me, take a look at the massively dysfunctional regimes of the last century—Hitler's, Stalin's, Mao's, Pol Pot's—which were predicated upon the formal and explicit exclusion of God from the public conversation.

One of the most significant contributions of the Bible to politics is precisely the placing of kings "under God." Israelite kings were not like Egyptian Pharaohs or Babylonian divine-rulers—absolute in judgment and godlike in sovereignty. Rather, they ruled at the pleasure of God and according to God's purposes, and accordingly, when they ran counter to the divine will, they were placed, quite properly, under judgment.

Take a look at the bitter denunciations of wicked kings by Isaiah, Jeremiah, Amos, Ezekiel, Daniel, and John the Baptist. The prophets, speaking for God, excoriated Israel's leaders for their idolatry and their indifference to the suffering of the weak and the poor. It is precisely this biblical intuition that shaped the thinking of the political philosophers of the eighteenth century, who put in place the whole set of checks and balances to which we have become accustomed. The bottom line is this: when the true God is marginalized, someone else or something else—the army, the press, the government, a single leader—plays the role of God, and that is dangerous indeed. I want ours to be a nation under God, not primarily out of pious considerations, but for my own safety's sake!

This is just one of the many frightening faces of an ideological secularism that we have increasingly allowed to dominate public life in America. Curiously, about midway through the final round of the US Open, Johnny Miller, the always-entertaining color commentator for NBC Golf, inadvertently suggested one reason for this dominance. A colleague asked Johnny why Ken Venturi, who won the Open at the Congressional Club in 1964, had played two rounds on Saturday in the blazing Washington heat. Miller explained that, in those days, golfers didn't play on Sunday for it was the Sabbath day. His simple answer brought me back to my own childhood, when Sunday did indeed have a distinctive texture: businesses were closed, sporting activities were suspended, and almost everyone went to church. The honoring of the Sabbath—stipulated in the third of the Ten Commandments—is a way to remind us of the Lordship of God, and hence it is a supremely effective means to hallow the country. It is sad that we have largely lost any sense of Sunday's difference: it is now more or less another weekend day off. It's sad, yes, but if my argument above is right, it's also more than a little frightening.

"Reduction to a Singleton" and the Sovereignty of Choice

IN MY CAPACITY AS THEOLOGIAN, teacher, and culture commentator, I've been reading articles on ethical matters for years and have grown relatively inured to the expression of even the most outrageous points of view. But a couple years ago, I came across a piece that was so shocking and so egregious that I was compelled, as I read it, to put the magazine down several times and just shake my head in disbelief. It was an article in *The New York Times Sunday Magazine* called "The Two Minus One Pregnancy," dealing with the phenomenon of "reducing" (love the Orwellian language) a pregnancy from two children to one. Evidently for years obstetricians had been willing to eliminate one or more children if a woman was pregnant with triplets or quadruplets, but now, at the behest of an increasing number of mothers, doctors are commencing to (again, I'm using the dreadfully antiseptic language from the article) "reduce to a singlet," which is to say, to eliminate one of two unborn and perfectly healthy twins.

The piece begins with the story of "Jenny," a forty-five year woman, who had, for years, been taking fertility drugs and enduring ovulation injections in order to have a child. To her chagrin, she found herself, as a result, pregnant with twins and decided that, given her age and precarious financial situation, she just couldn't cope with two infants at once. And so she found herself one day on the examination table, turning her head away as the obstetrician approached her abdomen with a long needle, aiming it arbitrarily at one of the two developing babies. Her justification for this procedure is breathtaking in its irrationality: "If I had conceived these twins naturally, I wouldn't have rejected this pregnancy, because you feel like there's a natural order…But we created this child in such an artificial manner…and somehow making a decision about how many to carry seemed to be just another choice."

Another woman, carrying a boy and a girl, decided to eliminate the male because "she already had a son." This sort of discrimination based on gender is, apparently, common among those seeking reductions, calling to mind the gender-specific abortion practices in China, a country now experiencing a serious imbalance between men and women.

"Shelby," a woman from Savannah, Georgia, submitted to artificial insemination with her husband's sperm while he was deployed with the Army in Iraq. To her dismay, she conceived triplets. Frantically, she complained to her doctor: "This is not an option for us! I want only one!" Her regular physician referred her to a doctor in Atlanta who "did reductions" but that doctor told her that he wouldn't reduce "below two." She finally found a doctor who would destroy two of her babies. The only instruction she gave him was to choose one child who would be healthy. She didn't want to make the decision based on gender because she wanted to make things "as ethically okay for me as I could." Big of her, of course. The daughter to whom she gave birth is now two and half years old, and Shelby assures us that, when her daughter is old enough, she will tell her about the reduction so as teach her little girl that "women have choices, even if they're sometimes difficult." I would love to be a fly on the wall for that little conversation: "Honey, I chose to have two of your siblings murdered so that I could have an easier time raising you. And I hope that you will feel empowered one day to do the same, if you so choose." I'm sure that will lead to some tender mother-daughter bonding.

The article also references the therapists who help women deal with the pesky feelings of guilt that this "Sophie's choice" induces. Dr. Stone, a Mt. Sinai doctor, says that she often recommends that couples involved in reductions see a therapist, "so they can be at peace with whatever they decide." And Dr. Donna Steinberg, a Manhattan-based psychologist who specializes in treating infertility patients, blithely explains that the guilt that some couples feel flows from "outsiders" who don't appreciate the complexity of the struggle and wonder "how is that possible?" Well, yes, Dr. Steinberg, outsiders might just imagine how the murder of a perfectly healthy unborn child for the flimsiest of reasons is possible.

What one notices from beginning to end of this article is the absolute primacy of choice that our society increasingly takes for granted. There must be no limit set to a woman's capacity for self-expression or self-creation, even if that choice involves the casual putting to death of her own children. We see here the playing out of the *Casey v. Planned Parenthood* principle. I'm referring to the notorious 1992 judgment of the US Supreme Court in an abortion-related case, which was articulated in part as follows: "At the heart of liberty is the right to define one's own concept of existence, of meaning, of the universe, of the mystery of human life." The objective utterly gives way to the prerogatives of the subject, for sovereign choice determines the meaning of existence itself! The words of the Supreme Court justices may have sounded harmlessly abstract in 1992, but we see the concrete application of those words in the dreadful stories I've just rehearsed. Inconvenient babies? Babies of the wrong gender? Babies that just don't fit into Mom's career plans? One more baby than Mom can possibly handle? No problem: just choose to dispose of them.

I might suggest to some of the women interviewed that their feelings of guilt are much more than annoying sensations, flowing from ignorant outsiders; they are actually the indications of a properly functioning conscience, which is to say, an instinct for what is objectively right and wrong, for those values that ought to shape choice and not be trumped by it.

Why It's Okay to Be Against Heresy and for Imposing One's Will on Others

In the same week, two prominent Catholic women—Kathleen Sebelius in an address to the graduates of Georgetown University's public policy school, and Maureen Dowd in a column published in *The New York Times*—delivered strong statements about the Church's role in civil society. Dowd's column was more or less a screed, while Sebelius's address was relatively measured in tone. Yet both were marked by some pretty fundamental misunderstandings, which have, sadly, become widespread.

Echoing an army of commentators from the last fifty years, Dowd exults in James Joyce's characterization of the Catholic Church (drawn, it appears, from the pages of *Finnegans Wake*) as "here comes everybody." The word "catholic" itself, she explains, means "all-embracing" and "inclusive," hence it is desperately sad that the Church, which is meant to be broad-minded and welcoming, has become so constricting. Whether it is disciplining liberal nuns or harassing pro-choice Catholic commencement speakers, the Church has abandoned the better angels of its nature and become intolerant. She concludes, "Absolute intolerance is always a sign of uncertainty and panic. Why do you have to hunt down everyone unless you're weak? But what is the quality of a belief that exists simply because it's enforced?" Not only is this narrow-minded aggression un-Catholic,

SEEDS OF THE WORD: FINDING GOD IN THE CULTURE

it's downright unpatriotic. "This is America. We don't hunt heresies here. We welcome them," she writes.

The problem here is a fundamental confusion between inclusiveness in regard to people and inclusiveness in regard to ideas. The Church is indeed all-embracing in the measure that it wants to gather all people to itself. The Bernini colonnade that reaches out like welcoming arms in front of St. Peter's Basilica in Rome is meant to carry precisely this symbolic valence. But the Church has never had such an attitude toward all ideologies and points of view. From the beginning, it has recognized that certain doctrines are repugnant to its own essential nature or contradictory to the revelation upon which the Church is constructed. This is precisely why, for the past two millennia, theologians, bishops, popes, and councils have consistently and strenuously battled heresies concerning central Catholic dogmas. They have understood that the adoption of these errors would fatally compromise the integrity of the Church.

Truth be told, any community must, if it is to survive, have a similar "intolerance." The Abraham Lincoln Society would legitimately oppose the proposal that its members ignore Lincoln and concentrate on the study of Winston Churchill; the U.S. Golf Association would find repugnant the suggestion that Pebble Beach be turned into a collection of baseball diamonds; and the United States of America indeed aggressively excludes those committed to the eradication of fundamental American principles. The Catholic Church is not a Voltairean debating society; it is a community that stands for some very definite things, which implies, necessarily, that it sets its back against very definite things. A Church that simply "welcomed" heresies would, overnight, cease to be itself.

We find another very common error in Secretary Sebelius's address to Georgetown. Deftly sidestepping the issue that has generated such controversy—the HHS demand that Catholic institutions provide insurance for procedures that Catholic morality finds objectionable—Sebelius cited John F. Kennedy's memorable 1960 address to Protestant ministers in Houston. Kennedy dreamed of an America "in which no religious body seeks to impose its will, either directly or indirectly, on the general populace." Over and again, from every quarter, one hears this call echoed today. But when you really think about it, you realize that it is so much nonsense.

What is so easily forgotten is that any law, any political movement, indeed any persuasive speech involves, in one way or another, the imposition of someone's will. In the mid-nineteenth century, William Lloyd Garrison and John Brown were certainly endeavoring to impose their wills regarding the abolition of slavery on the rest of the country. In 1862, with the publication of the Emancipation Proclamation, President Lincoln was most assuredly attempting to impose his will on many of his recalcitrant countrymen. Publicly protesting Jim Crow laws, marching through the streets of Selma and Montgomery, speaking in the cadences of Isaiah and Amos on the steps of Lincoln's Memorial in Washington, Dr. Martin Luther King was certainly trying to impose his vision on an America that was by no means entirely ready for it. Indeed, just a year after the "I Have a Dream" speech, King was delighted with the passage of strict civil rights legislation, which gave teeth to the proposals that he had long been making.

Now in all the examples that I've given, explicit legal moves were motivated by solidly religious conviction. If you doubt me in regard to Lincoln, I would recommend a careful rereading of his Second Inaugural Address. The point is this: none of it would have legitimately taken place in the America imagined by John F. Kennedy, an America in which no religious individual or institution tried to impose its will either directly or indirectly.

What many have sensed in the Obama administration is precisely an attempt to push religion qua religion out of the public conversation. Individuals, groups, and institutions are continually trying, for various reasons and to varying degrees of success, to impose their wills on people.

Fine. That's how it works. What isn't fair is to claim, arbitrarily, that religious individuals and institutions can't join in the process.

The Great Both/And of Catholic Social Teaching

FOR MANY ON THE LEFT, 2012 Vice Presidential candidate Paul Ryan was a menace, the very embodiment of cold, indifferent Republicanism. For many on the right, he was a knight in shining armor, a God-fearing advocate of a principled conservatism. Mitt Romney's choice of Ryan as running mate triggered the worst kind of exaggerated hoo-hah on both sides of the political debate. What was most interesting, from my perspective, was that Ryan, a devout Catholic, claimed the social doctrine of the Church as the principal inspiration for his policies. Whether you stand with *First Things* and affirm that such a claim is coherent or with *Commonweal* and affirm that it is absurd, Ryan's assertion prompts a healthy thinking-through of Catholic social teaching in the present economic and political context.

Ryan himself has correctly identified two principles as foundational for Catholic social thought, namely, subsidiarity and solidarity. The first, implied throughout the whole of Catholic social theory but given clearest expression in Pope Pius XI's encyclical *Quadragesimo Anno*, is that in the adjudication of matters political and economic, a preferential option should be given to the more local level of authority. For example, when seeking to solve a traffic flow issue in a suburb, appeal should be made to the municipal authority and not to the governor, much less to Congress or the president. Only when a satisfactory solution is not achieved by the local government should one move to the next highest level of authority, etc. This principle by no means calls into question the legitimacy of an overarching federal power (something you sense in the more extreme advocates of the Tea Party), but it does indeed involve a prejudice in favor of the local. The principle of subsidiarity is implied in much of the "small is beautiful" movement as well as in Tolkien's *Lord of the Rings*, which exhibits a steady mistrust of imperial power and a steady sympathy for the local, the neighborhood, the small business.

Now in Catholic social theory, subsidiarity is balanced by solidarity, which is to say, a keen sense of the common good, of the natural and supernatural connections that bind us to one another, of our responsibility for each other. I vividly remember former New York Governor Mario Cuomo's speech before the Democratic National Convention in San Francisco in 1984, in the course of which he effectively lampooned the idea that individual self-interest set utterly free would automatically redound to the general welfare. Catholic social thought does indeed stand athwart such "invisible hand" theorizing. It also recognizes that, always in accord with subsidiarity, sometimes the federal and state governments are the legitimate vehicles by which social solidarity is achieved.

Solidarity without subsidiarity can easily devolve into a kind of totalitarianism whereby "justice" is achieved either through outright manipulation and intimidation or through more subtle forms of social engineering. But subsidiarity without solidarity can result in a society marked by rampant individualism, a Gordon Gekko "greed is good" mentality, and an Ayn Rand/Nietzschean "objectivism" that positively celebrates the powerful person's dominance of the weak. Catholic social theory involves the subtle balancing of these two great principles so as to avoid these two characteristic pitfalls. It does, for example, consistently advocate the free market, entrepreneurial enterprise, and profit-making, and it holds out against all forms of Marxism and extreme socialism. But it also insists that the market be circumscribed by clear moral imperatives and that the wealthy realize their sacred obligation to aid the less advantaged. This last point is worth developing.

Thomas Aquinas teaches that ownership of private property is to be allowed, but that the *usus* (the use) of that privately held wealth must be directed toward the common good. This is because all of the earth and its goods belong, finally, to God, and must therefore be used according to God's purpose. Pope Leo XIII made this principle uncomfortably concrete when he specified, in regard to wealth, that once the demands of necessity and propriety have been met, the rest of what one owns belongs to the poor. And in saying that, he was echoing an observation of St. John Chrysostom: "If you have two shirts in your closet, one belongs to you; the other belongs to the man who has no shirt."

In his wonderful *Orthodoxy*, written over a hundred years ago but still remarkably relevant today, G.K. Chesterton said that Catholicism is marked through and through by the great both/and principle. Jesus is both divine and human. He is not one or the other; nor is he some bland mixture of the two; rather, he is emphatically one and emphatically the other. In a similar way, the Church is radically devoted to this world and radically devoted to the world to come. In the celibacy of its priests, it is totally against having children, and in the fruitful marriage of its lay people, it is totally for having children.

In its social teaching, this same sort of "bipolar extremism" is on display. Solidarity? The Church is all for it. Subsidiarity? The Church couldn't be more enthusiastic about it. Not one or the other, nor some bland compromise between the two, but both, advocated with equal vigor.

Gay Marriage and the Breakdown of Moral Argument

IN HIS CLASSIC TEXT *AFTER VIRTUE*, the philosopher Alisdair Mac-Intyre lamented, not so much the immorality that runs rampant in our contemporary society, but something more fundamental and in the long run more dangerous, namely, that we are no longer even capable of having a real argument about moral matters. The assumptions that once undergirded any coherent conversation about ethics, he said, are no longer taken for granted or universally shared. The result is that, in regard to questions of what is right and wrong, we simply talk past one another, or more often, scream at each other.

I thought of MacIntyre's observation when I read an article on the Supreme Court's consideration of the much-vexed issue of gay marriage. It was reported that, in the wake of the oral arguments, Justice Elena Kagan remarked, "Whenever someone expresses moral disapproval in a legal context, the red flag of discrimination goes up for me." Notice that the justice did not say that discrimination is the result of a bad moral argument, but simply that any appeal to morality is, ipso facto, tantamount to discrimination. Or to state it in MacIntyre's terms, since even attempting to make a moral argument is an exercise in futility, doing so can only be construed as an act of aggression. I will leave to the side the radical inconsistency involved in saying that one has an ethical objection (discrimination!) to the making of an ethical objection, but I would indeed like to draw attention to a very dangerous implication of this incoherent position.

If argument is indeed a nonstarter, the only recourse we have in the adjudication of our disputes is violence, either direct or indirect. This is precisely why a number of Christian leaders and theorists, especially in the West, have been expressing a deep concern about this manner of thinking. Any preacher or writer who ventures to make a moral argument against gay marriage is automatically condemned as a purveyor of "hate speech" or excoriated as a bigot, and, in extreme cases, he can be subject to legal sanction. This visceral, violent reaction is a consequence of the breakdown of the rational framework for moral discourse that MacIntyre so lamented.

A telltale sign of this collapse is our preoccupation, even obsession, with poll numbers in regard to this question. We are incessantly told that ever-increasing numbers of Americans—especially among the young—approve of gay marriage or are open to gay relationships. This is undoubtedly of great interest sociologically or politically, but in itself, it has nothing to do with the question of right or wrong. Lots of people can approve of something that is in fact morally repugnant, and a tiny minority can support something that is in fact morally splendid. For example, if polls were taken in 1945 concerning the rectitude of dropping atomic bombs on Japan in order to bring the war to a rapid conclusion, I am quite sure that overwhelming majorities would have approved. And if a poll had been taken in, say, 1825, concerning the legitimacy of slavery, I would bet that only a small minority of Americans would have come out for eliminating the practice. But, in either case, so what? Finally, an argument has to be made. In the absence of this, the citation of poll numbers in regard to a moral issue is nothing but a form of bullying: we've got you outnumbered.

Still another indication of the breakdown in moral argumentation is the sentimentalizing of the gay marriage issue. Over roughly the past twenty-five years, armies of gay people have come out of the closet, and this is indeed welcome. Repression, deception, and morbid self-reproach are never good things. The result of this coming out is that millions have recognized their brothers, sisters, aunts, cousins, uncles, and dear friends as gay. The homosexual person is no longer, accordingly, some strange and shadowy "other," but someone I know to be a decent human being. This development, too, is nothing but positive. The man or woman with a homosexual orientation must always be loved and treated, in all circumstances, with the respect due to a child of God. Nevertheless, it does not follow that everything a decent person does or wants is necessarily decent. Without a convincing argument, we cannot simply say that whatever a generally kind and loving person chooses to do is, by the very nature of the thing, right. This is why I am never impressed when a politician says that he is now in favor of gay marriage, because he has discovered that his son, whom he deeply loves, is gay. Please don't misunderstand me; I am sincerely delighted whenever a father loves and cherishes his gay son. However, that love in itself does not constitute an argument.

The attentive reader will have noticed that I have not proffered such an argument in the course of this article. That will have to be matter for another day. What I have tried to do is clear away some of the fog that obfuscates this issue, in the hopes that we might eventually see, with some clarity and objectivity, what the Catholic Church teaches in regard to sexuality in general and the question of gay marriage in particular.

Why Anti-Catholic Prejudice
Ought to Bother Everyone

Not long ago, two outrageously anti-Catholic outbursts took place in the public forum. The first was an article in the *US News and World Report* by syndicated columnist Jamie Stiehm. Ms. Stiehm argued that the Supreme Court was dangerously packed with Catholics, who have, she averred, a terribly difficult time separating church from state and who just can't refrain from imposing their views on others. Her meditations were prompted by Justice Sonia Sotomayor's daring to depart from feminist orthodoxy and to grant some legal breathing space to the Little Sisters of the Poor, who were objecting to the provisions of the HHS mandate. As even a moment's thoughtful consideration would reveal, this decision hadn't a thing to do with the intrusion of the "church" into the state, in fact just the contrary. Moreover, the appeal of American citizens (who happen to be Catholic nuns) and the decision of a justice of the Supreme Court in no way constitute an "imposition" on anyone. The very irrationality of Stiehm's argument is precisely what has led many to conclude that her intervention was prompted by the visceral anti-Catholicism that stubbornly persists in our society.

The second eruption of anti-Catholicism was even more startling. In the course of a radio interview, Gov. Andrew Cuomo blithely declared that anyone who is pro-life on the issue of abortion or opposed to gay marriage is "not welcome" in his state of New York. Mind you, the governor did not simply say that such people are wrongheaded or misguided; he didn't say that they should be opposed politically or that good arguments against their position should be mounted; he said they should be actively excluded from civil society! As many commentators have already pointed out, Governor Cuomo was thereby excluding roughly half of the citizens of the United States and, presumably, his own father Mario Cuomo, who once famously declared that he was personally opposed to abortion. Again, the very hysterical quality of this statement suggests that an irrational prejudice gave rise to it.

One does not have to search very far, of course, to find the source of this prejudice deep in the American national consciousness. Many of the founding Fathers harbored suspicions of Catholicism that came from their intellectual formation in both Protestantism and Enlightenment rationalism. Read John Adams's remarkable reaction to a Catholic Mass that he attended in Philadelphia to sense the texture of this prejudice. As the waves of immigrants from Ireland, Germany, and southern Europe arrived on American soil in the nineteenth century, many figures in the political and cultural establishment feared that an influx of Catholics would compromise the integrity of American society. Accordingly, they organized political parties the platforms of which were specifically and virulently anti-Catholic.

It is startling to realize that this political anti-Catholicism was not the exclusive preserve of yahoos and extremists. Prominent and mainstream figures such as Ulysses S. Grant and Woodrow Wilson were vehement in their opposition to the Catholic Church. Many have argued that the election of the Catholic John F. Kennedy to the presidency in 1960 signaled a sea change in American attitudes toward the Church, but we have to be cautious, for Kennedy represented, more or less, a privatized Catholicism that posed no real threat to the societal status quo.

What is particularly troubling today is the manner in which this deep-seated anti-Catholicism is finding expression precisely through that most enduring and powerful of American institutions, namely, the law. We are a famously litigious society; the law shapes our identity, protects our rights, and functions as a sanction against those things we find dangerous. Increasingly, Catholics are finding themselves on the wrong side of the law, especially in regard to issues of equality and sexual freedom. The HHS mandate is predicated upon the assumption that access to contraception, sterilization, and abortifacient drugs is a fundamental right, and therefore to stand against this, as the Church must, puts Catholics in opposition to the law. The same is true in regard to gay marriage. To oppose this practice is not only unpopular or impolitic, but, increasingly, contrary to legal statute. Already, in the context of the military, chaplains are encouraged and in some cases explicitly forbidden to condemn gay marriage, as this would constitute a violation of human rights.

This is why the remarks by Andrew Cuomo are especially chilling. That a governor of a major state—one of the chief lawmakers in our country—could call for the exclusion of pro-lifers and those opposed to gay marriage suggests that the law could be used to harass, restrict, and, at the limit, attack Catholics. Further, the attitude demonstrated by the son of Mario Cuomo suggests that there is a short path indeed from the privatization of Catholic moral convictions to the active attempt to eliminate those convictions from the public arena. I would hope, of course, that it is obvious how this aggression against Catholics in the political sphere ought deeply to concern everyone in a supposedly open society. If the legal establishment can use the law to aggress Catholics, it can use it, another day, to aggress anyone else.

RAYS OF TRUTH:
GOD IN THE CULTURE

We Have Here No Lasting City

THE COUNTRY IS STILL FEELING the effects of the 2009 economic crisis that impacted the stock market as well as the bond and credit markets. Many who are knowledgeable in the field say that the downturn, sometimes called the Great Recession, was as bad as the Great Depression of 1929, and they worry that its long-term consequences are largely unknown. Certainly an increase in unemployment, the foreclosure of many mortgages, a staggering loss of investments, and the collapse of numerous businesses are already stark realities. Many people have approached me to ask what spiritual wisdom and practical advice the Church has to offer in the face of such a financial disaster.

I would first point out that economics is seen by the Church as part of morality, since it is crucial to the maintenance of the common good. Furthermore, in the recent social teaching of the popes, the market economy has come in for special praise as an economic system that not only produces goods and services with admirable efficiency but that also honors the dignity of the human being as a free and self-directing agent. It is, the popes have argued, the economic form that corresponds to a democratic polity. Therefore, maintaining the health and viability of our economic system is of pressing ethical importance. We are all obliged, precisely as morally engaged persons, to work to ameliorate the situation on both the micro and macro level. More to it, the principle of subsidiarity—a master idea of Catholic social theory—dictates that the government can and should intervene in the economy when the latter's problems cannot be solved at the more local level. It seems to me that the steps taken by the federal government—from the bailout to the shoring up of regulations and investment safeguards—are altogether congruent with this principle.

But there is a deeper, more strictly spiritual dimension to this crisis. It has to do with the biblical conviction that "we have here no lasting city." This world is good, indeed very good, but it is, at the same time, fleeting, ephemeral, evanescent. The psalmist tells us that our lives are over "like a sigh" and that we are like "flowers which bloom in the morning but which by evening wither and fade." As his disciples gazed up admiringly at the splendor of the Jerusalem temple, Jesus commented that "not one stone will be left upon another, but all will be destroyed." These are not "pessimistic" observations; they are deeply realistic and finally liberating. The paradigmatic sin in the Bible is idolatry, defined as the deification of something or someone less than God. This spiritual mistake conduces to a whole series of crises both interior and exterior, for it upsets the fundamental order of things.

In the evocative language of the book of Genesis, the original sin (from which all human dysfunction has flowed) was an act of idolatry, Adam's hopeless attempt to turn his own ego into God. This Adamic distortion has taken many forms over the course of human history: the idolization of country, culture, political party, charismatic leader, or economic system. Elemental to the spiritual life is the awareness that all such earthly things are fleeting, and that one should, accordingly, place one's confidence only in the eternal God. Though it's hard for us to imagine, our political and economic system will one day fade away, and our status as the one great superpower will end. (Imagine how difficult it would have been for a Roman aristocrat in the year 150 to think that the Roman order would ever fade.) And this is why the shaking of the foundations can be, from a spiritual standpoint, a salutary reminder.

What practical advice can I give? First, cultivate the economic habits that foster both your own good and the common good. Though I'm oversimplifying a bit, a financial crisis is born of certain bad habits and practices: a willingness to live beyond one's means, to pile up dangerous amounts of debts, to act as though contractual agreements are not binding, to focus exclusively on one's own economic advantage. I would contrast these with the virtues placed through hard experience in the hearts of the generation that endured the Great Depression. Since we are so richly interconnected, our instincts for justice and economic responsibility can foster the common good.

Second, cultivate an attitude of detachment. This doesn't mean indifference to practical realities, but it does mean a willingness to let go of anything—including wealth—that is less than God. Recently, I read a story of a former Wall Street trader who has become an Eastern Orthodox monk. He now urges his former colleagues in the financial world to place a jar of dirt on their desks, to remind them of what is finally important. It's not a bad idea for all of us.

The Task of the Next Generation of the Catholic Commentariat

OVER THE LAST FEW YEARS, we have witnessed the deaths of a number of prominent commentators on things Catholic. William F. Buckley, was, of course, primarily a political observer, but he also frequently and incisively weighed in on ecclesial and theological matters. Tim Unsworth was a longtime writer on religion for the left-leaning *National Catholic Reporter.* And Cardinal Avery Dulles and Father Richard John Neuhaus—stalwarts on the Catholic right—went to their maker within a month of each other. The deaths of these major players in the religious commentariat prompts some reflections on the changing nature of the Catholic intellectual conversation in our country.

For the coterie of Catholics that is now fading from the scene, the dominant fact was the Second Vatican Council. That coming together of bishops, abbots, theologians, and members of the press was, as John O'Malley argued, "the greatest meeting of all time"; historian Barbara Tuchman characterized it as the most significant event of the twentieth century, surpassing in importance the two world wars and the dropping of the atomic bombs. It is not surprising in the least, therefore, that it preoccupied the minds and hearts of an entire generation of Catholic intellectuals. Vatican II has been described as "the Council of the Church," for ecclesiology and liturgy were its major themes. How does the Church worship? What is the nature and purpose of the Church? How is the Church governed and structured, and what is the correct manner of its relationship to the modern world? These were the central questions that beguiled the minds of the Council Fathers.

Some have argued that Paul VI's 1968 encyclical *Humanae Vitae* was even more determinative of the Catholic conversation than were the conciliar documents themselves, but discussions of that famous letter often turned on the fundamentally ecclesiological question of the range of the Magisterium's authority.

And so, in the wake of Vatican II, the commentariat turned with enthusiasm to a range of *ad intra* questions: women's ordination, the possibility of married priests, changes in the liturgy, developments in regard to the exercise of episcopal authority, sexual ethics, the nature of Catholic marriage, the adjustment of Catholic practices to modern styles, etc. To be sure, there were a variety of views on these matters, from hard left to hard right and every possibility in between, but the focus was on the household of the Church.

I remember these arguments well, since they dominated the years that I was coming of age. I recall the Church of the late sixties and seventies as a community at war with itself, struggling to get its own affairs in order. But through all of this, the members of the Vatican II generation—whether on the left or the right—seemed to hold to the basic narrative of Catholic Christianity. There did not appear to be major disagreement in regard to God's existence, the Trinity, the sacraments and the Eucharist, redemption, Mary and the saints, eternal life. The center held.

But my growing conviction is that, as the Vatican II generation fought with itself over intra-ecclesial matters, the basic story became less and less convincing to the culture. As the commentariat bickered about the household of the Church, they, perforce, spent little time presenting a compelling, coherent version of Catholicism to a world grown increasingly skeptical, secularized, and materialist. Mind you, I'm not suggesting for a moment that the questions they debated were unimportant or that they themselves were anything less than serious in their endeavors, but I am arguing that something extremely important was allowed to slip on their watch.

And therefore I believe that it is the task of the coming generation of Catholic intellectuals to offer a convincing apologetic for the basic narrative of the faith. To a scientific culture, we have to show how only a properly transcendent and intelligent cause can explain the contingencies and intelligibilities of the finite world. To a materialist culture, we have to show that, in the words of Pope Benedict XVI, the *Logos* is more metaphysically basic than mere matter. To a skeptical culture, we have to show that belief in the resurrection of Jesus is intellectually coherent and historically defensible. To a bored culture, we have to demonstrate that life in the Spirit is a high adventure, corresponding to the deepest longing of the human heart. The new Catholic commentariat has to return, I believe, to the style of the first preachers and teachers of the faith, those who were trying to beguile the bored and materialist culture of their own time with the impossibly good news of a God who raised his son from the dead.

As we say farewell to a generation of Catholic intellectuals, we realize that for the next generation, important work remains.

A-Rod and Augustine

I'VE BEEN A BASEBALL FAN since I was six years old, when my father took my brother and me to a Detroit Tigers game in the summer of 1966. I'll never forget the beauty of the intensely, almost garishly, green field and the crisp white uniforms of the home team players under the bright lights that night. I started with tee-ball when I was seven and moved through many years of Little League and Babe Ruth league, becoming in time a pretty good hitter and shortstop. When I was nine, in 1969, I moved with my family to Chicago and became (God help me) a Cubs fan, and learned very quickly what it was like to move from giddy hope to blackest despair. And I've always been an admirer of the great players that I've been privileged to see: Roberto Clemente, Ernie Banks, Brooks Robinson, Cal Ripken, Ryne Sandberg, Pete Rose, Greg Maddux, and many others.

In the summer of 1999, I was in Seattle, attending the first Mass of a student I had taught at Mundelein. Knowing my love for baseball, he had arranged to take me to a Mariners game, and the player I was most looking forward to seeing was Alex Rodriguez, A-Rod. He didn't disappoint. That night, he got, as I remember, three hits, but what has stayed in my mind was actually a strikeout, for as he swung at the third strike, he exhibited one of the most beautiful, balanced, and elegant swings I had ever seen.

I thought of that night a good deal as the revelations about Rodriguez's steroid use came forth. By his own admission, the great A-Rod joined the sad ranks of Ken Caminiti, Rafael Palmiero, John

Rocker, Mark Maguire, Roger Clemens, and of course Barry Bonds. Now there are any number of rather obvious moral observations that one can make concerning this scandal. One could say that these players have undermined the integrity of the game, that they have damaged their own bodies, that they have set a terrible example to young players, that they have lied under oath or pathetically ducked the question ("I'm not here to talk about the past"), that they have egregiously cheated on their fellow competitors, etc. And these observations would be absolutely valid. But when I look at the two most prominent players in this scandal—A-Rod and Barry Bonds—something else strikes me with particular power.

These two figures began using steroids—Bonds in 1998 and Rodriguez in 2001—when they were at the top of their games; when they were generally regarded as the best players in baseball. By 1998, Bonds was already a three-time MVP winner, and by 2001, A-Rod had been awarded the biggest contract in the history of professional sports. They both had sterling records, both were guaranteed a place in the Hall of Fame, both had more money than they could spend in ten lifetimes, both could out-hit, out-run, and out-play practically any player in the game. If they had been minor leaguers, desperately trying to break into the majors, or .250 hitters hoping for that extra boost that would keep them competitive for a few more years, we might understand. But why would these gods of baseball, these men who were, without artificial help, dominating their respective leagues, turn to steroids? It has been suggested that Bonds was jealous of the national frenzy around the Maguire-Sosa home run race in 1998, and that Rodriguez felt the pressure of living up to the expectations generated by his unprecedented contract. Fair enough. But I think that things go deeper than that.

St. Augustine spoke of "concupiscent desire," by which he meant a perversion of the will. We have, Augustine said, been wired for God ("Lord, you have made us for yourself") and therefore, nothing in this world will ever be able finally to satisfy us ("our hearts are restless until they rest in thee"). When we hook our infinite desire for God onto something less than God—pleasure, money, power, success, honor, victory—we fall into a perverted and ultimately self-destructive pattern. When money isn't enough (and it never is), we convince ourselves we need more and more of it; when honor isn't enough (and it never is), we seek honor desperately, obsessively; when athletic success isn't enough (and it never is), we will go to any extreme to assure more and more of it. This awful and frustrating rhythm, which Augustine called "concupiscent," we would call today "addiction." Barry Bonds and Alex Rodriguez were not addicted to steroids per se; they were addicted to success, and we know this because they were at the pinnacle of success and still didn't think it was enough.

One of the most liberating and salutary things that we can know is that we are not meant to be perfectly happy in this life. When we convince ourselves otherwise, we, necessarily, fall into one or more forms of addiction. Bonds and Rodriguez still felt, at the height of their success, a nagging sense of incompleteness.

That was not an invitation to take desperate measures; it was the invasion of grace.

Allowing the Mask to Slip

IN 2006, a young woman named Sycloria Williams came to an abortion clinic outside of Miami run by a Dr. Pierre Jean-Jacque Renelique. She was twenty-three weeks into her pregnancy, and she wanted to abort her child. The eighteen-year-old Williams was medicated in order to prepare her for the procedure, and then she waited for the doctor to arrive. But he was delayed so long that she gave birth to a baby girl. What followed beggars description. According to witnesses, a clinic employee, who had no medical background or license, took the child, placed her in a red biohazard bag and threw the bag into the dumpster behind the office. When Dr. Renelique finally arrived, he was told that the young woman had already given birth and that the baby had been disposed of. A few days later, police, following anonymous tips, found the decomposing remains of the child.

As this terrible tale came to light, there were cries of outrage on all sides. Predictably enough, pro-lifers expressed their deep dissatisfaction, but pro-choice advocates bemoaned the situation as well. The head of the Broward County chapter of the National Organization for Women said that she was deeply saddened that there still existed clinics where this kind of "botched abortion" could take place. Dr. Renelique himself was brought up for malpractice and his medical license was eventually revoked.

But here's what I find puzzling: given their convictions in regard to abortion, why should pro-choicers object to what happened in this case? And given the law of the land, why should the government or the medical establishment feel particularly compelled to take any punitive action against the doctor? Sycloria Williams came to that clinic for the express purpose of terminating the life of her child, and as far as pro-choicers are concerned, she was perfectly within her rights to do so. More to it, American law allows a mother to decide to end her pregnancy at any stage, as long as she is able to demonstrate that bringing the baby to term would threaten her (the mother's) physical or mental health. If things had gone according to plan, Dr. Renelique would have dismembered Ms. Williams's child in the womb, extracted the pieces of the child's body, and then disposed of them, presumably in a biohazard bag. Again, neither abortion advocates nor American law would have had any objection whatsoever to these steps.

But simply because the child was killed and disposed of after she was born, the police were alerted and a homicide investigation commenced; the Doctor's medical license was revoked and even pro-choicers expressed outrage. Can anyone explain the logic of this? Of course no one can, because this case vividly reveals the deep incoherence of the pro-choice position. It is, presumably, perfectly unobjectionable for a doctor to murder a baby while it still lives in her mother's womb, but horrifying for that same doctor to murder that same baby when, moments later, it emerges from her mother's body. I suppose that pro-choice advocates think some mystical transformation occurs in the birth canal, whereby a disposable lump of tissue becomes a person endowed with inalienable rights and worthy of the protection of the law. I find the statement of the Broward County NOW spokesman actually quite telling. She spoke of a "botched abortion," and what she meant was an abortion that showed itself publicly, that didn't take place in the darkness and privacy of a mother's body but that appeared in the full light of day for what it really is. Her complaint against the clinic employees was not that they had killed a human being, but that they had, embarrassingly enough, allowed the mask to slip.

An aspect of this story that I believe is worthy of note is that Ms. Williams herself, the mother of the discarded child, has brought charges against Dr. Renelique. One might be forgiven for finding this puzzling, since she came to the doctor precisely for the purpose of ridding herself of her baby. And one might not feel any particular sympathy with this woman. But the decisive factor seems to have been this: when the young mother actually looked into the face of her newborn baby, she realized that this tiny being was not a lump of tissue but a person. Significantly, she has given her murdered child a name.

Perhaps in God's mysterious providence, this terrible series of events has served a purpose: to make us feel, viscerally, the illogic of the pro-abortion position and to steel us, once more, to fight for innocent life.

Where are the "Nones" Coming From?

When the findings of the American Religious Identification Survey were published in 2008, they revealed several interesting trends. One of the most startling is that northern New England—once a bastion of both Protestant and Catholic Christianity—is now the most unchurched section of the country, a distinction formerly held by the Pacific Northwest. Another intriguing fact is that, due to massive Hispanic immigration, the center of gravity for American Catholicism has shifted from the great cities of the eastern seaboard to the Southwest and southern California (something) the Vatican recognized when it established Houston as a cardinatial see in 2007).

The survey shows that despite the exertions of Christopher Hitchens, Bill Maher, and their legion of media supporters, atheism has made very few inroads in the United States; only about 2% of Americans self-identify as either atheist or agnostic. The professional atheists would no doubt attribute this to the ignorance of most Americans, but in fact what it shows is that atheism is not only unattractive but deeply irrational. Though most believers couldn't state it with philosophical precision, they know instinctually that the contingency of the world has to be grounded, finally, in something non-contingent, and that the universal intelligibility of nature is the result of a creative intelligence. They know, in a word, that it is reasonable to believe in God.

But the statistic that I found most intriguing and alarming is this one: the group that has grown most vigorously since the last comparable survey is the "nones," that is to say, those who claim no religious affiliation at all. In 1990, only 8.2% of Americans claimed to belong to no church; in 2001, the number had risen to 14.2%, and in the 2008 poll, it increased to 15%. One of the analysts commented that the "nones" were the only "denomination" whose numbers increased in every state in the Union.

Now it is most important to note where the "nones" came from. They represent, disproportionately, a falling away from the mainstream Protestant churches. While the numbers of Roman Catholics and evangelical Protestants have remained fairly in recent surveys, the mainstream Protestant figures have plummeted: now only about 12% of Americans self-identify as Lutheran, Episcopalian, Presbyterian, Methodist, or United Church of Christ. And thereupon hangs a tale.

In the course of the twentieth century—and intensifying in the last forty years or so—the mainstream Protestant churches dramatically liberalized themselves. By this I mean that they abandoned, or at least softened, many of the doctrines of classical Christianity—Trinity, Incarnation, sin, redemption, heaven, and hell—and embraced a kind of soft "spirituality." They also heartily endorsed the social justice program of political liberalism without providing anything close to a properly theological justification for it. The result is that they became, more often than not, a faint echo of the political and psychological convictions of the secular culture.

I have a friend who converted to Catholicism from Quakerism about ten years ago. He said that what prompted his conversion (at least in part) was that when his fellow Quakers rose to speak at the their Sunday assembly, presumably at the urging of the Holy Spirit, their opinions were remarkably similar to those expressed on the editorial page of *The New York Times*! A fellow student of mine years ago in a hospital chaplaincy training program was a member of a mainstream Protestant church, and he said one day, with great pride, that the doctrinal statements of his denomination were kept in a loose-leaf binder, since they were always subject to change!

That kind of doctrinal indifferentism and lazy secularism is precisely the recipe that produces the "nones." John Henry Newman commented that one of the marks of a robust Christianity is "the power of assimilation," by which he meant the capacity to take in from its environment what is conducive to its flourishing and to resist what is detrimental to its well-being. In this sense, a healthy religion is like a healthy organism that ranges around its world confidently taking in what it can and holding off what it must. The surest sign that an animal is unhealthy is that one or both of these capacities breaks down, and the surest sign that it is dead is that it has lost its distinctiveness, becoming utterly absorbed by its environment. That absorption by the cultural environment is precisely the fate of those Christian churches that lost their power of assimilation and resistance. The "nones" are, for the most part, simply those who have acknowledged this fact.

An authentic Christianity never hunkers down behind defensive walls, because its purpose is to transfigure the culture. But if it is to accomplish this end, it must be clear about what it stands for and what, by implication, it stands against. We Catholics must be vigilant in this regard, lest more of our own join the swelling ranks of the "nones."

Covering Up the Name of Jesus

I'VE ALREADY EXPLORED how Notre Dame, the flagship Catholic university in the United States, presented an honorary degree (in law, of all things) to the most radically pro-abortion president in history. But shortly thereafter, Georgetown, the most prominent Jesuit university in the country, in order to satisfy the demands of the Obama White House, covered up all the religious symbols in its Gaston Hall when the President spoke there. Most egregiously, they placed black-painted wood over the golden letters *IHS* which were inconveniently situated directly over the president's lectern. These are the first three letters of the name of Jesus in Greek, *IHSOUS*, which were adopted five centuries ago by St. Ignatius of Loyola as a special emblem of his order, the Society of Jesus. The White House evidently wanted a background of flags and drapery for the president's policy speech and resolved that the *IHS* and other religious signage should be obscured.

Now the question of the right relationship between religion and politics in our society is a famously complex one, and I certainly don't blame Georgetown for inviting the president to give a policy address at its campus. When I was critical of Notre Dame's decision to present Obama with an honorary degree, my goal wasn't to close down the conversation and turn Catholic campuses into intellectual ghettos. I would have had no objection to the president coming to Notre Dame to debate, to argue, to discuss—even the matter of abortion. What I objected to was the honor that they were giving him. So there isn't the slightest problem with Georgetown offering itself as a forum for a serious presidential speech. But what a Catholic university should never do is to surrender its own identity or to make apologies for its own deepest commitments. A Catholic center of higher learning should never acquiesce in its own secularization in order to participate in the public conversation.

I must confess that I found Jesuit Fr. Thomas Reese's comment hard to take. Attempting to explain the situation, he said that Georgetown agreed with the White House that there shouldn't be anything to distract the attention of the audience from the President's words. So a priest of the Society of Jesus thinks that, at a Jesuit university, the name of Jesus is a distraction!

In point of fact, understanding Jesus is the key to this particular controversy and to the wider question of the church and the public square. The peculiar claim of the Church is that Jesus is not one religious figure among many, not one more in a long line of prophets and inspired teachers. Jesus is the Son of God, the incarnation of the *Logos*, which is to say, the very word by which God created the universe. The great theologians of our tradition clearly grasped the implication of this doctrine: Jesus, precisely as the *Logos* made flesh, is related to any and every expression of the *Logos* (mind or reason) in the culture. Every truth discovered by science or philosophy, every design apparent in nature, every instance of artistic beauty, every arrangement of justice is a reflection of what appears fully in Jesus. And this is why the Church, at its best, has always been the friend of the arts, of philosophy, of science, and of literature.

Furthermore, this is why the first universities—Bologna, Paris, Oxford, Cambridge—emerged precisely out of the milieu of the Church. In the thirteenth century, St. Bonaventure, professor at the University of Paris, composed an extraordinary text called *Christ the Center*, the gravamen of whose argument is that Jesus the *Logos* is at the heart of physics, mathematics, history, and metaphysics. In the mid-nineteenth century, John Henry Newman, in a series of lectures entitled *The Idea of a University,* made much the same assertion. The Jesus reverenced by the great tradition belongs, therefore, very much in the public sphere and around the table of intellectual conversation. In that context, he poses no threat to legitimate expressions of reason, and he serves as a trump to the unreason that can surface easily enough in the sciences, in politics, or in philosophy. A Catholic university worthy of the name is a place where Jesus the *Logos* has this essential regulating role.

What is particularly interesting (and troubling) about the Georgetown decision to cover up the name of Jesus is that it symbolizes something much broader, namely, the tendency of too many Catholic institutions to consider Jesus something of an embarrassment, a hindrance to the full immersion of Catholics in the secular society. The Christ who is the embodiment of Reason itself does not hinder, and should never embarrass, those who are seeking truth in any form.

A Secular Europe and the
Mission of the Church

As my Word On Fire team journeyed through Europe in 2009, filming for our ten-part documentary, *CATHOLICISM*, we traveled throughout France, Germany, and Poland, taking in some of the artistic and architectural glories of European Catholicism. We photographed at Notre Dame Cathedral and the Sainte Chapelle in Paris, at Chartres Cathedral, at the Unterlinden Museum in Colmar, which houses Grünewald's magnificent Isenheim altarpiece, at the imposing Cathedral of Cologne in Germany, and finally at Wawel Cathedral in Krakow. Our purpose was to use these works of art as an aesthetic accompaniment to my spoken elaboration of certain basic themes within the theology and spirituality of the Church.

As we were finishing our filming in the Sainte Chapelle, that jewel box of a Gothic building designed in the thirteenth century to house the relic of the crown of thorns, I turned to John Cummings, our cameraman, and said, "Well, what did you think of this place?" He replied, "It's amazing, but finally, it's one more empty church." John's comment, telling and insightful, has stayed in my mind. More often than not, the monuments of European Catholicism are like *objets d'art* in a dusty museum of culture, rather than expressions of a living faith. Mass attendance is notoriously low throughout Europe (Poland is the exception that proves the rule), and the dominant European attitude toward Christianity seems to be bored indifference.

Indeed, on a cold Sunday morning, our team attended Mass at Chartres Cathedral, and found that the liturgy was poorly attended and the average age of the participants was very high. At the Unterlinden Museum, we were privileged to have a very bright doctoral candidate as our guide. She spoke five languages fluently and was well versed in contemporary Italian literature and art, but she was so uninformed about Christianity that she felt obliged to ask me the meaning of the phrase, found on the altarpiece, "A virgin will give birth and we shall call him Emmanuel."

Now the reasons for this attenuation of Christianity in Europe are various, and the issue has been explored from numerous angles, especially in the last few decades. Many scholars have pointed to the modern critique of a Church grown far too cozy with political and cultural power. Others have pointed to the skepticism and atheism of Nietzsche, Marx, Comte, Freud, and Feuerbach, which gradually trickled down from the high culture to the popular level and became, in time, a sort of consensus view. Still others argue that the individualism, materialism, and consumerism at the heart of the modern worldview militate against a vibrantly imagined Christianity, especially in its Catholic expression.

I would like to add still another perspective. The orgy of violence that occurred in the heart of Europe in the twentieth century, including two world wars and two nearly successful attempts at genocide, ruptured something in the European spirit. Many wondered how, after such a cataclysm, belief in a loving God and in the human being fashioned after the divine image could be taken seriously. For these reasons, and many others beside, Europe suffered, to state it pithily, a loss of the sense of the transcendent. And the empty churches noticed by John Cummings are the consequence.

Having acknowledged this state of affairs, what precisely is the way forward? I believe we should recover a sense of the Church as witness. The Church's fundamental role in any culture and at any time is to bear witness to Jesus and his resurrection. When the first Christians proclaimed this message, they were met, for the most part, with opposition. We hear in the Acts of the Apostles that when Paul preached the resurrection on the Areopagus in Athens, most people scoffed and walked away. In the first few centuries of the Church's life, Christians faced, more often than not, hostility, and, in extreme cases, persecution unto death. After the time of Constantine, the Church found a much more hospitable cultural environment, and by the period of the High Middle Ages, its message had come dramatically to shape the whole of society. Chartres, Notre Dame, the Sainte Chapelle, the writings of Thomas Aquinas and Duns Scotus, and the *Divine Comedy* of Dante all come from this confident and vibrant period. With the rise of Protestantism and then secular modernity, the Church found itself situated much more ambiguously in relation to the wider culture, and, as we've seen in our own time, its message of Jesus' resurrection is met, at least in Europe, with a yawn.

So it goes, and so it has always gone. Cultural forms shift; opposition to the Church waxes and wanes; sometimes the Gospel is with the flow and sometimes it runs against the grain. Chartres was the finest flower of the Christian culture; and now it is mostly the haunt of tourists. But through it all, in season and out, either as a dominant force or, in the words of Benedict XIV, a "creative minority," the Church witnesses to Jesus Christ and his resurrection from the dead. In that, it finds, not necessarily success, but its identity.

Why Is Everyone Crazy
About Vampires?

You'd have to be living under a rock not to have noticed the prevalence of vampires in today's culture. One of the most popular television shows in recent years was *Buffy the Vampire Slayer*; Anne Rice's *Vampire Chronicles* continue to be widely read, and she released the latest installment, *Prince Lestat*, in 2014; HBO promoted a series about vampires called *True Blood*; Wesley Snipes starred in a trilogy of vampire films called *Blade*; and one of the most successful film series of late is *Twilight*, the story of teen mortals and teen vampires in love. How do we explain the seemingly endless fascination with the undead?

Obviously, clever marketing has a good deal to do with it, but I think there are deeper reasons as well. There is, in the spiritual order, a law analogous to the law of the conservation of energy, which I would express as follows: when the supernatural is suppressed, it necessarily finds expression in indirect and distorted form. What we have witnessed in the last fifty years or so is the attenuating, and in some circles, complete disappearance of the Biblical worldview. I've complained in the past about a bland, bored secularism that simply sets aside questions of the spiritual, the supernatural, and the transcendent. And this widespread bracketing of the religious dimension is abetted by a consumerist culture that teaches us in a thousand ways that sensual pleasure and wealth are the keys to happiness. For the secularist mind, God is, at best, a distant, indifferent force; Jesus is a guru of self-affirmation; and eternal life is a childish fantasy.

But in accord with the above-mentioned law, the supernatural will not be denied. The instinct for God and for a world that transcends the realm of ordinary experience is hardwired into us, and thus our desire, thwarted by the environing culture, will produce some distorted version of transcendence, some ersatz spirituality. Hence the world of vampires.

Let me analyze just one feature of this universe. Besides blood sucking, the distinguishing mark of vampires is immortality; they are the undead, the eternally young. Though the materialist ideology around us insists that we are no more than clever animals who will fade away at death, deep within us is the sure sense that we are more than that. There are in us, as Shakespeare's Cleopatra put it, "immortal longings," for we are linked, whether we like it or not, to the eternal God who stands outside of time. When the proper religious sense of immortality is suspended, we produce the weird ersatz of the vampire who cannot die. I say ersatz, because authentic immortality has nothing to do with endless life in this world; rather, it has to do with being brought outside of time into the eternal realm of God. But when we're starving spiritually, we find even thin gruel appealing.

Just recently, I came across a most illuminating remark by Anne Rice, the aforementioned author of the series of novels that effectively inaugurated the entire vampire craze. She said that the character of Louis, the tortured vampire who is famously interviewed in her first novel, was evocative of the many friends of hers from the sixties and seventies of the last century; people who had fallen into the morass of a post-Christian secularism. Like Louis, they knew they were caught up in something spiritually deadly, and again like the vampire, they could find no way out. The anguish of

Rice's vampire was parallel to the anguish of the secular generation, thirsty for the very thing that their culture had denied. What makes Rice's observation even more fascinating is that she herself followed that thirst and made her way through the secularist delusion of her generation and rediscovered Christ. Although, sadly, she eventually left the Church because of its sexual teachings, Anne Rice re-embraced the vividly imagined and intellectually profound faith of her youth and produced a multi-volume life of Jesus, told in the first person, and another text launched a new series of novels on angels.

Anne Rice's Catholicism brings to mind the Catholicism that played a central role in the original *Dracula* by Bram Stoker. Stoker, a nineteenth century Irishman, placed the vampire legend within the overarching biblical narrative of sin, grace, and redemption. In Stoker's telling, Dracula had cursed God and hence fallen into a hellish state (which helps to explain his aversion to the crucifix). Professor Van Helsing, a scientist and a devout believer (yes, the two can coexist!), brought the tortured vampire to salvation. Throughout the novel, Catholic themes abound: the Eucharist, the Mass, eternal life, etc. At the end of the nineteenth century, it was still possible to situate the vampire story within the far greater story of Christianity. What we witness today is a sad declension, whereby vampire tales are a bloodless substitute for robust Christianity.

Judge Judy, Simon Cowell, and the Lord God

WHILE TOOLING RECENTLY DOWN THE EXPRESSWAY, I noticed bill-boards advertising three separate television programs involving a judge: Judge Judy, Judge Mathis, and Judge Hatchett. As you know, these are only three of many more such shows that fill the airwaves of daytime TV. More to it, almost all of the "reality shows" that have sprung up in the last decade involve some sort of judgment. *Survivor* culminates with a gathering of the tribe and a solemn decision to vote someone off of the program. *Dancing with the Stars* is a fierce competition presided over by three judges, who objectively assess the performances of celebrity dancer-wannabes. And the premier tele-vision show of the past ten years, *American Idol*, features one of the most ruthless and infamous judges ever to appear in the popular culture: Simon Cowell.

Finally, even the most casual survey of TV talk shows reveals how central to their success is an act of judgment. Jerry Springer's audience is presented with some deeply dysfunctional individual, and, after sufficient prompting from the host, they erupt in shouts of vociferous disapproval. Dr. Phil's show reaches its high point when the good doctor bluntly tells some poor couple exactly what is wrong with their marriage and why they have to change their lives radical-ly. There are almost invariably tears of shame and regret.

Now here is what I find fascinating: this obsession with judgment exists in our culture side by side with an enormous stress on toleration and acceptance. We tell ourselves all the time that we are a nonjudgmental people; we pride ourselves on our open-mindedness; and if there is one value we would claim as absolute it might be: never do anything that would lower another person's self-esteem. Christina Aguilera sang in a popular song from a few years ago: "I am beautiful in every single way, and your words can't get me down." The greatest villain in the eyes of the self-esteem establishment is undoubtedly the Catholic Church. Again and again we hear that Catholicism, especially in matters of sex and lifestyle, is "judgmental" and "intolerant." I have encountered numerous people who (usually without realizing that I am a priest) refer to themselves as "recovering Catholics," comparing the harsh Church to a wounding disease. Perhaps I was premature in calling the Church the prime villain, for behind the Church is God himself, the supreme judge. In the atheist literature that is so prevalent today we hear over and again how cruel, manipulative, domineering, and demanding is the God of the Bible. Christopher Hitchens compared living under the regime of the judging God to living in a "spiritual North Korea."

Well, how do we read these two dimensions together? How do we make sense of both Christina Aguilera and Simon Cowell? A principle that I find extremely helpful is this: a repressed religious value does not go away; it comes up elsewhere in somewhat distorted form. Authentic judgment—which the self-esteem police have tried to eliminate—has its revenge, because, deep down, we know that judgment is indispensable to the development of a healthy personality and the maintenance of a rightly functioning society. What I mean by judgment is clear and unambiguous truth-telling, the placing of things, both good and bad, in the light that permits them to appear as they really are. Both Simon Cowell and Judge Judy are instructive. Simon regularly tells terrible singers that they are terrible and that they will never make it as professional entertainers. His interventions are often met with tears, obscene gestures, and angry words, but we watch Simon, not just because he's a master of the one-liner, but because he is, more often than not, right. And we know that his harsh words are actually going to benefit the pathetic performers whom he addresses. Judge Judy, having heard a plaintiff or defendant present his case, will often respond, "That doesn't make any sense, so it's probably a lie." Trained in the etiquette of self-esteem, we're flummoxed by this kind of directness, but we're also convinced that she's usually right and that her truth-telling, in the long run, benefits those whom she judges.

At the risk of sounding blasphemous, Simon Cowell and Judge Judy can tell us a good deal about God. It's true that the God of the Bible is presented consistently, and sometimes disconcertingly, as a judge. But this does not mean that he is vindictive; it means that he shines the light of his truth on human affairs. When that light falls on sin, deceit, injustice, and corruption, things get uncomfortable, but so be it. For only through such painful judgment do real healing and progress take place. The Church, in its formal teaching, is a servant of the divine judgment, and therefore a source of illumination and, finally, salvation.

Perhaps we might consider all of the judges whom we obviously love to watch to be minor icons of the Judge in whose light we ought to live.

Reading the Scandal
with Biblical Eyes

ONCE AGAIN WE'RE LIVING IN SCANDAL TIMES. The "Long Lent" of the sexual abuse scandal that the American Church endured in 2002 has now descended on the European Church. Once again, the news media are in a frenzy—CNN has blanket coverage, the *New York Times* is running regular stories, and thousands of blogs are buzzing. In preparation for a television interview about the sex-abuse scandal, I spent an entire day reading almost everything I could find in both the American and international press and found the process dismaying, depressing, and dispiriting. But what particularly struck me was this: though the sex-abuse scandal has been analyzed legally, institutionally, psychologically, and culturally, it has rarely been looked at biblically—even by Church representatives themselves. And this is tragic, for the Bible, the Word of God, is the definitive lens through which the whole of reality is most rightly read, and church men and women above all should know this.

What does a biblical reading of this never-ending scandal offer? First, we should not be surprised that people behave badly. The Bible clearly teaches that we human beings have been made in the image and likeness of God and that we are destined for eternal life with God. Nevertheless it teaches with equal clarity that we are fallen, marked by the original sin, which has compromised us in body, mind, and will. The scriptural narratives are remarkably honest about this. They make reference to rape, theft, murder, jealous rages, palace intrigue, naked ambition, family dysfunction, political corruption, adultery, and yes, sexual abuse. More to it, many of these crimes are committed by God's chosen instruments: Saul, David, Solomon, Jacob, Peter, and Paul, to name just a handful. An interviewer asked me just a few days ago, "How could this (the scandal) have happened?" and I responded, "Sin." I could have given a more textured answer, bringing in the psychological and institutional dimensions, but I believe I gave, from a biblical perspective, the most fundamental and clarifying response.

Second, the Church has enemies. St. Paul reminded us long ago that the Church of Jesus Christ is the new Israel, carrying on in transfigured form the mission of Israel to be a light to the nations, the enduring sign of God's existence and love. But it is a commonplace of the biblical narratives that Israel was not universally revered. Instead, it was enslaved by Egypt, harassed by the Philistines, overrun by the Assyrians, exiled by the Babylonians, conquered by the Greeks and the Romans. And Israel was often at war with itself: the prophets were regularly ignored, mocked, or even murdered by the people they were sent to address. The point is this: the message of God's love is not one that is necessarily received with enthusiasm by a sinful world; just the contrary.

Now only the blindest or most anti-Catholic of commentators would fail to see that, to a degree, enemies of the Church are operative in the coverage surrounding this scandal. The sexual abuse of children is an international epidemic, and it is present in every aspect of society. In the United States alone, there are approximately 39,000,000 victims of child sexual abuse, and around 50% of these were abused by family members. In the decade between 1990 and 2000, nearly 300,000 children in the American public school system were abused by teachers or coaches. Social workers in Africa report that in many countries on that continent, the numbers concerning the sexual abuse of young girls runs from "very, very high to astronomically high." And this is to say nothing of the multi-billion-dollar-a-year pornography industry in the United States, which disproportionately abuses young people, and the even more shocking—and highly profitable—sex trade involving kids. Moreover, the John Jay study showed that over a fifty year period, only 3-4% of Catholic priests were credibly charged with sex abuse, a figure below the national average, and in the year prior to writing this, precisely six cases of clerical sex abuse, in a Church of 65,000,000, were reported.

Yet, to watch the television networks or read the newspapers, one would think that the sexual abuse of children is a uniquely Catholic problem, one indeed facilitated by a wicked cabal of priestly and episcopal conspirators. There are some in the mainstream culture who are unhappy with many of the positions the Catholic Church has taken on sexual issues, especially abortion, and who would like to marginalize the Church's voice or eliminate it entirely from the public conversation. Biblically minded people should not find this the least bit surprising.

A third lesson provides a balance to the second. God regularly—and sometimes harshly—chastises his people Israel in order to cleanse them. On the biblical reading, God raises up figures who name the sins of the nation and call especially the leaders of the people to repentance and reform. Under this rubric, we might consider Samuel (who challenged Saul), Nathan (who called out David), Isaiah (who railed against the temple establishment), Jeremiah (who took the leadership of Israel to task), and Jesus himself (who had a few things to say about "whitewashed sepulchers"). Not everyone who brought the clergy sex scandal to light is an enemy of the Church; many should be construed as instruments of God's vengeance, who compelled a reluctant Church to come to grips with a problem that had been, for far too long, ignored, brushed under the carpet, or handled with pathetic incompetence. And for that matter, Yahweh sometimes used the enemies of Israel—Philistines, Babylonians, Romans, etc.—to work out his cleansing purposes. Might the Lord God be using the *Boston Globe* or the *New York Times* in much the same way?

I think that it's good to study this terrible phenomenon as thoroughly as we can, but we should never forget that the most clarifying perspective is the one provided by God's holy Word.

Biblical Wisdom
for Troubled Times

A WHILE BACK, I was scheduled to address the priests of the Archdiocese of Boston, but bad weather rolled into O'Hare, and my flight was cancelled. However, I'd like to share with you some of the insights I had intended to offer to the Boston priests. As you know, Boston was the epicenter of the clergy sex abuse scandal that came to light in 2002 and that continues to shake the Church around the country and around the world. I struggled rather mightily to prepare this talk, for I didn't want to dwell on the difficulties, and I wanted, above all, to give these priests a sense of hope, but I knew I had to make some reference to the scandal. I decided to take my own advice, per my previous essay, and look at the issue through biblical eyes.

I chose to focus on two texts from the Old Testament, the first from the opening chapters of the first book of Samuel and the second from the sixth chapter of the second book of Kings. As the first book of Samuel gets underway, we hear about Eli, the high priest at Shiloh. He is presented to us as blind, tired, and spiritually out of touch—an ineffective leader for Israel. More to it, he has two wicked sons, Hophni and Phineas, who are, like their father priests, but who are using their priesthood to take advantage of the people who come to them for help. We hear that many called out to Eli, urging him to discipline his sons, but he refused. Does any of this sound familiar:

corrupt priests who use their office to harm the people and a supervisor who miserably fails to correct them?

What followed upon this deep corruption was disaster for Israel. God permitted the Philistines to rout the Israelite army, killing 30,000 foot soldiers, killing Hophni and Phineas, and carrying the Ark of the Covenant off into captivity. This last outrage was probably the most devastating, since it was tantamount to ripping the heart out of the nation. We are told that a single soldier escaped from the field of battle, ran to Shiloh, and delivered the news to Eli. Upon hearing of the total catastrophe, the old man keeled over, broke his neck, and died. Does any of that sound familiar? The Church, which Paul calls "the new Israel," is passing through a catastrophic period, a Long Lent, a perfect storm. As the waves of the clergy sex abuse scandal wash over us, we wonder whether the Church will survive, and we feel, perhaps, that the heart of the Church has been ripped out. And it appears as though we are surrounded by armies of our enemies.

It is most important to note that, for the biblical authors, God is active in all things and at all times, both when Israel flourishes and when Israel suffers. God steadily loves his people, but that love appears in differing guises according to circumstances. The deaths of Eli and his sons, the wiping out of the Israelite army, the humiliation of the entire nation through the capture of the Ark, these were construed as the means by which Yahweh was cleansing and purifying the people, ridding them of sin and preparing them for renovation. The first book of Samuel opens with the cry of Hannah, a barren Israelite woman begging God for a child. With his customary pastoral sensitivity, Eli accused her of being drunk in church, but Hannah protested that she was passionately invoking God. Though Eli wouldn't listen, God did—and Hannah gave birth to Samuel, who, come of age, became the great prophet and re-founder of the nation, the one who rallied the people and anointed David as King.

The very best rubric under which to read the Old Testament texts is this: God bringing life out of death, opportunity out of impossibility. We see this motif over and over again—in the stories of Abraham, Jacob, Joseph, Moses, David, Isaiah, the Maccabees, etc. When things are, from the purely human standpoint, hopeless, God opens up a path. So in the story under consideration, even as God permits the painful cleansing of Israel, he is already preparing its salvation.

The questions I planned to pose to the priests of Boston— especially the younger brothers—were these: are there any Samuels among you? Are there any among you who are being raised up by God to be specially dedicated to him and to lead the renovation of the Church? Are you ready to endure the chastisement and accept the challenge?

The second biblical story I considered is a fairly obscure narrative dealing with the prophet Elisha. We hear that Elisha had raised the ire of the King of Aram and that the King had accordingly, surrounded the little town of Dothan, where Elisha lived along with a number of young aspiring servants of God. When one of Elisha's charges saw the assembled host, he turned to the prophet in terror and said, "Alas, master, what shall we do?" Elisha remained utterly calm and replied, "Do not be afraid, for there are more with us than are with them." A word that I've often used to describe what it feels like to go through the sex abuse crisis is "beleaguered." It feels as though the Church and the priesthood are surrounded by enemies, peering at us, questioning us, laughing at us, and suspecting the worst of us. And I confess to feeling often like Elisha's student as he gazed, horrified, at the army encamped against him.

Now what did Elisha see? What gave him such blithe confidence? He saw the power of the invisible world, the realm of the spirit, the kingdom of God. The creator of the entire universe is not something within the visible world; rather he is a spiritual power whose name is Love. When we call upon that love, we get in touch with the greatest force in existence, the power that mocks any of the powers of this world. There are always "more with us than are with them." I asked the beleaguered priests of Boston to believe this central biblical message and to act on their belief.

After Elisha made his statement, he asked the Lord to reveal to his young student what the prophet had seen. So God opened the young man's eyes and he saw that "the mountain was full of horses and chariots of fire all around Elisha." These are the spiritual forces: the angels, the saints, and the infinitely intense presence of God. I asked the elder priests of Boston to minister to their younger brothers as Elisha did to this student, passing on to them a spiritual vision, and teaching them to use the tools by which to access the transcendent powers. In this way, they will help them to find the courage to withstand, to resist, and to thrive.

Vatican II encouraged us to read the signs of the times. I intended to tell my brother priests that if we read our times with biblical eyes, we will face some terrible truths, but we will, finally, find hope.

Creative Nonviolence

WHEN IT COMES TO GUN VIOLENCE, the past few years have been pretty terrible. We wring our hands over the killings in the Holy Land, Iraq, and Afghanistan, but things are practically as bad in our own streets.

I won't enter into the details of the political discussion (I'm not really qualified to do so), but I would like to explore a religious dimension of the problem. I wonder how many have remarked that, with only a few exceptions, the murders that have taken place in our schoolyards and on our streets have been instances of Christians killing other Christians? In this regard, our home-grown mayhem is like the violence of the two great world wars of the last century, in which French, English, American, and Canadian Christians killed German, Austrian, Italian, and Russian Christians. How ironic and terrible all this was (and is), given that the figure who stands at the heart of the Christian faith advocated the path of nonviolence with great seriousness and told his followers that they should be known, above all, by the love they have one another. Stanley Hauerwas, whom *Time Magazine* named in 2001 as the "best theologian in America," once uttered this *cri de coeur*: "A modest proposal for peace: Christians should stop killing other Christians."

To be sure, the stubborn and tragic violence on our streets is the product of many causes: a breakdown in family structures, a compromising of relationships within the community, economic collapse, political fecklessness, etc. But I would suggest that it is also a failure of the Christian churches effectively to teach to their own people the way of nonviolence. The nonviolence that Jesus preached in the Sermon on the Mount is a canny and spiritually informed strategy for dealing with the problem of unjust aggression.

There are two classical responses to violence: fight or flight. Faced with a threat, we typically either fight back or run away—and sometimes this is all we reasonably can do. However, we also know that neither of these strategies is particularly efficacious in the long run. Fighting fire with fire usually just exacerbates the problem (as Gandhi said, "an eye for an eye, making the whole world blind"), and acquiescing to violence confirms the perpetrator's injustice.

What Jesus proposed was a third way: "If someone strikes you on the right cheek, turn and give him the other." No one in Jesus' time would have used the unclean left hand for any kind of social interaction. Therefore, to strike someone on the right cheek was to hit him with the back of the right hand, and this was a gesture of contempt, reserved for slaves and social inferiors. Faced with this kind of aggression, Jesus says, one should neither fight back nor flee; rather one should stand one's ground and turn the other cheek. He thereby signals to the aggressor that he refuses to live in that person's spiritual and psychological space. And he mirrors back the aggressor's aggression, shaming him into self-awareness and prompting conversion.

Naïve? Impractical? Tell that to Gandhi, Martin Luther King, and St. John Paul II, all of whom effected massive social changes through creative employment of Jesus' teaching. The Christian churches need to recover their confidence in this method and to teach it, at the very least, to their own congregants.

The Spiritual Value of
the BP Oil Leak

I GRANT, OF COURSE, that the BP oil leak of 2010 in the Gulf of Mexico was an environmental disaster, perhaps the worst since the Dust Bowl of the 1930s. But I also think it might carry a certain spiritual value. How would I explain this gnomic remark? Well, the gusher a mile below the surface of the ocean confounded everyone. BP executives looked and sounded befuddled; the crews using the most advanced technological tools to stem the tide of oil were ineffectual; our smartest scientists couldn't seem to come up with any solutions; and the President was stymied by his daughter's plaintive question, "Daddy, have you plugged the hole yet?" I don't point all this out in order to mock the scientists, businessmen, and politicians who, presumably, strived to solve the problem. I do so in order to draw attention to our profound vulnerability and our inescapable finitude.

At the dawn of the modern era, the English philosopher Francis Bacon declared that knowledge is power, by which he meant the power to control the forces of nature and make our lives more comfortable. And not long after Bacon, René Descartes urged European intellectuals to forget about religious abstractions and concentrate their energies on "the mastery of nature." These amount to the most followed marching orders in history, for from them have flowed what we characterize as the distinctively modern sciences and the technologies that have revolutionized human life. We have computers, televisions, nuclear weapons, operating rooms, antibiotics, electrical lights, airplanes, and automobiles, precisely because we listened to Bacon and Descartes. Now, I'm for all of these things (well, maybe not nuclear weapons), and I would never want to return to a pre-technological world. However, I agree with many of the postmodern philosophers who have pointed out how the very success of the scientific paradigm has conduced to a hyper-confidence, even an arrogance, on the part of modern people. We are so accustomed to solving our problems through the development and application of the right technology that we begin to think that we are, indeed, the masters of nature—and this is spiritually dangerous.

The classical and medieval philosophers spoke of the radical contingency of the world, by which they meant its fleeting, evanescent, non-self-explanatory quality. Things come and go. Nothing lasts forever. We don't last forever. And no amount of scientific or technological progress will change these stubborn facts. This is precisely why we must look outside the physical universe for final stability, meaning, purpose. As the Scripture has it, "only in God will my soul be at rest" (Ps 62:5). And this is why it is spiritually healthy when we self-declared masters of the universe occasionally get reminded of our own contingency and insufficiency. This reminding can come through sickness, through moral failure, through the fear of death—and perhaps even through a hole that we can't seem to plug.

Muslims, Christians, and Secularists

I HAD THE PRIVILEGE TO ADDRESS the annual Iftar Dinner, which was held at the Islamic Cultural Center in Niles, Illinois. This event— at the heart of which is a festive meal signaling the end of the daily Ramadan fast—brings Christians and Muslims together for fellowship, prayer, and conversation. I had been asked to reflect briefly on the topic of the future of religion in America. Given my religiously mixed audience, I decided to speak on the responsibility that all people of faith have in the presence of the growing threat of ideological secularism in our society. A 2008 Pew Forum study showed that the fastest-growing "religious" denomination in American is the "nones," those who claim no formal religious affiliation. It furthermore showed that there is no substantial difference in the attitudes of believers and nonbelievers in regard to a wide range of moral and political issues. What both of these data indicate is that secularism— the conviction that God, even if he exists, doesn't much matter—is on the rise.

I told my largely Muslim audience that, in the face of this threat, all religious believers must be, first, clear and public witnesses to the existence of God. Cardinal Souhard, the great post-war Archbishop of Paris, said that Christians should live their lives in such a way that they would make no sense unless God exists. People should be able to see by the way we behave and think that God is real. The Catholic theological tradition—informed in no small way by the work of Islamic philosophers and commentators—holds that God can be known through an appeal to the contingency, or non-self-sufficiency, of the world. Since nothing in nature or culture finally explains itself, we have to posit the existence of that which exists through the power of its own essence. Both the Muslim thinker Averroes and the Catholic master Thomas Aquinas held that this reality is the Creator God, attested to in both the Bible and the Qur'an. One of the features of both atheism and secularism is a tendency to deny precisely this contingency of the world and to see nature or culture as absolute. Healthy religion ought to point stubbornly to the fleeting, evanescent quality of the universe, and hence raise the minds and hearts of people to the transcendent God. I'm sure that no one needs reminding that the very idea of God is under attack today. The so-called "new" atheists—Richard Dawkins, Daniel Dennett, Sam Harris, and others—have ridiculed God as a "sky fairy" or an "invisible friend," a pathetic holdover from a superstitious time. We religious people have to oppose this through an appeal to our own rich intellectual traditions.

I then said that all the followers of the Abrahamic religions ought to affirm the unity of God. In the sixth chapter of the book of Deuteronomy, we find the great *Shema* declaration, "Hear, O Israel, the Lord your God is Lord alone"; and in the Islamic call to prayer, we hear five times a day that Allah is one; and the Nicene Creed commences with the declaration *credo in unum Deum* (I believe in one God). Some forty years ago, Joseph Ratzinger, later Pope Benedict XVI, asserted that belief in the oneness of God is inherently subversive, precisely because it implicitly undermines any false claimant to ultimacy. To say that there is only one God is to say that no culture, no individual, no political party, no ideology is absolute. And this declaration must be made publicly. The modern nation-states have preferred that religions remain private, and hence marginal and powerless, for in that condition they pose no challenge to the nation-state's primacy. But believers in the unity of God can have no truck with this arrangement, for it deprives them of their properly prophetic voice.

I argued, thirdly, that religious people ought to witness to the fact of creation. The Jewish, Islamic, and Christian traditions come together in saying that the universe was made, in its entirety, by the utterly self-sufficient God. This is actually quite astonishing, for it shows that the world is here as the result of an act of the purest love. Thomas Aquinas said that love is willing the good of the other as other, really wanting what is best for someone else. The God who has no need of the world can therefore relate to the world only with an utter lack of self-interest. Furthermore, the fact of creation shows that, whether we like it or not, we are all connected to one another, since we have all come forth from the same divine source. As St. Francis saw, even the sun and moon are brother and sister to us. Long before we decide to enter into political and social relationships through acts of the will, we are always already joined to each other by the deepest bonds. The path of compassion is but the ethical expression of this metaphysical conviction.

The greatest common enemy that all religious people have is ideological secularism. We have to oppose it by speaking publicly of the one creator God and by acting, consciously and intentionally, as the children of that God.

Kenneth Clark and the Danger
of Heroic Materialism

Lord Kenneth Clark is one of my intellectual heroes. Clark, who died in 1983, was the director of the National Gallery in London for many years and was generally recognized as one of the most insightful and influential art critics of the twentieth century. He burst into the popular consciousness in 1969 when his television program *Civilisation: A Personal View* became an unexpected international sensation. I watched this ten-part series (and devoured the accompanying book) when I was a teenager, and Clark's perspectives massively shaped my own thinking about history, aesthetics, and philosophy. When, a few years ago, I embarked on the production of a ten-part documentary about Catholicism, emphasizing both the truth and the artistic beauty of the Church, Kenneth Clark was my model and inspiration.

I recently watched the last few episodes of *Civilisation*, hoping to see if our series on Catholicism was anywhere near Clark's standard of excellence. What particularly struck me was the final episode, and Clark's rather bleak and prophetic summation to the entire series. The segment is entitled "Heroic Materialism," and it has to do with Western culture in the nineteenth and twentieth centuries. Lord Clark indicated a number of figures in both England and America who helped to produce the world that we know today, a civilization marked by industrialization, mechanization, the

    SEEDS OF THE WORD: FINDING GOD IN THE CULTURE

emergence of mega-cities, and the triumph of practical reason and science. There is no question but that this type of culture has given rise to a more convenient and easeful life; it would be hard for most of us even to imagine a world without electricity, automobiles, airplanes, and computers, and few of us would deny that these inventions have been, on the whole, a boon for the human race.

However, Clark points out that this contemporary culture is also marked by an undeniable soullessness and superficiality, evident perhaps most obviously in the ugliness, chaos, and confusion of our great metropolises. All of its virtues notwithstanding, Manhattan is a long way indeed from the spiritually ordered harmony of, say, Renaissance Florence or Medieval Chartres, or even nineteenth-century Paris. If our modern cities have an organizing principle it would be material gain, money-making, and this simply does not produce an aesthetically and morally pleasing way of life. As I've pointed out before, following the suggestion of Christopher Dawson and Joseph Campbell, the dominant buildings of contemporary cities are not religious or political edifices, but rather monuments to economic power: the Empire State Building, the John Hancock Center, the Aon Building, the Chrysler Building, etc. Even the most cursory glance at the skylines of our major cities reveals, as vividly as possible, what we consider of highest value.

But, concludes Clark, heroic materialism—however impressive and practically beneficial it might be—is never enough to satisfy the deepest longing of the human heart, and therefore never a sufficient organizing ideal for a human society. The Marxist narrative, he says, has been exposed as a fraud (pretty prophetic to say in 1969), but what we're left with as an alternative is the heroic materialism of Western capitalism, and, he insists, "that is not enough." This is not the too-easy moral equivalence approach that has seduced many in recent decades, but rather a striking anticipation of a central theme in the writings of Pope St. John Paul II. There was no more focused and energetic opponent of Communism and no more enthusiastic advocate of human rights-based democratic polity than John Paul II. Nevertheless, John Paul consistently criticized what he termed the "practical atheism" of the West, which is to say, its tendency to make material and scientific progress the ultimate values.

Throughout the *Civilisation* series, Kenneth Clark placed a stress on the role that Christian spirituality and theology played in the development of European culture. Neither Chartres nor Michelangelo, nor St. Francis, nor Dante, nor Shakespeare, nor T.S. Eliot, nor universities, nor monasteries, nor hospitals would be thinkable apart from Christianity. What Clark was bemoaning in the final episode was the fading away of the Christian story evident in the triumph of heroic materialism. Though many Christians remain in the West, he fears (and I would share this trepidation) that the Christian narrative has been occluded by a more powerful narrative—the story of material progress.

I believe that what is needed today is a compelling retelling of the Christian story. There is, in fact, no narrative more beautiful, more powerful, more fascinating than that which the Bible in its entirety presents: the Creator of the universe, out of love, has sent his only Son so that fallen human beings might be elevated to share the very life of God. That is a story which will sing to contemporary people just as surely as it sang to men and women of past ages. That is a story which will challenge the supremacy of heroic materialism or any other secularist ideology. That is a story which will create the culture anew. We just have to muster the courage, the intelligence, and the imagination necessary to tell it again.

Bob Dylan in China

KNOWING MY INTEREST IN ALL THINGS BOB DYLAN, a friend sent me an article penned by Maureen Dowd, columnist for *The New York Times*. It had to do with the maestro's unprecedented appearance in China, but it was far from an encomium. Dowd took Bob Dylan sharply to task for caving in to the Communist authorities, apparently agreeing to their demands not to sing any of his best-known anti-war and countercultural anthems from the sixties: "Blowin' in the Wind," "A Hard Rain's Gonna Fall," "The Times They Are A-Changin'," etc. How unlike the courageous young Dylan, she opined, who walked off the *Ed Sullivan Show* when the censors told him he couldn't sing "Talkin' John Birch Society Blues," a rather biting satire of the right-wing extremist group. Then again, she went on, didn't Dylan himself, in his much-lauded autobiography, *Chronicles Vol. I*, not admit that he was never much for the sixties counterculture and that he never sought to be the voice of a generation? Wasn't this latest episode just one more indication that the "real" Dylan was but a conventional entertainer, willing to go along with anyone or adopt any style in order to make money?

Well, it's never pleasant to see one of your heroes raked over the coals. My interest piqued and my dander up, I went to one of my favorite websites, BobLinks.com, which features set lists of every concert as well as amateur reviews by concert attendees, in order to see what Dylan actually played in China. Dowd was right in saying that Dylan did not play any of his classic "protest" songs, and for all I know he might have agreed with the Communist government not to play them. But the second I saw how he led off each concert, I laughed out loud, for I realized that Dowd had totally missed just how radical Bob Dylan was in China, indeed far more revolutionary than he would have been had he played his four thousandth version of "Blowin' in the Wind."

At each of his Chinese concerts, Dylan opened with a song from his explicitly Christian period, from the late seventies and early eighties. The first night, in Shanghai, he commenced the show with "Gotta Serve Somebody," a 1979 number that won Dylan a Grammy for best song. It is based on a passage from the 24th chapter of the book of Joshua. After the Israelites had completed their conquest of the Promised Land, Joshua assembled the people and posed to them a blunt choice: either you worship the Lord or you worship the gods of the people you have conquered. Then he says unambiguously, "As for me and my household, we will serve the Lord" (Josh 24:16). Dylan translates this into his distinctive poetry: "You might be the ambassador to England or France/ You might like to gamble, you might like to dance/ You might be the heavyweight champion of the world/ You might be a socialite with a long string of pearls/ but you're gonna have to serve somebody/ It might be the devil or it might be the Lord/ But you're gonna have to serve somebody." There it is, as stark as Joshua's challenge: either the true God or the dark power that lies behind all false claimants to ultimacy. To sing those lines in a country which has been, from the time of Mao-Tse-Tung, officially atheist, which has actively persecuted the Christian churches, putting uncounted thousands of Christians to death and throwing still more into prison—well, I don't know, Ms. Dowd, but that's pretty revolutionary in my book.

And in Beijing the next night, Dylan opened his concert with another song from his first Christian album, a sprightly little number called "Gonna Change My Way of Thinkin'." The next to last stanza of that blues tune is this: "Jesus said be ready, You know not the hour which I come/ Jesus said be ready, You know not the hour which I come/ He said, 'He who is not for me is against me'/ Just so you'd know where he was comin' from." For my money, to sing those lines in a country where absolute authority has been claimed by an oppressive state, which has been willing to murder scores of millions of people who stood in its way, is about as countercultural, challenging, subversive, and revolutionary as you can get.

Anyone that knows the work of Bob Dylan knows that the songwriter has been deeply religious his whole career long. His explicitly political protest songs were rooted in the prophetic tradition of ancient Israel and almost without exception called the judgment of God on wicked rulers and unscrupulous financiers. What was that "hard rain a-gonna fall" if not the flood of Noah? And what was that "wind" in which the answers were blowin' if not the Holy Spirit? In his Christian period, all of this became explicit and straightforward—and it was with two of these Christian songs that he decided to challenge Chinese society. In doing so, he was standing with St. Paul, who dared to speak of "Jesus the Lord" in a society in which "Caesar is Lord" was a signal of one's loyalty to the power structure.

With due respect to Maureen Dowd, the Bob Dylan who decided to proclaim, with the full blast of a rock band, the Lordship of Jesus Christ in Communist China has never been more truly revolutionary.

Celebrating the Death
of bin Laden?

OSAMA BIN LADEN WAS A WICKED MAN, responsible for the deaths of tens of thousands of innocent people on several continents, and responsible too for something more subtle and insidious: the terrifying of practically everyone on the planet. I believe that fearmongers deserve special opprobrium, since they produce that state of mind, which, as St. John tells us, is the opposite of love, for "perfect love casts out all fear." The memory of September 11th is like a nightmare that will forever haunt and nag and trouble the consciousness of mankind. It is impossible to doubt what President Obama said, namely, that the world is a better, safer place without the cruel and hateful man at the source of all this misery.

I heard the news of bin Laden's death when I was in Rome for the beatification of Pope John Paul II. I watched some of the coverage on the BBC and CNN, taking in the scenes of Americans celebrating at Ground Zero, at the Mets-Phillies game, and in front of the White House. I completely understood the feelings of jubilation and patriotic pride that they were exhibiting, and I will admit that I felt them too. There was indeed a keen sense that at least a measure of justice had been done in putting Osama bin Laden to death. And there was, too, just that wonderful release that comes when a great threat has been made to disappear. Some of the celebrations put me in mind of the unrestrained rejoicing at the end of World War II.

In the midst of all the shouting, however, another small voice was heard, that of Pope Benedict XVI. The Pope commented very simply that it is never right to celebrate the death of another human being, no matter how vile. I am quite sure that Pope Benedict was under absolutely no illusions regarding Osama bin Laden. He was not the least bit interested in exculpating him for his crimes. But he reminded Christians of a disturbing and deeply challenging truth that stands at the very heart of our moral tradition, namely, that we must love everyone, even our enemies. Jesus said, "Bless those who curse you; pray for you who maltreat you; if someone slaps you on the right cheek, turn and give him the other." This has nothing to do with sentimentality, nor is it a matter of being "soft" on crime. Original sin—the irreducible depravity that all of us experience in ourselves—is a fundamental Christian doctrine. But it is an acknowledgement that all of us are children of the one God and hence brothers and sisters to one another. We are connected, through God, by bonds that are deeper than the ties of nationality, culture, religion, or family. Whether we like it or not, we are implicated in each other.

And therefore our enemies are also our brothers and our sisters. Notice please, that I am not denying that we have enemies, real enemies, who are wicked, twisted, violent, and dangerous. But it is a Christian conviction that all of that evil is not telling the deepest truth about the enemy. The deepest truth is that he or she is a child of God, and thus worthy of our love. None of this implies, of course, that wicked people should not be arrested, brought to justice, punished, or even, in extreme cases, be killed. If, for example, in the process of bringing bin Laden to justice, our soldiers were fired upon, they had the right to return that fire. But it does indeed imply that the person so arrested, tried, imprisoned, or even put to death, should remain a beloved brother or sister.

How should this manifest itself? There are heroic examples of enemy love, such as the Amish couple who befriended and then defended in court the young man who had brutally killed their own son; or Cardinal Bernardin, who visited and anointed the man who had accused him falsely of sexual misconduct. But these are precious and rare. Something that all of us can do is to pray for those who maltreat us, offering them to God, expressing a spiritual solidarity with them. This is why I found it particularly moving that the American forces who buried Osama bin Laden at sea gave this terrible man a proper Islamic funeral service.

We should celebrate that the world is a safer place and that a wicked man has been brought to justice. But the Pope is right: we shouldn't celebrate that our enemy is dead. As hard as it is to say, we should pray for him as an act of love.

Why Are So Many Atheists
on the *CNN Belief Blog*?

When the *CNN Belief Blog*, which has graciously featured a few of my pieces, celebrated its first anniversary, its editors reflected on ten things that they've learned in the course of the year. The one that got my eye was this: that atheists are by far the most fervent commentators on matters religious. This completely coincides with my own experience as an Internet commentator and blogger. Every day, my website and YouTube page are inundated with remarks, usually of a sharply negative or dismissive nature, from atheists, agnostics, and critics of religion. In fact, some of my YouTube commentaries have been specifically targeted by atheist webmasters, who urge their followers to flood my site with "dislikes" and crude assessments of what I've said. And one of my contributions to the CNN site—what I took to be a benign article urging Christians to pray for Christopher Hitchens, then dying of cancer—excited literally thousands of angry responses from the haters of religion.

What do we make of this? I think we see, first, that atheists have come rather aggressively out of the closet. Following the prompts of Hitchens, Richard Dawkins, Sam Harris, Bill Maher, and many others, they have found the confidence to (excuse the word) evangelize for atheism. They are no longer content to hold on to their conviction as a private opinion; they consider religion dangerous and retrograde, and they want religious people to change their minds.

This fervor has led them, sadly, to employ a good deal of vitriolic rhetoric, but this is a free country, and their advocacy for atheism should not, of course, be censored. But it should be a wake-up call to all of my fellow religionists. We have a fight on our hands, and we have to be prepared, intellectually and morally, to get into the arena.

Most of the new atheists employ variations of the classical arguments of Ludwig Feuerbach, Karl Marx, Friedrich Nietzsche, and Sigmund Freud, namely, that religion is a pathetic projection born of suffering; that it is an infantile illusion; that it is dehumanizing; etc. How well do Christians know the theories of our intellectual enemies? Can we identify their blind spots and the flaws in their logic? Have we read the great Christian apologists—G.K. Chesterton, C.S. Lewis, Francis Schaeffer, Ronald Knox, Fulton Sheen—and can we wield their arguments against those who are coming at us? In my own Catholic Church, we sadly jettisoned much of our rich apologetic tradition in the years after Vatican II, convinced that it would be better to reach out positively to the culture. Well, at least part of that culture has turned pretty hostile, and it is high time to recover the intellectual weapons that we set aside.

Today's atheists also eagerly use the findings of contemporary science—especially in evolutionary biology and quantum physics—to undermine the claims of religion. Are the advocates of the faith ready to meet that challenge? How carefully have we read the scientific critics? And have we bothered to study the works of such deeply religious scientists as Fr. John Polkinghorne, Fr. George Coyne, Fr. Stanley Jaki, and Fr. Georges Le Maitre, colleague of Einstein and the formulator of the Big Bang theory of cosmic origins? We shouldn't imitate the Internet atheists in their nastiness, but we should certainly imitate them in our willingness to come forward boldly and show some intellectual teeth.

I'd like to make one other observation. The fierce and vocal presence of so many atheists on the *CNN Belief Blog*, and many other religious sites, also speaks to what I call "the Herod principle." The Gospels tell us that Herod Antipas arrested John the Baptist because the prophet had publicly challenged the king. Herod threw John into prison, but then, we are told, the king loved secretly to listen to the prophet, who continued to preach from his cell.

St. Augustine formulated an adage that beautifully sums up the essentials of Christian anthropology: "O Lord, you have made us for yourself; therefore our hearts are restless until they rest in you." A basic assumption of biblical people is that everyone is hard-wired for God in the measure that everyone seeks a fulfillment that cannot be had through any of the goods of this world. Long before Augustine, the psalmist prayed, "Only in God is my soul at rest." My wager, as a person of faith, is that everyone—and that includes Christopher Hitchens, Bill Maher, and Richard Dawkins—implicitly wants God, and hence remains permanently fascinated by the things of God. Though the fierce atheists of today profess that they would like to eliminate religious speech and religious ideas, secretly they love to listen as people speak of God. This goes a long way, it seems to me, toward explaining their presence in great numbers on religious blogs.

So I say to Christians and other believers: be ready for a good fight, and get some spiritual weapons in your hands. And I say to the atheists: I'll keep talking—because I know, despite all of your protestations and sputtering, that your hearts are listening.

The Acts We Perform,
the People We Become

From the 1950s through the late 1970s Karol Wojtyła (Pope St. John Paul II) was a professor of moral philosophy at the Catholic University of Lublin in Poland, specializing in sexual ethics and what we call today "marriage and family life." He produced two important books touching on these matters, *The Acting Person*, a rigorous philosophical exploration of Christian anthropology, and *Love and Responsibility*, a much more accessible analysis of love, sex, and marriage. These texts provided the foundation for the richly textured teaching of Pope John Paul II that now goes by the name "theology of the body." As was evident throughout his papacy, John Paul had a deep devotion to young people, and he wanted them to see the teaching of the Church in regard to sex, not as a burden, but as an invitation to fuller life. I would like to develop just one insight from John Paul's rich magisterium on sex and marriage, for I share the perennial concern of older people that too many young people are treating sex in a morally casual way.

Karol Wojtyła taught that in making an ethical decision, a moral agent does not only give rise to a particular act, but he also contributes to the person he is becoming. Every time I perform a moral act, I am building up my character, and every time I perform an unethical act, I am compromising my character. A sufficient number of virtuous acts, in time, shapes me in such a way that I can predictably and reliably perform virtuously in the future, and a sufficient number of vicious acts can misshape me in such a way that I am incapable of choosing rightly in the future. This is not judgmentalism; it is a kind of spiritual or moral physics, an articulation of a basic law.

We see the same principle at work in sports. If you swing the golf club the wrong way enough times, you become a bad golfer, that is to say, someone habitually incapable of hitting the ball straight and far. And if you swing the club correctly enough times, you become a good golfer, someone habitually given to hitting the ball straight and far.

John Paul put his finger on a problem typical of our time, namely, that people think that they can do lots of bad things while still remaining, deep down, "good persons," as though their characters are separable from the particular things that they do. In point of fact, a person who habitually engages in self-absorbed, self-destructive, and manipulative behavior is slowly but surely warping his character, turning himself into a self-absorbed, self-destructive, and manipulative person. Viewed from a slightly different angle, this is the problem of separating the "self" from the body, as though the "real person" hides under or behind the concrete moves of the body. Catholic philosophy and theology have battled this kind of dualism for centuries, insisting that the self is a composite of spirit and matter. In fact, it is fascinating to note how often this gnostic conception of the person (to give it its proper name) asserts itself, and how often the Church has risen up to oppose it.

Now apply this principle to sexual behavior. Study after study has shown that teenagers and college students are participating more and more in a "hookup" culture, an environment in which the most casual and impersonal forms of sexual behavior are accepted as a matter of course. As recently as twenty-five or thirty years ago, there was still, even among teenagers, a sense that sexual contact belonged at least in the context of a "loving" or "committed" relationship, but today it appears as though even this modicum of moral responsibility has disappeared. And this is doing terrible damage to young people. Dr. Leonard Sax, a physician and psychiatrist, explored the phenomenon of the hookup culture in his book *Why Gender Matters*, a text I would warmly recommend to teenagers and their parents. He described that tawdry moral universe in some detail, and then he remarked that his psychiatrist's office is filled with young people—especially young women—who have fallen into debilitating depression, anxiety, and low self-esteem. Dr. Sax theorized that these psychological symptoms are a function of a kind of cognitive dissonance. The wider society is telling teenagers that they can behave in any way they like and still be "good people," but the consciences of these young people are telling a different story. Deep down, they know that selfish and irresponsible behavior is turning them into selfish and irresponsible people—and their souls are crying out. Their presence in Dr. Sax's waiting room witnesses to the truth of John Paul's understanding of the moral act.

I might sum up John Paul's insight by saying that moral acts matter, both in the short run and in the long run. For weal or for woe, they produce immediate consequences, and they form characters. And so I might venture to say to a young person tempted to engage in irresponsible sexual behavior: please realize that, though you may not immediately appreciate it, the particular things you choose to do are inevitably shaping the person you are becoming.

If You Want to Be a Good Person,
It Does Matter What You Believe

A TEAM OF SOCIOLOGISTS led by Catholic University professor William D'Antonio published a survey that received quite a bit of media attention, for it showed that many Catholics disagree with core doctrines of the Church and yet still consider themselves "good Catholics." For instance, 40% of the respondents said that belief in the real presence of Jesus in the Eucharist is not essential to being a faithful Catholic. Perhaps the most startling statistic is that fully 88% of those surveyed said "how a person lives is more important than whether he or she is a Catholic." In a follow up piece in *The Chicago Sun-Times*, a reporter asked a number of people on the street for their reaction to these findings. One man said, "I'm a very good Catholic because I follow what's in my heart, more than what the Church tells me to do..."

As even the most casual student of societal trends knows, this sort of cavalier attitude toward doctrine is rampant, at least in the West. I dare say that most people in Europe or North America would hold some version of the following: as long as, deep down, you are a good person, it doesn't much matter what you believe. The intellectual pedigree of this popular idea can be traced back at least to the eighteenth-century German philosopher Immanuel Kant, who held that religion is fundamentally reducible to ethics. All other forms of religious life and practice—dogmas, rituals, liturgies, sacraments, etc.—are meant, Kant thought, simply to contribute to upright moral behavior. In the measure that they fulfill this purpose, they are acceptable, but in the measure that they contribute nothing to ethics, they become irrelevant, even dangerous.

I would argue that what is truly dangerous is precisely the bifurcation between doctrine and ethics that Kant inaugurated, and that has become so ingrained in the contemporary imagination. For though our culture rarely admits it, so many of the ethical norms that we take for granted are deeply rooted in very definite doctrinal claims of the Judeo-Christian traditions. When the dogmas are ignored or declared irrelevant, the normativity of the moral claims is, sooner or later, attenuated.

I would imagine that, if pressed, most people in our society would characterize "being a good person" as treating others with love, honoring the dignity, freedom, and inherent worth of their fellow human beings. And most would agree that ethical violations—stealing, lying, sexual misbehavior, infidelity, cheating, doing physical harm, etc.—are correctly seen as negations of love.

But what is love? Love is not primarily a feeling or an instinct; rather, it is the act of willing the good of the other as other. It is radical self-gift, living for the sake of the other. To be kind to someone else so that he might be kind to you, or to treat a fellow human being justly so that he, in turn, might treat you with justice is not to love, for such moves are tantamount to indirect self-interest. Truly to love is to move outside of the black hole of one's egotism, to resist the centripetal force that compels one to assume the attitude of self-protection. But this means that love is rightly described as a "theological virtue," for it represents a participation in the love that God is. Since God has no needs, only God can utterly exist for the sake of the other. All of the great masters of the Christian spiritual tradition saw that we are able to love only inasmuch as we have received, as a grace, a share in the very life, energy, and nature of God.

So far we've looked at the subjective side of love. But what of its object? Why, precisely, are we convinced that our fellow human beings are in possession of rights, dignity, and inherent worth? This conviction has become so ingrained in us, so taken for granted, that we forget how peculiarly theological it is. Every human being, regardless of considerations of race, education, intelligence, strength, or accomplishment, is a subject of inestimable value because he or she has been created by God and destined by God for eternal life. Take God out of the equation, and human dignity rather rapidly evanesces. If you doubt me on this score, I would invite you to look to societies in which belief in a Creator God was not operative. In classical Greece, the society of Plato and Aristotle, only a certain handful of people—aristocratic, virtuous, propertied, and well-educated—were seen as worthy of respect. Everyone else was expected to do as he or she was told. Infants deemed imperfect could be exposed, and a startlingly large number of people were consigned to slavery. And in the secular totalitarianisms of the last century, societies in which God was systematically denied, human dignity was so little respected that the piling up of tens of millions of corpses was seen as an acceptable political strategy—Lenin's "cracking of some eggs to make an omelet."

In our commitment to love and human dignity, we are, whether we know it or not, operating out of a theological consciousness. When the doctrines and practices that support religious consciousness are dismissed—as they so often are in contemporary secularism—the moral convictions born of that consciousness are imperiled. This is the massively important point missed by those who so blithely say, "It doesn't matter what you believe, as long as you're a nice person."

Why I Loved to Listen to Christopher Hitchens

I HAVE, OVER THE YEARS, playfully accused some of my atheist inter-locutors of being "secret Herods." The Biblical Herod arrested John the Baptist but nevertheless took pleasure in listening to John preach from his prison cell. So, I've suggested, the atheists who come to my website and comment so acerbically and so frequently on my Inter-net videos are, despite themselves, secretly seeking out the things of God. I will confess to having a certain Herod syndrome in re-verse in regard to Christopher Hitchens. Though he was certainly the most outspoken and biting critic of religion in the last fifty years, and though he often infuriated me with this cavalier and insulting dismissals of what I hold most dear, I will admit that I loved to listen to him.

I think I watched every Hitchens debate that I could find on YouTube. I subscribed to *Vanity Fair* largely because Hitchens was a regular contributor. I read every one of his books—including plow-ing through his paving-stone sized collection of essays called *Argu-ably*—and I delighted in watching him thrust and parry with news interviewers from across the political spectrum, who just could never seem to get a handle on him. Part of the attraction was what the an-cient Romans called *gaudium de stilo* (delight in style). No one wrote quite like Christopher Hitchens. Whether he was describing an up-rising on the streets of Athens, or criticizing the formation of young men in the British boarding schools of the 1950s, or defending his support of the Iraq war, or begging people to let go of what he took to be their childish belief in God, Hitchens was unfailingly intelligent, perceptive, funny, sarcastic, and addictively readable. Another part of the appeal was that his personality was always massively present in what he wrote. There was absolutely nothing detached about a Hitchens book, article, or speech. Rather, his aggressive, inquisitive, cocksure, irritated, delightfully alert self was consistently on display. Also, Hitchens and I liked a lot of the same people and topics: Evelyn Waugh, contemporary politics, religion, and above all, Bob Dylan. But what I appreciated most about Christopher Hitchens was his passion for God—which I realize might require a bit of explanation!

One of the fundamental mistakes that Hitchens and his fellow new atheists consistently made in regard to religion is their misconstrual of what serious believers mean by the word "God." Time and again, the new atheists mocked God as a "sky fairy" or an "invisible friend," and they argued that religious belief was tantamount to accepting the existence of "a flying spaghetti monster," a wild mythological fantasy for which there is not a shred of evidence. Or they ridiculed religious philosophers for proposing, over and again, a pathetic "god of the gaps," a supernatural cause fitted awkwardly into a schema of explanation that science would eventually clarify in its own terms.

In all of these ways, however, they missed their mark. For the classical theological tradition, God is not a being in the world, one object, however supreme, among many. The maker of the entire universe cannot be, himself, an item within the universe, and the one who is responsible for the nexus of causal relations in its entirety could never be a missing link in an ordinary scientific schema. Thomas Aquinas makes the decisive point when he says that God is not *ens summum* (highest being) but rather *ipsum esse* (the sheer act of being itself). God is neither a thing in the world, nor the sum total of existing things; he is instead the unconditioned cause of the conditioned universe, the reason why there is something rather than nothing. Accordingly, God is not some good thing, but Goodness itself; not some true object, but Truth itself; not some beautiful reality, but Beauty itself. And this helps us to see how Christopher Hitchens, despite his protestations, actually loved God.

What you couldn't miss in Hitchens's writing and speaking was a passion for justice, a deep desire to defend those who were denied their rights. This comes through from his first book on Cyprus and Greece to his articles in defense of his friend Salman Rushdie to his later essays and speeches on the Iraq war. Where does this passion come from? What makes sense of it? If there is no God, which is to say, no unconditioned justice, no absolute criterion of good and evil, why precisely would someone burn with righteous indignation at violations of justice? If we are here simply by dumb chance, if all of us will one day die and simply fade away, if the earth will one day be incinerated and the universe spins away without purpose and in utter indifference to human cruelty and human nobility, why would anyone finally bother? Wouldn't in fact Dostoyevsky be right in saying that if there is no God everything is permitted? My point is that the very passion for setting things right, which burned so brightly in Christopher Hitchens, is a powerful indicator that he was, whether he acknowledged it or not, connected to unconditioned justice. And that connection brought him very close indeed to what serious believers mean by God.

Soon after Hitchens revealed that he had been diagnosed with a very aggressive form of cancer, I wrote a piece for the *CNN Belief Blog* in which I urged my fellow Christians to pray for him. The article, which I considered rather benign, awakened a furious response on the part of Hitchens's allies. More than two thousand respondents told me, effectively, to leave Hitchens alone and not impose my "medieval mumbo-jumbo" on their hero. I didn't abide by their recommendation. I prayed for Hitchens throughout his illness, and I pray for him now—a man religious despite himself.

Andrew Sullivan's
Nonthreatening Jesus

A cover story for *Newsweek* magazine, printed during Holy Week and penned by political and cultural commentator Andrew Sullivan, concerns the "crisis" that is supposedly gripping Christianity. Weighed down by its preoccupation with doctrines and supernatural claims, which are incredible to contemporary audiences, compromised by the corruption of its leadership, co-opted for base political ends, Christianity is verging, he argues, on the brink of collapse. The solution Sullivan proposes is a renewal of Christianity; a return to its roots and essential teachings. And here he invokes, as a sort of patron saint, Thomas Jefferson, who as a young man literally took a straight razor to the pages of the New Testament and cut out any passages dealing with the miraculous, the supernatural, or the resurrection and divinity of Jesus. The result of this Jeffersonian surgery is Jesus the enlightened sage, the teacher of timeless moral truths concerning love, forgiveness, and non-violence. Both Jefferson and Sullivan urge that this Christ, freed from churchly distortions, can still speak in a liberating way to an intelligent and non-superstitious audience.

As the reference to Jefferson should make clear, there is nothing particularly new in Sullivan's proposal. The liberation of Jesus the wisdom figure from the shackles of supernatural doctrine has been a preoccupation of much of the liberal theology of the last two hundred years. Hence, Friedrich Schleiermacher turned Jesus into a religious genius with a particularly powerful sense of God; Rudolf Bultmann converted him into the prototype of the existentialist philosopher; Immanuel Kant transformed him into the supreme teacher of the moral life. And this approach is very much alive today. Deepak Chopra and Eckhart Tolle, to give just two examples among many, present Jesus, not as the God-man risen from the dead, but rather as a New Age guru.

The first problem with this type of theorizing is that it has little to do with the New Testament. As Jefferson's Bible makes clear, the excision of references to the miraculous, to the resurrection, and to the divinity of Jesus delivers to us mere fragments of the Gospels. Matthew, Mark, Luke, and John were massively interested in the miracles and exorcisms of Jesus, and they were positively obsessed with his dying and rising. The Gospels have been accurately characterized as "passion narratives with long introductions." Further, the earliest Christian texts that we have are the epistles of St. Paul, and in those letters that St. Paul wrote to the communities he founded, there are but a tiny handful of references to the teaching of Jesus. What clearly preoccupied Paul was not the moral doctrine of Jesus, but the resurrection of Jesus from the dead. And in the evangelical preaching of the first disciples—preserved in the Acts of the Apostles—we find, not articulations of Jesus' ethical vision, but rather affirmations of the resurrection. St. Peter's "you killed the author of life, but God raised him from the dead, and to this we are witnesses" (Acts 3:15) is absolutely typical. And from this followed as a consequence the affirmation of the Lordship of Jesus. One of the commonest phrases in the writings of Paul is *Iesous Kyrios* (Jesus is Lord), which carried a very provocative connotation indeed—for a watchword of Paul's time and place was *Kaiser kyrios* (Caesar is Lord), meaning that the Roman emperor was the one to whom final allegiance was due. In saying *Iesous Kyrios*, Paul was directly challenging that political and social status quo, which goes a long way toward explaining why he spent a good deal of time in jail!

And this leads to the second major problem with a proposal like Sullivan's: it offers absolutely no challenge to the powers that be. It is precisely the bland and harmless version of Christianity with which the regnant culture is comfortable. Go back to Peter's sermon for a moment. "You killed him," said the chief of Jesus' disciples. The "you" here includes the power structures of the time, both Jewish and Roman, which depended for their endurance in power on their ability to frighten their subjects through threats of lethal punishment. "But God raised him." The resurrection of Jesus from the dead is the clearest affirmation possible that God is more powerful than the corrupt and violent authorities that govern the world—which is precisely why the tyrants have always been terrified of it. When the first Christians held up the cross—the greatest expression of state-sponsored terrorism—they were purposely taunting the leaders of their time by saying, "You think that frightens us?" The opening line of the Gospel of Mark is a direct challenge to Rome: "The beginning of the good news about Jesus Christ, the Son of God" (Mark 1:1). "Good news" (*euangelion* in Mark's Greek) was a term used to describe an imperial victory. The first Christian evangelist is saying, not so subtly, that the real good news hasn't a thing to do with Caesar. Rather, it has to do with someone whom Caesar killed and whom God raised from the dead. And just to rub it in, he refers to this resurrected Lord as "Son of God." Ever since the time of Augustus, "Son of God" was a title claimed by the Roman emperor. Not so, says Mark. The authentic Son of God is the one who is more powerful than Caesar.

Again and again, Sullivan says that he wants a Jesus who is "apolitical." Quite right—and that's just why the cultural and political leaders of the contemporary West will be perfectly at home with his proposal. A defanged, privatized, spiritual teacher poses little threat to the status quo. But the Son of God, crucified under Pontius Pilate and risen from the dead through the power of the Holy Spirit, is a permanent and very dangerous threat. That's why I will confess that I smiled a bit at Andrew Sullivan as I read his article. Like the young Thomas Jefferson, I'm sure he thinks he's being very edgy and provocative. Au contraire, in point of fact.

How to Solve the Bully Problem

It is very difficult indeed to watch the documentary *Bully* without experiencing both an intense sadness and a feeling of helplessness. The film opens with the heartbreaking ruminations of a father whose son committed suicide after being brutally bullied by his classmates.

We hear a number of similar stories throughout the film, and we also are allowed to watch and listen as very real kids are pestered, belittled, mocked, and in some cases, physically assaulted just because they are, in some sense, different. The most memorable figure in the movie is a young man, around 12, named Alex. He seems to be a good-natured kid, happy in the embrace of his family, but because he's a bit uncoordinated, geeky, and odd-looking (his brutal nickname is "fishface"), his fellow students mercilessly pick on him. Alex's daily ride on the school bus is like something out of Dante's *Inferno*.

What would be funny, if it weren't so tragic, is the cluelessness of the school officials (and of the adults in general) who should be doing something about the problem. We get to watch the vice principal of Alex's school as she deals with aggressive students, and as she tries to mollify Alex's parents. What we hear is a pathetic mixture of bromides, self-serving remarks, boys-will-be-boys platitudes, and, worst of all, a marked tendency to blame the victim. When the parents complain about the bus that Alex rides, the vice principal vapidly comments, "Well, I rode that bus once, and the children were like angels." I mean, is she really naïve enough to think that their behavior in the presence of the vice principal is even vaguely typical? I will admit, however, that I sympathized with her confusion when, at one point, she gazed into the camera lens and sighed, "I just don't know what to do." A lot of the adults in the documentary seemed to share that sentiment.

Well, I know someone who knows what to do. Some time ago, I reviewed a book by Dr. Leonard Sax called *Why Gender Matters*, an incisive study of why boys and girls benefit from very different approaches to education and character formation. Dr. Sax sent me a copy of his 2007 study titled *Boys Adrift: The Five Factors Driving the Growing Epidemic of Unmotivated Boys and Underachieving Young Men*. As the subtitle indicates, the book examines the problem of the "slacker dude," the teenager who would rather watch video games than attend class or the twentysomething who would rather lounge around his parents' home than start an ambitious career. To get all of the details, please peruse Dr. Sax's informative and eminently readable book in its entirety.

But with the problem of bullying in mind, I would like to focus on one chapter of *Boys Adrift*, titled "The Revenge of the Forsaken Gods." Echoing in many ways the reflections of Joseph Campbell and Richard Rohr, Dr. Sax bemoans the fact that our culture has largely forgotten the subtle art of transforming boys into men. Despite (or perhaps because of) our scientific predilection, we think that this process just happens naturally. Our "primitive" ancestors knew that it did not, and this is why they developed sophisticated rituals of initiation, designed to shock boys out of their natural narcissism and habits of self-protection into moral and spiritual maturity.

Whether we are talking about the Navajo, Masai warriors, or Orthodox Jews, traditional cultures understand that boys have to be brought through a period of trial—some test of skill and endurance—during which they learn the virtues of courage and self-sacrifice. Sometimes, these initiation rituals are accompanied by a kind of ceremonial scarring, for the elders want the boys to know, in their bodies, that they've been tested and permanently changed. Sax astutely observes that many of the great American authors—Faulkner, Hemingway, Dos Passos, Studs Terkel, James Dickey—wrote passionately and persuasively about this very topic. Many great films, from *The Hustler*, *On the Waterfront*, and *Rebel Without a Cause* to *Braveheart* and *Gladiator*, dramatically display the process by which a boy becomes a heroic man of selflessness and courage.

The principal element in the initiation process—whether real or fictionally presented—is a mature man who embodies the virtues to which the boy aspires. Finally, men of valor, charity, ambition, and grace transform boys into men of valor, charity, ambition and grace. When this mentoring dynamic is lost, Dr. Sax argues, the result is boys adrift and young men taking their cues from Eminem, 50 Cent, Akon, and the Situation.

Now you might be wondering what all this has to do with the phenomenon of bullying. One reason why boys turn into bullies is that they have no one around to turn them into men. Boys are filled with energies meant to be channeled in a positive direction—toward protecting the innocent and building up society. Without strong male role models and without a disciplined process of initiation into maturity, these energies remain either unfocused (as in the case of slackers) or directed toward violence and the exploitation of the weak (as in the case of bullies). Dr. Sax comments that you might not be able to turn a bully into a flower child, but with the right male mentoring, you could certainly turn him into a knight.

If a son of yours is either bullied or becoming a bully, I would strongly recommend that you read *Boys Adrift* and, above all, that you introduce your son to a strong, morally upright, focused and courageous male mentor—fast.

Savvy Headhunters and
the Hookup Culture

I FIRST CAME ACROSS THE TERM "hookup culture" in Leonard Sax's thought-provoking and disturbing book *Why Gender Matters*. But the phenomenon itself I found beautifully depicted in an earlier novel—Tom Wolfe's *I Am Charlotte Simmons*. As Sax specifies, the hookup mentality—prevalent among even some very young people but especially among university students—dictates that casual sexual encounters involving absolutely no expectation of relationship, or even psychological engagement, are perfectly acceptable. Sax, a psychiatrist specializing in family therapy, learned of the hookup world from the veritable army of young women suffering from depression and anxiety who were streaming into his office. And through the figure of Charlotte Simmons—an innocent girl from North Carolina who utterly lost her way morally and psychologically at a prestigious university where casual sex and drugs were far more important than learning—Wolfe showed the debilitating effects of this self-absorbed and hedonistic culture.

Now it would seem self-evident that such permissiveness, though prevalent, is morally problematic and something to be decried rather than celebrated. But an article titled "Boys on the Side" in *The Atlantic* offers a dissenting opinion. According to author Hanna Rosin, the hookup mentality is, in point of fact, a great boon to women. She allows that lots of books and studies have pointed out the dark side of the hookup culture, including the deep frustration and humiliation that can follow from transient sexual encounters, but she insists that steady questioning of typical young women today would reveal that none of them really wants a return to traditional morality. She argues, "For most women, the hookup culture is like an island they visit, mostly during their college years and even then only when they are bored or experimenting or don't know any better. But it is not a place where they drown." Why aren't they destroyed by this sexual licentiousness? Rosin explains, "The most patient and thorough research about the hookup culture shows that over the long run, women benefit greatly from living in a world where they can have sexual adventure without commitment or all that much shame, and where they can enter into temporary relationships that don't get in the way of future success." One might think that prevalence of casual sex would produce women who are sexual victims, but Rosin contends that precisely the opposite is the case. Young women who choose a variety of sexual partners and who assiduously steer clear of pesky relationships are "managing their romantic lives like savvy headhunters." Instead of being manipulated by powerful men, young ladies are happily becoming adept at manipulation. And here is Rosin's grand conclusion: "The hookup culture is too bound up with everything that's fabulous about being a young woman in 2012—the freedom, the confidence, the knowledge that you can always depend on yourself."

Now I would like you to concentrate on that last statement. Notice how every virtue that Rosin cites—freedom, confidence, self-reliance—is a subjective disposition. No one in his right mind would contend that those attitudes are anything but good, but they are good precisely in the measure that they order a person to some objective value that lies outside of her subjectivity. We savor freedom because it is the condition for the possibility of pursuing the good in a responsible way; we think that confidence and self-reliance are worthwhile because they enable one to achieve the good easily and joyfully. But if the question of the objectively valuable is bracketed, then those subjective dispositions lose their orientation and devolve, in point of fact, into something quite destructive.

What struck me throughout Rosin's article was the complete absence of a reference to the objectively valuable in regard to sexual behavior. The purpose of sex? The meaning of the sexual act? The proper ethical, or dare I say religious, setting for sexuality? Never mentioned—and apparently irrelevant. All that seems to matter is that young people—especially young women—have the opportunity to define themselves sexually however they want, to "manage" their sexual activity "like savvy headhunters." Can I suggest that that last phrase is telling indeed? When the realm of the objectively valuable is marginalized, the subject will inevitably fall back on herself, stewing in her own juices. And let's be honest, left to our own devices, the vast majority of us would do what is most convenient and most selfish. (The Church, by the way, refers to this natural tendency toward self-absorption as the principle effect of original sin.) In the arena of sexuality, the one-sided stress on freedom and self-reliance will lead, in very short order, to manipulation, domination, and indifference to relationship. But when the sexual impulse is ordered according to the objective values of love, commitment, marriage, and the call of God, then it is transfigured into something radiant and rare.

The hookup culture is all about sexual freedom. However, it would be wise to remember a line from Bob Dylan, "Freedom, just around the corner from you/ but with truth so far off, what good would it do?" Sexual liberty without objective value produces a lot of savvy headhunters, but they will wind up in Dr. Sax's office suffering from a deep sadness of the heart.

Sex, Love, and God: The Catholic Answer to Puritanism and Nietzcheanism

MANY OF THE CATHOLIC CHURCH'S TEACHINGS are vilified in both the high and popular cultures, but none more than its doctrines concerning marriage and sexuality. Time and again, the Church's views on sex are characterized as puritanical, life-denying, and hopelessly outdated—holdovers from the Bronze Age. Above all, critics pillory the Church for setting unreasonable limits to the sexual freedom of contemporary people. Church leaders, who defend traditional sexual morality, are parodied as versions of Dana Carvey's "church lady"—fussy, accusatory, secretly perverse, and sex-obsessed.

Let me respond first to the charge of puritanism. Throughout the history of religion and philosophy, a puritanical strain is indeed apparent. Whether it manifests itself as Manichaeism, Gnosticism, or Platonic dualism, the puritanical philosophy teaches that spirit is good and matter is evil or fallen. In most such schemas, the whole purpose of life is to escape from matter, especially from sexuality, which so ties us to the material realm. But authentic biblical Christianity is not puritanical. The Creator God described in the book of Genesis made the entire panoply of things physical—planets, stars, the moon and sun, animals, fish, and even things that creep and crawl upon the earth—and found all of it good, even very good. Accordingly, there is nothing perverse or morally questionable about bodies, sex, sexual longing, or the sexual act. In fact, it's just the contrary. When, in the Gospel of Mark, Jesus himself is asked about marriage and sexuality, he hearkens back to the book of Genesis and the story of creation: "At the beginning of creation God made them male and female; for this reason a man shall leave his father and mother and the two shall become as one. They are no longer two but one flesh" (Mark 10:6-8). That last sentence is, dare I say it, inescapably "sexy." Plato might have been a puritan, and perhaps John Calvin too, but Jesus most certainly was not.

So given this stress on the goodness of sex and sexual pleasure, what separates the Christian view from, say, the "Playboy" philosophy? The simple answer is that, for biblical people, sexuality must be placed in the wider context of love, which is to say, willing the good of the other. It is fundamental to Catholic spirituality and morality that everything in life must be drawn magnetically toward love, must be conditioned and transfigured by love. Thus, one's business concerns must be marked by love, lest they devolve into crass materialism; and one's relationships must be leavened by love, lest they devolve into occasions for self-interested manipulation; even one's play must be directed toward love, lest it devolve into mere self-indulgence. Sex is no exception to this rule. The goodness of sexual desire is designed, by its very nature, to become an ingredient in a program of self-forgetting love, and hence to become something rare and life-enhancing.

If you want to see what happens when this principle is ignored, take a long, hard look at the hookup culture prevalent among many young—and not so young—people today. Sex as mere recreation, as contact sport, as a source only of superficial pleasure, has produced armies of the desperately sad and anxious, many of whom have no idea that it is precisely their errant sexuality that has produced such deleterious effects in them. When sexual pleasure is drawn out of itself by the magnetic attraction of love, it is rescued from self-preoccupation.

Now there is a third step as well, for human love must be situated in the context of divine purpose. Once Jesus clarified that male and female are destined to become one flesh, he further specified that "What God has joined together" no human being should put asunder. When I was working full time as a parish priest, I had the privilege of preparing many young couples for marriage. I would always ask them, "Why do you want to be married in the Church?" After some hesitation, the young people would invariably respond with some version of "Well, we're in love," to which I would respond, "I'm delighted that you're in love, but that's no reason to be married in the Church!" My point was that entering into a properly sacramental marriage implied that the bride and groom realized that they had been brought together by God and precisely for God's reasons, that their sexuality and their mutual love were in service of an even higher purpose. To make their vows before a priest and a Catholic community, I would tell them, was tantamount to saying that they knew their relationship was sacramental—a vehicle of God's grace to the wider world. This final contextualization guaranteed that sexuality—already good in itself and already elevated by love—had now something truly sacred.

Our culture has become increasingly Nietzchean, by which I mean obsessed with the power of self-creation. This is why toleration is the only objective value that many people recognize, and why freedom, especially in the arena of sexuality, is so highly prized. It is furthermore why attempts to contextualize sex within higher frameworks of meaning are so often mocked as puritanism or fussy antiquarianism. Thank God that, amidst the million voices advocating self-indulgent sexuality, there is at least the one voice of the Catholic Church shouting "No,"—a no in service of a higher "Yes!"

The Adventures of Classical Morality

ONE OF THE MOST SIGNIFICANT FAULT LINES in Western culture opened up in the sixteenth and seventeenth centuries, when what we now know as the "modern" world separated itself from the classical and medieval worlds. The thinking of Descartes, Spinoza, Leibniz, Kant, Newton, Jefferson, and many others represented a sea change in the way Western people looked at practically everything. In almost every telling of the story, this development is presented as an unmitigated good. I rather emphatically do not subscribe to this interpretation. It would be foolish indeed not to see that tremendous advances, especially in the arenas of science and politics, took place because of the modern turn, but it would be even more foolish to hold that modernity did not represent, in many other ways, a severe declension from what came before. This decline is particularly apparent in the areas of the arts and ethics, and I believe that there is an important similarity in the manner in which those two disciplines went bad in the modern period.

Classical philosophy and science sought to understand things in terms of Aristotle's four causes: material (what something is made of), formal (a thing's essential structure), efficient (how it got the way it is), and final (its purpose or destiny). The founders of modernity became suspicious of our capacity to know form (for things seem to be in constant flux) and finality (for it just wasn't clear where the universe was going). Accordingly, they put a great stress on the remaining two Aristotelian causes, the material and the efficient. And this is precisely why the distinctively modern sciences—with their exclusive focus on what things are made of and how they got in their present state of being—developed the way they did.

But this elimination of formal and final causality and the hyper-stress on material and efficient causality had profound effects outside of the physical sciences. A classical sculptor, painter, or architect was trying to imitate the forms that he found in nature, and thereby to create something objectively beautiful. It is by no means accidental, for instance, that architects from the classical period through the High Renaissance designed buildings that mimicked the dimensions and features of the human body. One reason that Michelangelo's architecture is so deeply satisfying to us is that it was grounded in that artist's particularly profound grasp of the body's rhythms and proportions. Thomas Aquinas defined art as *recta ratio factibilium* (right reason in regard to the making of things), and the rectitude he had in mind was none other than an understanding of the forms that God had already placed in nature. But a modern artist, unconvinced that objective form ought to provide a norm for her work, tends to see art as the objectification of subjectivity. The self-expression of the artist—the efficient cause of the work, if you will—is more important than any conformity of that work to a formal norm. This approach was beautifully and succinctly summed up by the Dadaist painter Marcel Duchamp: "Whatever an artist spits out is art." With that statement, we have reached the polar opposite of *recta ratio factibilium*.

The marginalizing of final causality had a deep and deleterious effect on the way moderns tend to think about morality. Classical moral thinkers—from Plato and Aristotle to Augustine and Thomas Aquinas—considered the ethical act in terms of its purpose or finality. What made an act good was its orientation toward its proper end. Thus, since the end of the speech act is the enunciation of the truth, speaking a lie is morally problematic, and since the end of a political act is the enactment of justice, unjust legislating is unethical, etc. If art is *recta ratio factibilium*, then ethics, for Aquinas, is *recta ratio agibilium* (right reason in regard to action), the rectitude of the reason in this context coming from conformity to finality. But with final causality relegated to the margins, morality became a matter of self-expression and self-creation. The extreme instance of this attitude can be found in the writings of Friedrich Nietzsche and Jean-Paul Sartre. The nineteenth-century German Nietzsche opined that the supreme morality—beyond good and evil—was the ecstatic self-assertion of the superman, and the twentieth-century Frenchman Sartre held that the "authentic" person is the one who acts in accord with his or her own deepest instincts. Sartre famously argued that existence (unfettered freedom) precedes essence (who or what a person becomes). And that is the polar opposite of a *recta ratio agibilium* ordered to objective finality.

If you think that all of this seems hopelessly obscure and irrelevant to the contemporary situation, then think again. Even the most radical ideas of the moderns in regard to morality have trickled down, through a network of professors, teachers, script writers, television personalities, singers, bloggers, etc. to reach the ordinary person today. And this, I would submit, is what makes the Catholic position on ethics so hard to understand. The modern person instinctually says, "Who are you to tell me what to do?" or "Who are you to set limits to my freedom?" And the Catholic instinctually says, "Order your freedom to an objective truth that makes you the person you are meant to be."

It would be the stuff of another chapter to explore, even with relative adequacy, the manner in which this dilemma might be resolved, but might I suggest that the fundamental problem with modern ethics (as with modern art, generally speaking) is that it is boring. The self-asserting and self-expressing ego never really gets anywhere, never breaks out of its own clean, well-lighted space. But the human subject, enraptured by the objective good, sets out on a journey away from the narrow confines of the self and becomes an adventurer.

Sympathy for the Devil

SOME YEARS AGO, *The New Yorker* ran a cartoon that perfectly lampooned the loopy ideology of "inclusion" that has come to characterize so much of the Christian world. It showed a neat and tidy church, filled with an attentive congregation. The pastor was at the podium, introducing a guest speaker. "In accordance with our policy of equal time," he said, "I would like now to give our friend the opportunity to present an alternative point of view." Sitting next to him, about to rise to speak, was the devil, dressed perfectly and tapping the pages of his prepared text on his knee.

I was put in mind of that cartoon when I read a sermon delivered by Katharine Jefferts Schori, the Presiding Bishop of the Episcopal Church in America. Addressing a congregation in Curaçao, Venezuela, Bishop Jefferts Schori praised the beauty of (what else?) diversity, but lamented the fact that so many people are still frightened by what is other or different: "Human beings have a long history of discounting and devaluing difference, finding it offensive or even evil." Now I suppose that if one were to make the right distinctions—differentiating between that which is simply unusual and that which is intrinsically bad—one might be able coherently to make this point.

But the bishop moved, instead, in an astonishing direction, finding an example of the lamentable exclusivity she is talking about in the behavior of the Apostle Paul himself. In the sixteenth chapter of the Acts of the Apostles, we find the story of Paul's first visit to the Greek town of Philippi. We are told that one day, while on his way to prayer, Paul was accosted by a slave girl "who had a spirit of divination and brought her owners a great deal of money by fortune-telling" (Acts 16:16). This demon-possessed child followed Paul and his companions up and down for several days, shouting, "These men are slaves of the Most High God, who proclaim to you a way of salvation." Having finally had enough of her, Paul turned to the young woman and addressed the wicked spirit within her, "I order you in the name of Jesus Christ to come out of her" (Acts 16:18). And the demon, we are told, came out of her instantly.

Up until this incident in Venezuela, the entire Christian interpretive tradition read that passage as an account of deliverance; the story of the liberation of a young woman who had been enslaved both to dark spiritual powers and to the nefarious human beings who had exploited her. But Bishop Jefferts Schori read it as a tale of patriarchal oppression and intolerance. She preached, "But Paul is annoyed, perhaps, for being put in his place, and he responds by depriving her of her gift of spiritual awareness. Paul can't abide something he won't see as beautiful or holy, so he tries to destroy it." The bishop correctly pointed out that the girl was saying true things about Paul and his friends, but demons say true things all the time in the New Testament. Think of the dark spirits who consistently confess that Jesus is the Holy One of God. That a Christian bishop would characterize the demonic possession of a young girl as something "beautiful and holy" simply beggars belief.

But things get even more bizarre. We are told in Acts that the girl's owners are furious that Paul has effectively robbed them of their principal source of income and that they therefore stir up controversy and get him thrown in prison. But on the bishop's reading, Paul is just getting what he deserved: "That's pretty much where he put himself by his own refusal to recognize that she too shares in God's nature, just as much as he does—maybe more so!" The bishop seems to rejoice that a mid-first-century Philippian version of the liberal thought police had the good sense to imprison the patriarchal Paul for his deep intolerance of fallen spirits!

That night in prison, we are told, Paul and Silas sang hymns of praise to God and preached the Gospel to their jailers. Jefferts Schori read this, strangely, as Paul coming to his senses at last, remembering God, dropping the annoyance he felt toward the girl, and embracing the spirit of compassion. Wouldn't it be a lot simpler and clearer to say that Paul, who had never "forgotten God," quite consistently showed compassion both toward the possessed girl and the unevangelized jailor, delivering the former and preaching the Gospel to the latter?

What is at the root of this deeply wrong-headed homily is a conflation of early twenty-first century values of inclusion and toleration with the great Biblical value of love. To love is to will the good of the other as other. As such, love can involve—indeed, must involve—a deep intolerance toward wickedness and a clear willingness to exclude certain forms of life, behavior, and thought. When inclusivity and toleration emerge as the supreme goods—as they have in much of our society today—then love devolves into something vague, sentimental, and finally dangerous.

How dangerous? Well, we might begin to see the devil himself as beautiful and holy. You see why this sermon reminded me of that *New Yorker* cartoon?

Your Life Is Not About You

Time Magazine's cover story "The Childfree Life" generated a good deal of controversy and commentary. The photo that graced the cover of the edition pretty much summed up the argument: a young, fit couple lounge languidly on a beach and gaze up at the camera with blissful smiles—and no child anywhere in sight. What the editors want us to accept is that this scenario is not just increasingly a fact in our country, but that it is morally acceptable as well, a lifestyle choice that some people legitimately make. Whereas in one phase of the feminist movement, "having it all" meant that a woman should be able to both pursue a career and raise a family, now it apparently means a relationship and a career without the crushing encumbrance of annoying, expensive, and demanding children.

There is no question that childlessness is on the rise in the United States. Our birthrate is the lowest in recorded history, surpassing even the crash in reproduction that followed the economic crash of the 1930s. We have not yet reached the drastic levels found in Europe (in Italy, for example, one in four women never give birth), but childlessness has risen in our country across all ethnic and racial groups, even those that have traditionally put a particular premium on large families.

What is behind this phenomenon? The article's author spoke to a variety of women who had decided not to have children, and found a number of different reasons for their decision. Some said that they simply never experienced the desire for children; others said that their careers were so satisfying to them that they couldn't imagine taking on the responsibility of raising children; still others argued that in an era when bringing up a child costs upward of $250,000, they simply couldn't afford to have even one baby. The comedian Margaret Cho admitted, bluntly enough, "Babies scare me more than anything." A researcher at the London School of Economics weighed in to say that there is a tight correlation between intelligence and childlessness: the smarter you are, it appears, the less likely you are to have children!

In accord with the tenor of our time, those who have opted out of the children game paint themselves, of course, as victims. They are persecuted, they say, by a culture that remains relentlessly baby-obsessed and, in the words of one of the interviewees, "oppressively family-centric."

Patricia O'Laughlin, a Los Angeles-based psychotherapist, specializes in helping women cope with the crushing expectations of a society that expects them to reproduce. As an act of resistance, many childless couples have banded together for mutual support. One such group in Nashville comes together for activities such as "zip-lining, canoeing, and a monthly dinner the foodie couple in the group organizes." One of their members, Andrea Reynolds, was quoted as saying, "We can do anything we want, so why wouldn't we?"

What particularly struck me in this article was that none of the people interviewed ever moved outside of the ambit of his or her private desire. Some people, it seems, are into children, and others aren't, just as some people like baseball and others prefer football. No childless couple would insist that every couple remain childless, and they would expect the same tolerance to be accorded to them from the other side. But never, in these discussions, was reference made to values that present themselves in their sheer objectivity to the subject, values that make a demand on freedom. Rather, the individual will was consistently construed as sovereign and self-disposing.

And this represents a marked transformation in cultural orientation. Up until very recent times, the decision whether or not to have children would never have been simply "up to the individual." Rather, the individual choice would have been situated in the context of a whole series of values that properly condition and shape the will: family, neighborhood, society, culture, the human race, nature, and ultimately, God. We can see this so clearly in the initiation rituals of primal peoples and in the formation of young people in practically every culture on the planet until the modern period. Having children was about carrying on the family name and tradition; it was about contributing to the strength and integrity of one's society; it was about perpetuating the great adventure of the human race; it was a participation in the dynamism of nature itself. And finally, it was about cooperating with God's desire that life flourish: "And you, be fruitful and multiply, teem on the earth and multiply in it" (Gen 9:7). None of this is meant to be crushing to the will, but liberating. When these great values present themselves to our freedom, we are drawn out beyond ourselves and integrated into great realities that expand us and make us more alive.

It is finally with relief and a burst of joy that we realize that our lives are not about us. Traditionally, having children was one of the primary means by which this shift in consciousness took place. That increasingly this liberation is forestalled and that people are finding themselves locked in the cold space of what they sovereignly choose, I find rather sad.

Hannah Arendt's Moral Lesson

THE APPEARANCE OF AN ART HOUSE FILM on the philosopher Hannah Arendt has sparked renewed interest in an old controversy. In 1961, Arendt went to Jerusalem as a correspondent for *The New Yorker* magazine to cover the trial of Adolf Eichmann, the notorious Nazi colonel accused of masterminding the transportation of millions of Jews to the death camps. Arendt was herself a Jew who had managed to escape from Nazi Germany and who had been, years before, something of an ardent Zionist. But she had since grown suspicious of the Israeli state, seeing it as un-self-critical and indifferent to the legitimate concerns of the Palestinians. I think it is fair to say, therefore, that she came to the trial with a complicated set of assumptions and a good deal of conflicting feelings.

As the trial unfolded, Arendt was massively put off by what she saw as the grandstanding of the prosecutors. Their irresponsible, even clownish, antics were, she concluded, the public face of the Israeli state, which had determined to make of the Eichmann proceedings a show trial. But what struck her most of all was Eichmann himself. Sequestered in a glass box for his own protection, squinting behind owlish spectacles, screwing up his mouth in an odd, nervous tic, trading in homespun expressions, pleading that he was just a middle-level bureaucrat following orders, Eichmann was neither impressive nor frightening nor sinister. Arendt never doubted that Eichmann was guilty of great wickedness, but she saw the Nazi functionary as the very incarnation of what she famously called "the banality of evil." One of the distinctive marks of this banality Arendt characterized as *Gedankenlosigkeit,* which could be superficially rendered in English as "thoughtlessness," but which carries more accurately the sense of "the inability to think." Eichmann couldn't rise above his own petty concerns about his career, and he couldn't begin to "think" along with another, to see what he was doing from the standpoint of his victims. This very *Gedankenlosigkeit* is what enabled him to say, probably with honesty, that he didn't feel as though he had committed any crimes.

The film, called *Hannah Arendt,* very effectively portrays the firestorm of protest that followed Arendt's account of the Eichmann trial. Many Jews, both in Israel and America, thought by characterizing Eichmann the way she did, she had exonerated him and effectively blamed his victims. I won't descend into the complexity of that argument, which rages to some degree to the present day. But I will say that I believe Arendt's critics missed the rather profound metaphysical significance of what the philosopher was saying about the Nazi bureaucrat. In a text written during the heat of bitter controversy surrounding her book, Arendt tried to explain in greater detail what she meant by calling evil banal: "Good can be radical; evil can never be radical, it can only be extreme, for it possesses neither depth nor any demonic dimension, yet—and this is its horror!—it can spread like a fungus over the surface of the earth and lay waste the entire world."

The young Hannah Arendt had written her doctoral dissertation under the great German philosopher Karl Jaspers, and the topic of her work was the concept of love in the writings of St. Augustine. One of the most significant intellectual breakthroughs of Augustine's life was the insight that evil is not something substantial, but rather a type of non-being, a lack of some perfection that ought to be present. Thus, a cancer is evil in the measure that it compromises the proper functioning of a bodily organ, and a sin is evil in the measure that it represents a distortion or twisting of a rightly functioning will. Accordingly, evil does not stand over and against the good as a kind of coequal metaphysical force, as the Manichees would have it. Rather, it is invariably parasitic upon the good, existing only as a sort of shadow. J.R.R. Tolkien gave visual expression to this Augustinian notion in his portrayal of the Nazgul in *The Lord of the Rings*. Those terrible and terrifying threats, flying through the air on fearsome beasts, are revealed, once their capes and hoods are pulled away, to be precisely nothing, emptiness. And this is exactly why, to return to Arendt's description, evil can never be radical. It can never sink down into the roots of being; it can never stand on its own. It has no integrity, no real depth or substance. To be sure, it can be extreme, and it can, as Arendt's image suggests, spread far and wide, doing enormous damage. But it can never truly *be*. And this is why, when it shows up in raw form, it looks, not like Goethe's Mephistopheles or Milton's Satan, but rather like a little twerp in a glass box.

Occasionally, in the course of the liturgical year, Catholics are asked to renew their baptismal promises. One of the questions, to which the answer "I do" is expected, is this: "Do you renounce the lure of evil, so that sin may have no mastery over you?" Evil can never truly be beautiful, for beauty is a property of being; it can only be glamorous or alluring, superficially attractive.

The great moral lesson articulated by both Augustine and Hannah Arendt is that we must refuse to be beguiled by the glittering banality of wickedness, and we must consistently choose the substance over the shadow.

Cosmos and One More Telling
of the Tired Myth

SETH MACFARLANE, well known atheist and cartoonist, is the executive producer of the 2014 remake of *Cosmos*. The first episode featured, along with the science, an animated feature dealing with the sixteenth-century Dominican friar Giordano Bruno, who was burned at the stake by Church officials. A brooding statue of Bruno stands today in the Campo de' Fiori in Rome on the very spot where the unfortunate friar was put to death. In MacFarlane's cartoon, Bruno is portrayed as a hero of modern science, and Church officials are, without exception, depicted as wild-eyed fanatics and unthinking dogmatists. As I watched this piece, all I could think was *Here we go again.*

Avatars of the modern ideology feel obligated to tell their great foundation myth over and over, and central to that narrative is that both the physical sciences and liberal political arrangements emerged only after a long twilight struggle against the reactionary forces of religion, especially the Catholic religion. Like the effigies brought out to be burned on Guy Fawkes Day, the bugbear of intolerant and violent Catholicism has to be exposed to ridicule on a regular basis.

I will leave to the side for the moment the issue of liberal politics' relation to religion, but I feel obliged, once more, to expose the dangerous silliness of the view that Catholicism and the modern sciences are implacable foes. I would first observe that it is by no means accidental that the physical sciences in their modern form emerged when and where they did, that is to say, in the Europe of the sixteenth century. The great founders of modern science—Copernicus, Galileo, Tycho Brahe, Descartes, Pascal, etc.—were formed in Church-sponsored universities, where they learned their mathematics, astronomy, and physics. Moreover, in those same universities, all of the founders would have imbibed the two fundamentally theological assumptions that made the modern sciences possible, namely, that the world is not divine—and hence can be experimented upon rather than worshipped—and that the world is imbued with intelligibility—and hence can be understood. I say that these are theological presumptions, for they are both corollaries of the doctrine of creation. If God made the world in its entirety, then nothing in the world is divine; and if God made the world in its entirety, then every detail of the world is marked by the mind of the Creator. Without these two assumptions, the sciences as we know them will not, because they cannot, emerge.

In fact, from the intelligibility of the universe, the young Joseph Ratzinger (later Pope Benedict XVI) constructed an elegant argument for the existence of God. The objective intelligibility of the finite world, he maintained, is explicable only through recourse to a subjective intelligence that thought it into being. This correspondence is reflected in our intriguing usage of the word "recognition" (literally, to think again) to designate an act of knowledge. In employing that term, we are at least implicitly acknowledging that, in coming to know, we are re-thinking what has already been thought by the creative intelligence responsible for the world's intelligibility. If Ratzinger is right, religion, far from being science's enemy, is in fact its presupposition.

Secularist ideologues will relentlessly marshal stories of Hypatia, Galileo, Giordano Bruno, and others—all castigated or persecuted by Church people who did not adequately grasp the principles I have been laying out. But to focus on these few exceptional cases is to grossly misrepresent the history of the relationship between Catholicism and the sciences.

May I mention just a handful of the literally thousands of Catholic clerics who have made significant contributions to the sciences? Do you know about Fr. Jean Picard, a priest of the seventeenth century, who was the first person to determine the size of the earth to a reasonable degree of accuracy? Do you know about Fr. Giovanni Battista Riccioli, a seventeenth-century Jesuit astronomer and the first person to measure the rate of acceleration of a free-falling body? Do you know about Fr. George Searle, a Paulist priest of the early twentieth century who discovered six galaxies? Do you know about Fr. Benedetto Castelli, a Benedictine monk and scientist of the sixteenth century who was a very good friend and supporter of Galileo? Do you know about Fr. Francesco Grimaldi, a Jesuit priest who discovered the diffraction of light? Do you know about Fr. George Coyne, a contemporary Jesuit priest and astrophysicist who for many years ran the Vatican Observatory outside of Tucson? Perhaps you know about Fr. Gregor Mendel, the Augustinian monk who virtually invented modern genetics, and about Fr. Teilhard de Chardin, a twentieth-century Jesuit priest who wrote extensively on paleontology, and about Fr. Georges Lemaître, the formulator of the Big Bang theory of cosmic origins? Or Jesuit brother and Vatican astronomer Guy Consolmagno who, in 2014, became the first clergyman to be awarded the prestigious Carl Sagan Medal "for outstanding communication by an active planetary scientist to the general public"?

Can we please, once and for all, dispense with the nonsense that Catholicism is the enemy of the sciences? When we do, we'll expose the Seth MacFarlane telling of the story for what it really is: not scientific history but the basest sort of anti-Catholic propaganda.

SEEDS OF THE WORD: FINDING GOD IN THE CULTURE

Bill Maher and Not Understanding
Either Faith or the Bible

I DON'T KNOW WHAT POSSESSES ME to watch *Real Time with Bill Ma-her*, for Maher is, without a doubt, the most annoying anti-religion-ist on the scene today. Though his show is purportedly about poli-tics, it almost invariably includes some attack on religion, especially Christianity. Even during an interview with former President Jimmy Carter, whom Maher very much admires, the host managed to get in a sharp attack on Carter's faith. Not long ago, his program included a brief conversation with Ralph Reed, the articulate gentleman who used to run the Christian Coalition and who is now a lobbyist and activist on behalf of faith-related causes.

For the first three or four minutes, Reed and Maher dis-cussed the social science concerning children raised in stable vs. unstable families, and Reed was scoring quite a few points in favor of the traditional understanding of marriage. Sensing that he was making little headway, Maher decided to pull the religion card, and from that point on things went from bad to worse. Maher said, "Now you're a man of faith, which means someone who consciously sus-pends all critical thinking and accepts things on the basis of no evi-dence." Astonishingly, Reed said, "Yes," at which point, I shouted at the TV screen: "No!" Then Maher said, "And I believe that you take everything in the Bible literally," and Reed replied, "Yes," at which point I said, "Oh God, here we go again."

Maher then did what I knew he would do; he pulled out a sheet of paper which included references to several of the more morally outrageous practices that the God of the Bible seems to approve of, including slavery. Pathetically, Reed tried to clear things up by distinguishing the chattel slavery of the American south from the slavery practiced in the classical world, which amounted to a kind of indentured servitude. "Oh I get it," Maher responded, "God approves of the *good* kind of slavery." The audience roared with laughter. Reed lowered his head. Maher smirked and the cause of religion took still another step backward.

I would like, in very brief compass, to say something simple about each of the issues that Maher raised. Faith, rightly understood, does not involve any surrender of one's critical intellectual powers, nor is it tantamount to the acceptance of things on the basis of no evidence. What Bill Maher characterizes as "faith" is nothing but superstition, credulity, or intellectual irresponsibility. It is an ersatz "knowing" that falls short of the legitimate standards of reason. Real faith is not infra-rational but rather supra-rational, that is to say, not below reason but above reason and inclusive of it. It is beyond reason precisely because it is a response to the God who has revealed himself, and God is, by definition, beyond our capacity to grasp, to see, fully to understand. It involves darkness, to be sure, but the darkness that comes, not from an insufficiency of light, but from a surplus of light. If you are ever tempted to agree with Bill Maher on the nature of faith, I would invite you to read any page of Augustine, Thomas Aquinas, John Henry Newman, C.S. Lewis, or G.K. Chesterton, and honestly ask yourself the question, "Does this sound like someone who has suspended his critical faculties?"

As for the Bible, the moment you say, as Ralph Reed did, that you take the entirety of the Scriptures literally, you are hopelessly vulnerable to the kind of critique that Bill Maher raises. In its marvelous statement on biblical interpretation, *Dei Verbum*, Vatican II says that the Bible is the Word of God in the words of men. That laconic statement packs a punch, for it clarifies why the fundamentalist strategy of scriptural interpretation is always dysfunctional. God did not dictate the Scriptures word for word to people who received the message dumbly and automatically. Rather, God spoke subtly and indirectly, precisely through human agents who employed distinctive literary techniques and who were conditioned by the cultures in which they found themselves and by the audiences they addressed. Thus one of the most basic moves in Scriptural exegesis is the determination of the genre in which a given biblical author was operating. Are we dealing with a song, a psalm, a history, a legend, a letter, a Gospel, a tall tale, an apocalypse? Therefore, to ask, "Do you take the Bible literally?" is about as helpful as asking, "Do you take the library literally?"

A further implication of *Dei Verbum*'s statement is that there is a distinction between, as William Placher put it, "what is in the Bible and what the Bible teaches." There are lots of things that are indeed in the pages of the Scriptures but that are not essential to the overarching message of the Scriptures. They are things that were in the cultural milieu of the human authors but that are not ingredient in the revelation that God intends to offer. A good example of this would be the references to slavery that Maher cited. The institution of slavery was taken for granted in most ancient cultures, and is therefore it is not surprising that biblical authors would refer to it or even praise it, but attention to the great patterns and trajectories of the Bible as a whole reveals that the justification of slavery is not something that "the Bible teaches," which is precisely why the fight against slavery in the Western culture was led by people deeply shaped by the Scriptures.

There is much more, obviously, that can be said concerning these two complex areas of theology. Suffice it to say, the kind of conversation that Bill Maher and Ralph Reed had is decidedly not the best way forward.

Attack on Christians
in the Middle East

THOUGH YOU WOULD NEVER GUESS IT from the paucity of coverage in the major news media, there is a fierce persecution of Christians going on in the Middle East. In Egypt, convents and churches are being burned to the ground, and Copts, members of one of the most ancient Christian communities, are being routinely harassed, tortured, and arrested. In Iraq, the ISIS group, hoping to reestablish a "caliphate" across the northern sector of the Middle East, is brutally persecuting Christians. In mid-2014, an ultimatum was issued in Mosul, where Christians have been living for over 1,600 years, that believers in Jesus have to pay a stiff fine, leave the country, or be put to death. And the sheer shock of these extreme instances can allow us to overlook the fact that in Saudi Arabia Christians are not permitted to build churches or to practice their faith publicly in any way.

Moreover, Muslim persecution of Christianity is not limited to the Middle East. Islamist radicals have been attacking Christians in Indonesia, India, and the Philippines for quite some time. Perhaps the most extreme examples of this persecution are the attacks launched by the Islamist group Boko Haram in Nigeria. This terrorist sect has burned churches, wantonly killed innocent Christians at worship, and, most recently, kidnapped hundreds of Christian girls whose crime was attending school.

It is easy enough to condemn these actions as deeply inhumane, but I would like to press the critique a bit further, drawing attention to the work of Pope Francis's two immediate predecessors. Pope St. John Paul II was the most vocal defender of human rights in the twentieth century. Across the world and in hundreds of different venues, he insisted that respect for fundamental human rights must be the key to a just political order. And of all the human rights—to life, liberty, a just wage, access to the ballot—the most basic, he taught, was the right to religious freedom. This is because the spiritual aspiration of the human heart is what defines us as human beings. The violation of that most sacred of "spaces" is, therefore, the most offensive, the most heinous and dehumanizing. To use the threat of force to compel someone to change his religious beliefs—which we are regularly seeing in the Middle East—is not only criminal but wicked.

It is also deeply irrational—a point made by Pope Benedict XVI in his address at the University of Regensburg in September of 2006. In that controversial speech, Pope Benedict drew attention to a little-known dialogue between the fourteenth-century Byzantine emperor Manuel II Paleologus and a Muslim interlocutor. The Emperor pointed out that the idea of spreading the faith through violent conquest, which is recommended in the Qur'an, is supremely irrational. Faith is a function, not of the body, but of the soul, and therefore coercion through bodily persecution cannot even in principle awaken authentic faith. One must, instead, be skilled in arguments that would appeal to the mind: "to convince a reasonable soul, one does not need a strong arm, or weapons of any kind, or any other means of threatening a person with death." In a word, the idea of the holy war is not *syn logon* (according to the word or reason). And here is the decisive point: what is unreasonable is out of step with God's own nature, since God, on the Christian reading, is identified with the *Logos*—"In the beginning was the Word, and the Word was with God, and the Word was God."

However, in Muslim teaching, Allah's nature is so transcendent that it goes beyond any and all categories, including that of reason. Pope Benedict cites the noted French Islamic scholar R. Arnaldez, who points out that Allah is not even bound by his own word, so that if he so chose, he could recommend idolatry as morally praiseworthy. This elevation of the divine will over the divine mind, called voluntarism in the West, is, for Benedict, the source of enormous confusion and mischief. Most notably and dangerously, it opens the door to the idea of divinely sanctioned violence.

Now I fully realize that many Christians over the centuries have done terrible things in the name of God, and that the overwhelming majority of Muslims are peaceful and nonviolent. But I think it is clear that when Christians act in such a way, they are unequivocally at odds with their own conception of God. Is the same true of Muslims? I am still waiting for a compelling answer from the Muslim camp to the question posed by Pope Benedict. At the time, of course, Islamist radicals responded by killing a number of innocent Christians—certainly a curious way of refuting the notion that divinely sanctioned violence is irrational!

In the meantime, I believe that all people of good will ought to pray for both the victims and their persecutors, for the best way to honor God is through an act of compassion. The same God who is identified with the *Logos* is, according to the first letter of John, also identified with Love.

The Modern Areopagus

In October 2014, my media ministry Word On Fire marked a milestone: 10,000,000 views on our YouTube channel. This achievement fills me with gratitude both to God and to the many people who have taken the time to watch one or more of the videos that I've produced over the past several years. It also provides the occasion for me to reflect a bit on both the pitfalls and the advantages of evangelizing through new media.

When we commenced our outreach through YouTube, we did so in the manner of an experiment. YouTube had just come into being at that time, and it largely featured crude, homemade videos of cats jumping off the roof and babies gurgling for their mother's camcorder. I thought that we should try to invade this space with the Gospel, and so I resolved to make short video commentaries on movies, music, current affairs, cultural happenings, etc. We had absolutely no idea whether anyone would watch, and at first, our offerings garnered just a small audience. I distinctly remember being thrilled when one of our videos managed to pass the 500 views mark for the first time.

But over the months and years, word spread, and we began to build an audience. The first video of ours to go viral was my response to Bill Maher's awful movie *Religulous*. In the course of a few weeks, it was seen by 100,000 people, and it continues to perform well, even to the present. In fact, the atheists have been my most active friends on the Internet. Whenever I do a video on Maher or

Christopher Hitchens or Richard Dawkins or Stephen Hawking, I get a strong reaction and lots of views.

One of the features of YouTube that I appreciate the most is its interactivity. At first, I didn't realize that people could comment on videos—but I quickly found out. Most of the responses, I have to admit, are negative. There are an awful lot of people in the virtual world who hate God, religion, the Catholic Church, priests, etc., and they come after me with some energy. But after getting over the initial shock of reading such vitriol, I have actually come to enjoy the give-and-take with my detractors. In fact, on a number of my forums, quite lengthy and sometimes quite sophisticated arguments have unfolded, somewhat in the manner of Platonic dialogues.

YouTube provides pretty thorough demographics of one's viewership, and so we have been able to determine that the vast majority of our viewers are young men in their twenties and thirties—the very group that the Church has a notoriously hard time reaching. That the Internet allows me to engage young men who would never darken the doors of a Catholic church or come to a church-sponsored event is a source of great encouragement to me.

The format that I have chosen is the short video commentary (eight to ten minutes), based usually on a column that I have prepared for publication in the print media. Early on, some communications "experts" advised me to lose the Roman collar and appear in civilian clothes, so as to attract the more secular audience. I never took that advice, thank God. I always want it to be clear that I am a Catholic priest speaking on behalf of the Catholic Church—and I don't think young people are the least bamboozled by awkward attempts at "relevance." Just the contrary.

Some of my academic colleagues have always been skeptical that any serious communication of the faith can take place in such a circumscribed and popular forum. They maintain that nothing shy of a thirty-page, heavily-footnoted paper can do justice to a complex question. I was trained as an academic, and have spent nearly twenty-five years teaching and writing just such papers and books, but I emphatically dissent from a position that would effectively remove the Catholic voice from the wider cultural forum. John Henry Newman, G.K. Chesterton, Ronald Knox, C.S. Lewis, and Fulton Sheen all wrote substantive but accessible articles for the mainstream press, and YouTube is a comparable arena today. If intellectually serious believers absent themselves from the wider conversation and retreat to their libraries and classrooms, the public space will belong to the atheists and secularists.

As to my general approach, I have tended toward what Cardinal Dolan of New York calls "affirmative orthodoxy," which is to say, emphasizing what the Church is for rather than what it is against. As I said at the beginning of this book (and hence its title), I have also adopted the patristic method of seeking out *semina Verbi* (seeds of the Word), hints and echoes of the Gospel that can be found, often in distorted form, in the high and low contemporary culture.

As I have argued in previous chapters, I believe that Spider-man, Superman, *True Grit's* Rooster Cogburn, *Gran Torino's* cranky Walt Kowalski, *The Shawshank Redemption's* Andy Dufresne, and Bilbo the hobbit all convey some dimension of Jesus Christ. And I have maintained that both Christopher Hitchens's essays and the *Twilight* films speak inchoately but surely of the longing of the human heart for God.

We find ourselves at a moment in the history of communication comparable to the early sixteenth century. The printing press constituted a revolution not only in communication technology as such but more specifically in the propagation of the Gospel. Something very similar, but even more explosive, is at work today. The social media provide tools for the announcing of the Good News that

For orders and information, please contact the publisher.

P.O. Box 170
Des Plaines, IL 60016
1-866-928-1237
sales@wordonfire.org
www.wordonfire.org

Paul, Augustine, Aquinas, Pascal, Newman, and even Fulton Sheen never dreamed possible.

The best way that I can celebrate the 10,000,000 views on YouTube is to invite many others to join me in our modern Areopagus in declaring Christ from the rooftops and to the ends of the world.